THE HYPOCRITICAL HEGEMON

A volume in the series

Cornell Studies in Money
edited by Eric Helleiner and Jonathan Kirshner
A list of titles in this series is available at *cornellpress.cornell.edu*

THE HYPOCRITICAL HEGEMON

How the United States Shapes
Global Rules against Tax Evasion
and Avoidance

Lukas Hakelberg

CORNELL UNIVERSITY PRESS   **ITHACA AND LONDON**

Cornell University Press gratefully acknowledges support for publication from the "Combatting Fiscal Fraud and Empowering Regulators—COFFERS" project (European Union Horizon 2020 research and innovation programme grant agreement No. 727145). This support allowed electronic versions of this book to be open access.

First published 2020 by Cornell University Press

Library of Congress Cataloging-in-Publication Data

Names: Hakelberg, Lukas, 1985– author.
Title: The hypocritical hegemon : how the United States shapes global rules against tax evasion and avoidance / Lukas Hakelberg.
Description: Ithaca [New York] : Cornell University Press, 2020. | Series: Cornell studies in money | Includes bibliographical references and index.
Identifiers: LCCN 2019028606 (print) | LCCN 2019028607 (ebook) | ISBN 9781501748011 (paperback) | ISBN 9781501748028 (epub) | ISBN 9781501748035 (pdf)
Subjects: LCSH: Tax evasion—United States. | Tax evasion—European Union countries. | Taxation—Political aspects—United States. | Taxation—Political aspects—European Union countries. | Tax evasion (International law) | Tax administration and procedure—International cooperation. | Banks and banking, Foreign—Law and legislation—United States. | Confidential communications—Banking—European Union countries.
Classification: LCC HV6341 .H34 2020 (print) | LCC HV6341 (ebook) | DDC 364.1/3380973—dc23
LC record available at https://lccn.loc.gov/2019028606
LC ebook record available at https://lccn.loc.gov/2019028607

Contents

List of Illustrations   vii

Note on Terms   viii

Preface   ix

Acknowledgments   xv

1. Change and Stability in Global Tax Policy   1

2. Power in International Tax Politics   25

3. Countering Harmful Tax Practices   49

4. The Swift Return of Tax Competition   66

5. The Emergence of Multilateral AEI   82

6. The BEPS Project: Long Live Arm's Length   106

7. From Hegemony to Transatlantic Tax Battle?   131

Notes   149

References   155

Index   185

Figures

1.1. Foreign Financial Wealth in Secrecy Jurisdictions before FATCA (Percentage of Total)   8

1.2. The Share of Financial Services in OECD Secrecy Jurisdictions' Gross Value Added   9

Tables

1.1. CRS Adoptions among Major Secrecy Jurisdictions as of January 15, 2018   2

2.1. Measures of Financial Market Size in Developed and Emerging Economies 28

2.2. Foreign Portfolio Investment from Major Secrecy Jurisdictions in December 2009   29

2.3. Measures of Consumer Market Size for Major Economies in 2013   31

2.4. Royalty and License Fee Payments Received by Major Corporate Tax Havens in 2013   32

2.5. Interaction of Explanatory Factors in Determining Government Preferences   42

2.6. Combinations of Government Preferences and US Strategic Choice   43

5.1. AEI Adoptions among Major Secrecy Jurisdictions   99

Note on Terms

This book makes heavy use of the terms *tax haven, secrecy jurisdiction, tax evasion*, and *tax avoidance*, for which the academic literature does not provide consensual definitions (Palan, Murphy, and Chavagneux 2010). In this book, the term *tax haven* refers to countries that act as secrecy jurisdictions, corporate tax havens, or—very often—both. Secrecy jurisdictions provide foreign investors with legal constructs for the concealment of their identities. These legal constructs include bank secrecy (laws prohibiting the dissemination of information on account holders), trusts (legal arrangements separating the economic from the beneficial ownership of an asset portfolio), and anonymous shell companies (corporations that can be registered without identifying their beneficial owners). Corporate tax havens either impose no or minimal taxes on foreign profits or exempt certain types of revenue such as royalty or interest payments from the corporate tax base. Accordingly, a secrecy jurisdiction mainly abets tax evasion, which occurs when a household conceals financial wealth and related capital income from the tax office at its place of residence, whereas a corporate tax haven abets tax avoidance, which refers to the shifting of taxable profits from high-tax to low-tax countries without corresponding shifts in the underlying economic activity. Of course, all of these terms represent ideal types meant to facilitate systematic analysis. Many countries have been secrecy jurisdictions and corporate tax havens at the same time. Although corporations can legally avoid taxes, some may still engage in criminal tax evasion. Likewise, households can legally avoid taxes, especially when they own companies.

Preface

On 22 May 2013, Austria succumbed to the European Union's Orwellian system. Instead of protecting the civic rights of Austrian citizens, Werner Faymann, the Austrian chancellor, abandoned the country's freedom and sovereignty. At least in the hyperbolic rhetoric of Heinz-Christian Strache, the leader of Austria's right-wing populist party FPÖ (Freedom Party of Austria), this is what the chancellor's decision to end bank secrecy came down to. What had actually happened? The day before Strache aired his accusations at an urgently summoned parliamentary session, the EU's heads of state and government had agreed to extend the automatic exchange of information (AEI) on foreign-held bank accounts by the end of the year. Data reported from banks to tax authorities would no longer be limited to interest payments, and Austria and Luxembourg, the two countries that had resisted the information exchange for decades, would finally participate. In Austria, this decision implied the abolition of constitutionally enshrined bank secrecy provisions prohibiting the dissemination of client data and thereby increasing the country's attractiveness to tax evaders. In fact, I would learn much later that Austrian bank secrecy was the real reason my grandmother took me and my sister on annual hiking trips to Kleinwalsertal, an alpine valley on the border with Germany, during the 1990s. We—the two unsuspecting children—were covering the repatriation of savings our grandfather had hidden there from the German fisc decades earlier.

Why did Werner Faymann end Austrian resistance to the automatic exchange of information in 2013? Owing to the unanimity requirement for decisions on direct taxation, his government could have blocked the corresponding directive in the Council of the European Union. Austrian finance ministers had done so many times before. After all, bank secrecy had made the country the second-largest recipient of deposits from nonresident households in the Eurozone behind Luxembourg. This meant good business for Austrian private banks and turned peripheral regions like the Kleinwalsertal from agricultural zones into small financial centers. Moreover, the country's citizens had become firmly attached to the concept. Interview partners from across Austria's political spectrum told me that the public considered bank secrecy a "holy cow" not to be touched. Still, Faymann sharpened his butcher's knife just a few weeks before general elections in September, providing Strache's Eurosceptic FPÖ with a welcome opportunity to deplore another shift of Austrian sovereignty to Brussels.

In this book, I argue that the end of bank secrecy in Austria, and in all other traditional secrecy jurisdictions for that matter, ultimately results from a credible threat of sanctions issued by the United States. This threat was contained in a little-noticed law attached to the Obama administration's second stimulus package after the financial crisis: the Foreign Account Tax Compliance Act (FATCA). FATCA obliges foreign banks to routinely report US clients and their capital income to the Internal Revenue Service. If a bank fails to comply, the agency is allowed to withhold 30 percent of the payments this institution receives from US sources. Because of the US market's dominant role in international finance, no foreign bank could afford such a steep penalty. Accordingly, foreign banks began to lobby their home governments to abolish secrecy provisions preventing the banks' compliance with FATCA. By dismantling the legal barriers to the dissemination of bank account information, however, secrecy jurisdictions also became vulnerable to information requests from third countries. Because of a most-favored-nation clause contained in an EU directive, Austria and Luxembourg were, for instance, obliged to also exchange information with other EU member states after signing FATCA agreements with the United States. Owing to similar constraints, all of the world's traditional secrecy jurisdictions had joined a multilateral agreement on automatic information exchange by 2018.

This breakthrough stands in sharp contrast to conventional wisdom on international tax politics. According to a contractualist narrative, international capital mobility creates prohibitive enforcement costs. As soon as a tax haven makes concessions on secrecy or tax rates, so the logic predicts, investors will move their assets to a location that continues to offer the desired benefits. The payoff to remaining a tax haven thus increases with the number of governments complying with global standards. Hence, the last tax haven will benefit so much that it becomes impossible for other governments to offer equivalent side payments. In contrast, FATCA achieved global compliance with US demands through an almost costless sanctions threat. Likewise, a constructivist narrative suggests, shared international norms should protect tax havens from interventions by the international community. Since all governments wanted respect for their national sovereignty, especially when exercising their tax prerogative, they shied away from curtailing this right for others. Yet FATCA forced scores of governments to revise or repeal domestic laws, including—as in the Austrian case—their constitutions, and imposed significant adjustment costs on their economies.

Against this background, I provide a new narrative highlighting the ability of a great power like the United States to overcome the structural and normative constraints emphasized by previous accounts. Through credible sanction threats, linking market access to compliance with tax policy demands, the great power wrestles costly concessions from less powerful states, including the most sophisticated tax havens. After all, the income that zero-tax jurisdictions help to hide or divert is usually earned in major economies. If that income can no longer be channeled out tax free, the tax haven loses its raison d'être from the perspective of the investor. Accordingly, the tax haven depends even more on unhindered access to major markets than on secrecy provisions or tax breaks. At the same time, an investor will have difficulty circumventing regulation by a great power through divestment or a change of location. By definition, a great power accounts for a significant share in global demand, so withdrawing from its market comes with important opportunity costs. If the great power decides to apply its rules unequivocally to all outside investors, also choosing a different conduit for an investment will not protect the investor from its regulatory reach. Finally, the United States controls access to the world's reserve currency. Since international transactions are most often denominated in US dollars, even banks without significant US exposure need access to the currency and corresponding clearing infrastructure.

By preventing tax havens from abetting tax evasion and avoidance, however, the great power may also remove competitors for foreign investment. In fact, the Obama and Trump administrations have consistently refused to reciprocate the automatic reporting of account information they impose on everyone else. Tax evaders who used to hide their wealth in Switzerland have reacted by shifting their assets into trusts registered in secretive US states such as Nevada or South Dakota. Accordingly, the value of foreign deposits in the US has rapidly increased since the passage of FATCA, whereas it has sharply declined in most traditional secrecy jurisdictions. Although the US may thus have become the most important secrecy jurisdiction for EU residents, member states have been unable to wrestle reciprocity from the US government. The common market and consensus on automatic exchange of information with each other apparently do not suffice to match US power. The reason is that the EU suffers from regulatory dispersion in tax matters. Every decision on direct taxation, including the blacklisting of tax havens and the implementation of economic sanctions, still has to be made unanimously. Hence, a single veto is enough to prevent countermeasures from the entire EU. Unless member states centralize regulatory authority with the European Commission, the United States will thus be able to sustain its hypocritical stance on financial transparency.

If the US government has the power to tackle tax evasion by US residents with foreign accounts by imposing hypocritical standards on the rest of the world, however, a second puzzle emerges. Next to the enforcement of financial transparency, the Obama administration had also promised countermeasures to corporate tax avoidance at the outset of the administration's first term. Moreover, the administration had an opportunity to press for change in negotiations over the base erosion and profit-shifting (BEPS) project launched in 2013 by the Organisation for

Economic Co-operation and Development (OECD). Still, the administration
ended up defending the international tax system's status quo against reform proposals from European governments. Thereby, the Obama administration perpetuated an orthodox interpretation of the fundamental principles of international tax
law, which allow multinationals to geographically separate taxable income from
underlying economic activity. Why did the Obama administration use US power
to curb tax evasion by US households but not to limit tax avoidance by US multinationals?

To understand when the United States enforces and when it obstructs progress
in the global fight against tax dodging, we need to analyze the nation's domestic
politics. The easiest way for a government to maximize the sum of tax revenue and
domestic production is regressive tax reform. Such reform shifts the tax burden
from mobile capital to immobile labor and consumption. Since workers and consumers cannot usually exit the country as easily as investment, this strategy mini-
mizes the risk of losing tax base to higher tax rates. Since the rich earn a larger share
of their income from capital than the poor, whereas the poor spend a larger share of
their income on consumption than the rich, however, this strategy also shifts the
tax burden from the strongest onto the weakest shoulders and exacerbates income
inequality. Therefore, voters with a preference for redistribution often oppose
regressive tax reform. A Democratic government is thus more likely to support progressive tax reform that puts the largest burden on the strongest shoulders. For this
strategy to be effective, however, the administration needs to prevent the most
potent taxpayers—wealthy individuals and profitable corporations—from shifting
their wealth and income abroad. Hence, a Democratic administration should be in
favor of countermeasures to tax evasion and avoidance.

But this support is not enough for countermeasures to materialize. Affected
interest groups may wield enough power in the political process to block proposals increasing their effective tax burden. This power depends on their ability
to access policymakers, credibly threaten them with divestment, and convince
them of the legitimacy of their tax avoidance schemes. A multinational corporation could, for instance, threaten to cut jobs in a policymaker's electoral district
if she supports higher taxes on its foreign income. Alternatively, the corporation
could stress the legality of its tax-planning strategy, shifting the blame for tax
avoidance toward legislators writing incoherent tax codes. In contrast, wealthy
individuals who evade taxes by underreporting their foreign income break the
law. Despite their access to policymakers, these individuals may thus find it difficult to openly state their case. Tax-evading individuals should thus wield less
power in the political process than tax-avoiding multinationals. Accordingly, a
Democratic administration should adapt its position to opposition from tax-
avoiding multinationals but not to opposition from tax-evading individuals.

When we look at international tax policy from this perspective, we understand why FATCA creates new reporting requirements for foreign banks but none for US financial institutions. The Obama administration wanted to curb offshore tax evasion by US taxpayers. Simultaneously keeping US wealth managers from abetting tax evasion by foreign taxpayers would have provoked resistance from the financial sector, endangering the survival of the entire legislative project. Hence, the United States forced all other governments to deliver data but spared domestic banks from a meaningful increase in financial transparency. Likewise, we understand better why the Obama administration defended the international tax system's status quo against European attempts to curb base erosion and profit-shifting at the OECD. After its own attempts at keeping US multinationals from deferring tax payments on their foreign profits had failed, reforms proposed by European governments could have attributed some of that untaxed income to their coffers. Hence, the Obama administration decided that minimizing the foreign tax burden of US multinationals was still better than having European governments increase their tax take at the expense of the United States. Accordingly, US multinationals started to pay taxes on their foreign profits only once the Trump administration provided tax-haven conditions itself, reducing the applicable tax rate from 35 to 10.5 percent.

Does this narrative imply that international countermeasures to tax evasion and avoidance can never be implemented against the will of powerful interest groups in the United States? Since market power is decisive in international tax politics, this book suggests that bargaining dynamics will change only once the EU centralizes regulatory authority over international tax matters. Centralization would enable member states to request compliance from foreign banks and corporations as a bloc. If access to the common market was at stake, even US banks and multinationals should be willing to report account data or pay tax on their local business profits. The European Commission's state aid investigations into selective tax advantages granted to Amazon, Apple, or McDonald's may effect progress in this direction. By instructing EU tax havens to claw back forgone tax payments from privileged corporations, the Commission creates uncertainty over the legality of their sweetheart deals. As this reduces EU tax havens' attractiveness as destinations for profit-shifting, they lose their competitive advantage over other member states and may eventually become more interested in common rules.

Acknowledgments

Before entering the main discussion, I would like to thank the many bright people who took the time to read and discuss my work on its road toward publication. Without their valuable input, this book would not have been possible. First and foremost, I was very fortunate to work with Adrienne Héritier at the European University Institute (EUI). She provided orientation when needed and always asked exactly the right questions to help me improve my work. Philipp Genschel reassured me of the merit of a power-based approach to the politics of international taxation and motivated me to better explain why the European Union has been unable to harness the power of the common market. Thomas Rixen has been an incredible source of knowledge on the international tax system. He provided me with the opportunity to join the "Combatting Fiscal Fraud and Empowering Regulators" (COFFERS) project and made sure I found the time to revise my manuscript for publication amid our common work on the interaction between national and international tax policy. In this context, I gratefully acknowledge support for research and publication from the COFFERS project under the European Union's Horizon 2020 research and innovation program's grant agreement no. 727145. Patrick Emmenegger's feedback motivated me to dive deeper into the technicalities and legislative history of the qualified intermediary program and engage with the concept of structural power.

During my time at the EUI, recurrent discussions with Max Schaub, Elie Michel, Philip Rathgeb, Donagh Davis, Ludvig Lundstedt, Katharina Meissner, Magnus Schöller, Sven Steinmo, and Pepper Culpepper provided important suggestions and food for thought. Since then, this manuscript benefited from the engaging criticism of my colleagues at the University of Bamberg and in the COFFERS consortium, namely Valeska Gerstung, Frank Bandau, Leo Ahrens, Fabio Bothner, Simon Linder, Rasmus Christensen, Duncan Wigan, Markus Meinzer, and Leonard Seabrooke. At conferences where parts of this work were presented, I had the opportunity to engage in fruitful debates with Wouter Lips, Loriana Crasnic, Vincent Arel-Bundock, and Martin Hearson. Moreover, I'm particularly indebted to the forty-two individuals who took time off their schedules to tell me about their work in the international tax sphere and thereby provided the decisive empirical underpinning of this work. Likewise, I am very grateful to Sarah and Damien for hosting me during my field research in Washington, DC; to Sophie and Klaus for hosting me in Vienna; and to Sara and Moritz for hosting me in Paris.

I have also enjoyed the privilege of working with an excellent team of editors at Cornell University Press. Roger Malcolm Haydon provided straightforward guidance on how to make my argument more accessible for a general audience and organized an extremely efficient review process. Eric Helleiner showed incredible commitment, probably reading four versions of this manuscript in full, and always providing elaborate and extremely constructive comments. In combination with the thought-provoking criticism and helpful suggestions from two anonymous reviewers, his feedback guided me in revising the book's overall framing and structure, in checking my arguments and definitions for consistency, and in improving my discussion of the sources of state power.

My deepest gratitude goes to my family. My parents, Christiane and Jürgen, have unconditionally supported my intellectual journey since the beginning and shared my grandparents' tax evasion story when they felt it could help my research. My sister, Marike, has always helped out when time constraints threatened to overpower me, even taking time off at work to ease the conflict between my parental and academic duties. Finally, I'm infinitely grateful to my wife, Linda-Marie, for her everlasting love and support, for giving encouragement and kicks to the backside at the right time, and for soothing my brittle nerves for so many years. Last but not least, my most affectionate gratitude goes to my son, Paul, for making me happy every single day. I dedicate this book to Linda and him.

THE HYPOCRITICAL HEGEMON

CHANGE AND STABILITY IN GLOBAL TAX POLICY

On October 29, 2014, fifty-one governments gathered in Berlin to abolish bank secrecy. At the seventh meeting of the Global Forum on Transparency and Exchange of Information for Tax Purposes (Global Forum), they signed a multilateral agreement committing signatories to automatically inform one another of bank accounts held by their respective citizens and other local residents. Since then, an additional fifty governments have joined the agreement, including all jurisdictions that have traditionally figured on tax haven blacklists for refusing to grant administrative assistance to foreign tax authorities (see table 1.1). Since 2018, these governments have been bound by contract to implement a common reporting standard (CRS) developed by the Organisation for Economic Cooperation and Development (OECD). The CRS obliges governments to adopt rules requiring financial institutions to regularly report all capital income held by nonresident individuals and entities, as well as their account balances. In addition, domestic banks need to look through interposed trusts or shell companies when determining the beneficial owner of a new account, and also have to review ownership data for existing accounts containing more than $250,000. Global Forum members will monitor every signatory's CRS implementation in regular peer reviews and publish corresponding country reports (OECD 2014e, 2014g).

For countries formally known for their financial secrecy, the adoption of the CRS was a fundamental regulatory change. In order to comply, they had to dismantle secrecy laws, which had previously prevented the automatic reporting of client information from banks to tax authorities. The affected countries had defended such legal provisions for decades, and some had even given these provisions constitutional status. Switzerland, for instance, upgraded the breach of bank secrecy from civil to criminal offense when the French government raided the Paris offices of several Swiss banks in 1932 and refused any judicial cooperation on that basis (Guex 2000). Likewise, Austria added a provision to its constitution according to which parliament could change the bank secrecy law only with a two-thirds majority shortly before the country submitted its application for European Union (EU) membership in 1989. This should protect the secrecy provisions against requests for cooperation in tax matters (Bundesministerium für Finanzen 1988). Indeed, when the EU introduced the automatic exchange of information (AEI) on interest payments, Austria and Luxembourg were granted a temporary opt-out because of their bank secrecy laws. When the remaining member states attempted to end the opt-out, the two countries exploited the unanimity requirement for EU decisions on taxation to veto a corresponding directive six times in a row between 2009 and 2012 (Hakelberg 2015a).

TABLE 1.1   CRS Adoptions among Major Secrecy Jurisdictions as of January 15, 2018

| | OECD CRS STANDARD | |
JURISDICTION	SIGNED MULTILATERAL AGREEMENT	PASSED IMPLEMENTING LEGISLATION
Austria	yes	yes
Bahamas	yes	yes
Bahrain	yes	yes
Belgium	yes	yes
Bermuda	yes	yes
Cayman Islands	yes	yes
Curaçao	yes	yes
Guernsey	yes	yes
Hong Kong	yes (China)	yes
Isle of Man	yes	yes
Jersey	yes	yes
Luxembourg	yes	yes
Macao	yes (China)	yes
Panama	yes	yes
Singapore	yes	yes
Switzerland	yes	yes

Note: Major secrecy jurisdictions include all countries identified as offshore financial centers by the Bank for International Settlements (BIS) for "dealing primarily with nonresidents and/or in foreign currency on a scale out of proportion to the size of the host economy" (BIS 2016a, 59) and those OECD members (Austria, Belgium, Luxembourg, Switzerland) that had refused to participate in the AEI on interest payments introduced by the EU in 2003 (Rixen and Schwarz 2012).

Sources: BIS (2016b); OECD (2017a, 2018b).

Their governments' success in defending bank secrecy at the international level enabled Austrian, Luxembourgian, and Swiss banks to boost their business with foreign clients. During the first decade of the twenty-first century, Swiss financial institutions managed almost half of the world's households' offshore financial wealth, amounting to $2 trillion or 9 percent of global gross domestic product (GDP) (Zucman 2013, 33). At the same time, Austrian and Luxembourgian banks were the largest recipients of cross-border deposits from households residing in other Eurozone countries. In 2010, Luxembourg reported €20 billion, Austria €9 billion, and Germany—the EU's largest economy—merely €8 billion in bank deposits from the remaining member states of the currency union (Hakelberg 2015b, 411). This influx of foreign capital led to impressive growth rates in the financial sectors of the recipient countries but also made them highly dependent on investment from nonresidents. For instance, foreign financial wealth managed by Swiss banks equaled three times the amount of domestic wealth in 2007 (Zucman 2013, online appendix). Yet this influx was essentially driven by the promise of confidentiality, which foreign investors could exploit for tax evasion purposes among other things.[1] The latest research suggests that 80 percent of the portfolios held by Scandinavian clients with the Swiss branch of HSBC had not been declared to tax authorities by their owners during the 2000s (Alstadsæter, Johannesen, and Zucman 2017b). Likewise, US Senate investigations revealed that 90 percent of the accounts held by US clients with Union Bank of Switzerland (UBS) and Credit Suisse over the same time period had not been declared to the Internal Revenue Service (IRS) (Levin and Coleman 2008; Levin and McCain 2014). Still, the Austrian, Luxembourgian, and Swiss governments ended up conceding their financial sectors' key competitive advantage by adopting the CRS.

In addition to the economic costs, this decision also came with important political costs. For citizens in financially discreet countries, bank secrecy and its defense had often become part of their national identity. Many Austrians, for instance, believed in a narrative according to which bank secrecy had been introduced to restore trust in the country's financial system and regularize black market activity after World War II. A high level of privacy, so the story goes, should motivate Austrians to entrust their savings to local banks instead of hiding money in their mattresses.[2] As citizens became increasingly accustomed to the inability of the state to gather information on their accounts, bank secrecy attained the status of a "holy cow" in Austrian politics. No party dared to touch it for fear of the electoral consequences.[3] Likewise, many Swiss were proud of their bank secrecy law, which they wrongly believed was introduced to protect the assets of German Jews persecuted by the Nazis.[4] Policymakers exploited these narratives, despite their shaky empirical foundations, to raise popular support for bank secrecy. In policymakers' view, bank secrecy was a legitimate particularity rooted in historical circumstances that had nothing to do with the poaching of tax base from neighboring countries. In domestic politics, defending bank secrecy against outside pressure thus meant to preserve a national characteristic (Blocher 2006; Strache 2013). Nonetheless, the Austrian and Swiss governments expended considerable political capital to overcome domestic opposition to the CRS.

Given their previous defense of bank secrecy and the important economic and political costs linked to its abolition, *why did tax havens eventually agree to automatically exchange account information with foreign governments?* In this book, I argue that the end of bank secrecy in traditional secrecy jurisdictions is the result of coercion by the United States. On March 18, 2010, the US Congress passed the Obama administration's second stimulus package after the financial crisis. Attached to this package was a little-noticed law that contained a credible threat of sanctions against secrecy jurisdictions: the Foreign Account Tax Compliance Act (FATCA). The act obliges foreign financial institutions to automatically report US clients and their capital income to the IRS. If a bank fails to comply, the agency is granted authority to withhold 30 percent of the payments this institution receives from US sources (Mollohan 2010). Since the United States controls the world's largest financial market as well as central financial infrastructure like clearing houses and other interbank settlement systems, no foreign bank was willing to divest from the United States to circumvent the new reporting requirements. Instead, foreign banks began to lobby their home governments to abolish bank secrecy and other provisions preventing their compliance with FATCA (Emmenegger 2017; Grinberg 2012).

By dismantling the legal barriers to the dissemination of bank account information, however, secrecy jurisdictions also became vulnerable to information requests from third countries. Because of a most-favored-nation clause contained in an EU directive, Austria and Luxembourg were, for instance, legally obliged to exchange information with other EU member states after signing FATCA agreements with the US Treasury. Likewise, Switzerland could no longer fend off the EU's request to participate in its AEI system after it had agreed to automatically report information on bank accounts held by US residents to the IRS. By making this concession, the Swiss government had ended its principled defense of bank secrecy. Hence, Switzerland's traditional legal argument against the provision of administrative assistance to its European neighbors was no longer tenable. For financial institutions in Switzerland and other former secrecy jurisdictions, their governments' decision to transmit account data to more than one foreign government created several challenges. If other secrecy jurisdictions did not accept the AEI, former secrecy jurisdictions could lose hidden capital to foreign competitors still providing secrecy benefits. If foreign governments requested different types of information, former secrecy jurisdictions' compliance burden would increase. Therefore, traditional secrecy jurisdictions joined major developed economies in calling for a level regulatory playing field: that is, governments around the world should apply a single global AEI standard based on FATCA. Against this background, the OECD developed the CRS and the multilateral agreement for its implementation (see chapter 5).

Yet a fundamental limitation remains. After imposing the AEI on the rest of the world, the Obama administration eventually refused to reciprocate the reporting of account information under its bilateral FATCA treaties and did not sign the multilateral agreement binding governments to the CRS (cf. OECD 2018b; US Treasury 2012a). Consequently, US banks currently have to follow much weaker transparency standards than banks in other countries. For instance, US banks are still under no obligation to look through trusts when determining account ownership (cf. FinCEN 2016). Unlike in countries respecting the CRS, in the United States foreign account holders can thus remain anonymous when they put their financial wealth in trust. Accordingly, the number of corresponding contractual relationships registered in secretive US states such as Nevada or South Dakota has rapidly increased since the multilateral adoption of the CRS (Scannell and Houlder 2016). Likewise, the value of foreign deposits in US banks has grown substantially, whereas the traditional secrecy jurisdictions listed in table 1.1 have incurred important losses (Hakelberg and Schaub 2018). In fact, Casi, Spengel, and Stage (2018) show that deposits from the EU and other OECD countries in the United States grew by 9 percent between 2014—when traditional secrecy jurisdictions adopted the CRS—and 2017. Concomitantly, such deposits diminished by 14 percent on average in the group of formerly secretive countries they study, including Guernsey, Hong Kong, the Isle of Man, Jersey and Macau.

Although the United States may thus replace Switzerland as the most important secrecy jurisdiction for European investors, the EU, which matches US market power when acting in unison (see chapter 2), has not yet managed to wrestle full reciprocity from the Obama and Trump administrations. The reason is that member states, which found consensus on AEI within the EU, still disagree on including the United States in their blacklist of tax havens facing collective sanctions (cf. Council of the European Union 2017; European Commission 2016e). Because of the unanimity requirement in tax matters discussed earlier, the veto of a single government is enough to prevent this decision, and several export-dependent member states, including Germany, fear an inclusion of the United States could provoke retaliatory measures in the trade arena.[5] Since internal division has prevented the EU from checking their hypocrisy, successive US governments have thus been able to uphold a highly redistributive international AEI regime, inviting committed foreign tax evaders to shift their hidden financial wealth from traditional secrecy jurisdictions into the United States. While Austrian tax advisers have, in response, deplored a loss of business to US competition,[6] one of their American colleagues rebuffed European criticism of FATCA's lack of reciprocity simply by stating that "fair is what you can get away with, and the United States has the power to defend this outcome."[7]

Coercion Transcends Structural and Normative Constraints

The unexpected end of bank secrecy in traditional secrecy jurisdictions reflects the ability of a great power like the United States to unilaterally effect fundamental change in international tax policy through coercion. This interpretation stands in sharp contrast to the two established narratives to international tax policy: the contractualist and the constructivist perspective. From the contractualist perspective, an international agreement must be based on the common interest of the signatory states. Otherwise, disadvantaged governments will either refuse to cooperate or defect from the agreement (Dehejia and Genschel 1999; Rixen 2008). If this approach were still correct, tax havens would expect joint gains from the multilateral AEI and participate voluntarily. From the constructivist perspective, shared regulative norms, including the respect for national sovereignty, have traditionally prevented powerful governments from forcing tax havens to remove domestic legal hurdles to the dissemination of account information (Webb 2004; Sharman 2006b). If this reading continued to apply, the US sanctions threat contained in FATCA should have been preceded by normative change legitimizing the use of coercion against tax havens. To exclude the possibilities that tax havens' participation in the multilateral AEI results from voluntary consent or normative change instead of coercion, I will thus show two things in this section. First, the structural constraints precluding a common interest in countermeasures to tax evasion were still in place when the US Congress passed FATCA. Second, there was no need for normative change, because regulative norms have never consistently prevented the US from interfering with the legal systems of tax havens.

Structural Constraints to Cooperation from Tax Havens

The contractualist narrative of international tax policy identifies two structural constraints preventing governments from reaching agreement on countermeasures to tax evasion: an asymmetric prisoner's dilemma and a weakest-link problem. The asymmetric prisoner's dilemma results from the uneven distribution of benefits from tax competition between small and large countries. Relative to their small domestic capital stock, small countries can attract a lot of foreign capital with a tax cut. Hence, they can compensate for tax revenue lost to a lower tax rate with tax revenue generated from a broader tax base. In contrast, large countries can—relative to their large domestic capital stock—only attract a small amount of foreign capital with a tax cut. As large countries find it more difficult to compensate for a lower tax rate with a broader tax base, they lose the tax competition for capital to small countries. Accordingly, large countries have an interest in international tax coordination, whereas small countries prefer tax competition (Genschel and Schwarz 2011; Wilson 1999). Since most governments assert a right to tax the worldwide income of individuals resident within the government's territory, however, the crucial prerequisite for the competitiveness of small tax haven countries is secrecy. The low tax rates they offer apply only if the taxable capital income of a foreign account-holder remains hidden from the tax authorities in her country of residence.

Whereas the asymmetric prisoner's dilemma results from interest heterogeneity between small and large countries, the weakest-link problem prevents large countries from changing the preferences of small countries through side payments. Since small countries gain less revenue from tax competition than large countries lose, because of the small countries' lower rates, at first sight there seems to remain scope for a mutually beneficial agreement, in which large countries compensate small countries for refraining from tax competition. For the agreement to be effective, however, all of the world's tax havens would have to participate. Otherwise, tax evaders seeking low rates and secrecy could simply transfer their financial wealth to the remaining uncooperative jurisdictions. If large countries offered a compensatory deal, tax havens would thus have an incentive to drag their feet. The longer they stay out of an expanding coalition of cooperating governments, the more they benefit from reduced competition in the tax haven market, and the more expensive their compensation becomes for large countries (Elsayyad and Konrad 2012). From the contractualist perspective, the expectation of an exponential rise in enforcement costs, sometimes created by cautionary tales of capital flight disseminated by the financial industry, causes otherwise powerful governments of large countries to shy away from initiatives against tax evasion (Dehejia and Genschel 1999; Rixen 2013).

If the asymmetric prisoner's dilemma and weakest-link problem had somehow disappeared before the United States issued a credible threat of sanctions through FATCA, enabling secrecy jurisdictions to voluntarily agree to the AEI, we would thus have to observe at least one of three things: (1) a reduction in the benefit secrecy jurisdictions reap from abetting tax evasion reflected in an outflow of foreign financial wealth or a shrinking contribution of financial services

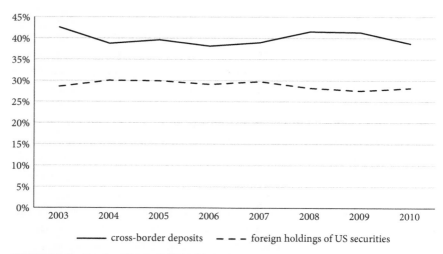

FIGURE 1.1. Foreign Financial Wealth in Secrecy Jurisdictions before FATCA (Percentage of Total)

Note: Cross-border deposits reflect deposit liabilities of banks in the respective reporting country to all foreign households and nonfinancial corporations. Foreign holdings of US securities include all forms of equity and all debt securities issued in the United States and held or managed by households, corporations, or financial institutions in a foreign country. Secrecy jurisdictions include all countries identified as offshore financial centers by the BIS for "dealing primarily with nonresidents and/or in foreign currency on a scale out of proportion to the size of the host economy" (BIS 2016a, 59), and those OECD members (Austria, Belgium, Luxembourg, Switzerland) that had refused to participate in the AEI on interest payments introduced by the EU in 2003 (also see table 1.1.). Sources: BIS (2018); US Treasury (2017a).

to a tax haven's overall economic performance; (2) a decrease in the importance foreign depositors in secrecy jurisdictions attach to financial secrecy, removing the link between information reporting and capital flight; or (3) an offer of side payments from large countries to secrecy jurisdictions despite the high expected cost of these payments.

To assess the first point, I draw on the two most widely used data sources in research on the relevance of secrecy jurisdictions in global financial relations: cross-border deposits from households and nonfinancial corporations reported by the Bank for International Settlements (BIS) and foreign holdings of US securities reported by the US Treasury (cf. Alstadsæter, Johannesen, and Zucman 2017b; Desai and Dharmapala 2010; Huizinga and Nicodème 2004; Johannesen and Zucman 2014). As figure 1.1 illustrates, the share of secrecy jurisdictions in the global total of both measures remained constant during the eight years preceding the adoption of FATCA. Whereas secrecy jurisdictions' share of worldwide cross-border deposits fluctuated around 40 percent, secrecy jurisdictions accounted for a third of all foreign holdings of US securities during this time period. We can thus conclude that secrecy jurisdictions' popularity among foreign

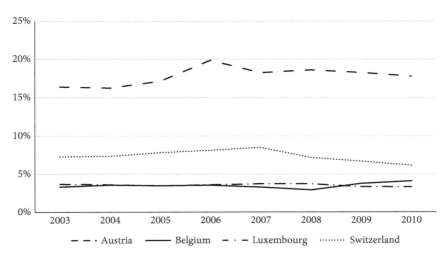

FIGURE 1.2. The Share of Financial Services in OECD Secrecy Jurisdictions' Gross Value Added

Note: Gross value added (GVA) is defined as an industry sector's output minus intermediate consumption. The sum of GVA over all sectors plus taxes on products minus subsidies on products gives a country's gross domestic product (GDP). The chart is limited to OECD secrecy jurisdictions because GVA data of comparable detail are not available for the remaining jurisdictions included in table 1.1. Previous research suggests, however, that the economic dependence of small island havens on the provision of financial services is much higher (Christensen, Shaxson, and Wigan 2016).

Source: Eurostat (2018).

depositors wishing to earn a lowly taxed return on US securities had not deteriorated before the adoption of FATCA. Likewise, data on countries' main GDP aggregates reported by Eurostat, the EU's statistics office, suggest that even in relatively large secrecy jurisdictions with rather diversified national economies, the provision of financial services continued to make an important contribution to national economic performance despite the financial crisis of 2008. In Luxembourg, the share of financial services in gross value added (GVA) increased from 16 percent in 2003 to 18 percent in 2010. In Austria and Switzerland, the corresponding shares declined only marginally, from 4 to 3 percent and from 7 to 6 percent, respectively, over the same time period (see figure 1.2). Accordingly, dependence on the financial sector had not declined significantly in any of these countries before FATCA.

To assess the second point, I draw on previous research on the relationship between the level of financial secrecy provided by a given country, and its stock of financial wealth. Huizinga and Nicodème (2004) find, for instance, that a country's adoption of domestic information reporting from banks to tax authorities increases the value of resident households' foreign deposits by 28 percent. That is, many depositors prefer moving their savings abroad to disclosing their capital income to their local tax office. Likewise, Johannesen and Zucman (2014) show that a secrecy jurisdiction's signature of a bilateral Tax Information Exchange Agreement (TIEA) reduces the value of cross-border deposits from the treaty partner's households by 22 percent. This result is striking since TIEAs, which were promoted by the OECD just before the emergence of AEI as the new global standard, merely provide for information exchange upon request. To receive administrative assistance from the treaty partner, a tax authority needs to provide prior evidence of tax evasion by a clearly identified individual. Since this type of evidence is exactly what tax authorities are usually lacking, a secrecy jurisdiction's consent to information exchange upon request does not increase the risk of detection for tax evaders (Eccleston and Woodward 2014; Genschel and Rixen 2015). Still, they showed a substantial reaction. Instead of withdrawing their deposits from the secrecy jurisdiction entering into a TIEA with their home country, however, most tax evaders merely shifted formal account ownership to a trust or shell company registered in a second secrecy jurisdiction. This behavior explains why overall foreign deposits in secrecy jurisdictions remained constant despite the observed reduction in deposits from countries with a bilateral TIEA relationship (Johannesen and Zucman 2014). We can thus conclude that tax evaders remained highly sensitive even to tiny changes in the level of financial secrecy when FATCA was adopted.

Finally, the historical record shows that secrecy jurisdictions have not been compensated for participating in the AEI either before or after the US Congress passed FATCA (cf. Eccleston and Gray 2014; Eggenberger and Emmenegger 2015; Palan and Wigan 2014). The first reason is that compensating secrecy jurisdictions is a "hard political sell for democratically elected governments" (Genschel and Schwarz 2011, 354). After all, large-country governments would spend the money of honest taxpayers to compensate secrecy jurisdictions for ceasing to serve the dishonest. Accordingly, compensation has never been seriously debated in negotiations over tax cooperation at the OECD (Sharman 2006b, 153–54). The second reason is that compensatory arguments rely on the implicit assumption that governments compete for tax revenue, which could be replaced by handouts from large countries. It seems more realistic, however, to assume that governments compete for tax base, because incoming foreign capital not only increases tax revenue in secrecy jurisdictions but also raises economic activity, wages, and employment—which, in turn, cause increased revenue from the taxation of labor and reduced spending on unemployment benefits (Genschel and Seelkopf 2015). These positive spillover effects are most likely more important than the increased revenue from capital taxation itself, meaning that handouts represent a poor alternative. While large countries are thus highly unlikely to offer compensation, secrecy jurisdictions are just as unlikely to accept it.

In sum, a substantial part of secrecy jurisdiction's economic output continued to depend on the exploitation of large stocks of foreign financial wealth during the first decade of the twenty-first century. The size of these stocks was a function of the level of financial secrecy offered to foreign depositors, and large countries did not offer secrecy jurisdictions compensation for becoming more transparent. Accordingly, their governments expected significant economic losses from replacing bank secrecy with the routine reporting of foreign account-holders to the tax authorities of their home countries. For instance, the Luxembourgian statistics office predicted a decline of 5 to 10 percent in the financial sector's contribution to GVA, leading to a 0.5 percent decline in overall employment, before Xavier Bettel, the country's prime minister, signed the multilateral AEI agreement (Adam 2014). Likewise, the Swiss Federal Council, the country's executive organ, expected economic losses from the AEI's "relatively high implementation costs for financial institutions," and a "certain outflow of assets managed in Switzerland on behalf of foreign private clients" that may not be compensated by new inflows (Schweizerischer Bundesrat 2015, 52). Hence, we can conclude that secrecy jurisdictions did not accept the AEI to benefit from joint gains but rather did so despite expecting significant costs. Since cooperation leaves them worse off than the status quo ante, cooperation cannot result from voluntary consent.

Normative Constraints to Bullying Tax Havens

Against this background, coercion suggests itself as a plausible alternative. According to the constructivist narrative of international tax policy, however, an alliance of tax havens and libertarian lobbyists has in the past mobilized the regulative norm of nonintervention to prevent the OECD and United States from enforcing tax cooperation. This argument is based on the analysis of the OECD campaign against "harmful tax competition" (HTC) launched in 1998 to prevent tax havens from poaching foreign tax base through the provision of financial secrecy and preferential tax regimes. To pressure tax havens into compliance with the OECD demands, including the exchange of account information upon request, OECD members threatened tax havens with collective sanctions. In response, the governments of several tax-competitive island states argued that using coercive means against fragile developing countries was inappropriate and inconsistent with the OECD's central missions of promoting cooperation and sustainable growth. In parallel, right-wing American think tanks persuaded the incoming Bush administration that the OECD campaign infringed upon fiscal sovereignty and replaced efficiency-enhancing international competition with a global tax cartel. From the constructivist perspective, these arguments drew their force from the apparent mismatch between the OECD's identity as an impartial provider of expertise and the use of coercive power, and the positive connotation of competition among the Bush administration's senior officials. Hence, the United States and the OECD were persuaded to delay and eventually rule out the use of sanctions against tax havens in 2003 (Sharman 2006b; Webb 2004).

Only six years later, however, the Obama administration developed FATCA, which did exactly what the regulative norm of nonintervention was supposed to rule out: on pain of significant penalties, the act obliges all foreign banks, including those from tax havens, to report US account-holders to the IRS, thereby imposing legal amendments on foreign countries and undermining their competitiveness in the attraction of hidden wealth. From the constructivist perspective, the adoption of FATCA must thus have been preceded by normative change legitimizing the use of economic sanctions against tax havens. Yet as I will further elaborate in chapters 3 and 4, the historical record shows that the norm of nonintervention never consistently prevented the US government from interfering with the legal systems of tax havens, including during the time period from which constructivist scholars draw the bulk of their empirical evidence. In fact, the persuasiveness of the normative arguments emphasized by the constructivist narrative varied considerably with the US administration's political orientation and the legality of the tax minimization strategies targeted by economic sanctions. Instead of normative change, a change in government paired with a strong focus on criminal tax evasion were decisive for the adoption of FATCA.

As mentioned above, the constructivist narrative recognizes the importance of the US administration's political orientation. According to Webb (2004, 813), the Republican administration of George W. Bush was "ideologically predisposed to accept the critiques of the right-wing coalition that had formed in the US to oppose the [OECD campaign against harmful tax competition.]" In fact, tax competition was an important justification for the Bush administration's domestic tax policy agenda. From its perspective, taxes on corporate profits and capital income had to be cut to preserve US competitiveness in the attraction of investment. Hence, senior officials perceived support for an OECD project framed by libertarian lobbyists as a socialist plot against international competition as incompatible with the Bush administration's general approach to tax reform (see chapter 4). When the administration's party ideology did not resonate with the normative arguments deployed in favor of tax havens, however, the US also did not shy away from interfering with their legal systems. In contrast to the Bush administration, the Clinton administration had defended the progressivity of the income tax during its tenure. In the Clinton administration's view, tax evasion undermined the tax system's perceived fairness, thereby reducing the readiness of ordinary citizens to voluntarily comply with the tax code. Since preventing secrecy jurisdictions from abetting tax evasion by US citizens was perfectly compatible with this tax policy agenda, arguments mobilizing the norm of nonintervention in defense of tax havens gained little traction with Democratic officials. Accordingly, the Clinton administration did use coercive pressure against noncooperative jurisdictions (see chapter 3).

To begin with, the Clinton Treasury Department backed the OECD's sanctions threat in public statements and through the inclusion of agreed-on defensive measures among the revenue proposals attached to its last budget (Associated Press 2000b; US Treasury 2000). While US support lasted, several major tax havens, including Bermuda and the Cayman Islands, committed to applying the OECD standard for information exchange upon request (Government of Bermuda 2000; Governor of the Cayman Islands 2000). More important, however, the Clinton administration introduced the qualified intermediary (QI) program for foreign financial institutions wishing to exempt their clients from withholding taxes on the return to US securities. In order to become a QI and benefit from the exemption, banks had to report US clients and their income from US sources to the IRS and withhold US taxes on payments to foreigners (IRS 2000). Although the program contained a gaping loophole—the absence of a requirement to look through legal entities when identifying account owners allowed foreign banks to hide their US clients behind shell companies (Levin and Coleman 2006)—the QI program still forced several governments to create exemptions from their secrecy provisions. For instance, the Swiss finance ministry issued a regulation freeing compliance officers responsible for the implementation of the QI program from their obligations under the country's bank secrecy law, an act of administrative overreach later criticized by the federal council (Schweizerischer Bundesrat 2012).

Yet the salience of arguments mobilizing the norm of nonintervention varied not just with the US government's political orientation. Much to the chagrin of right-wing American think tanks, even the Bush administration did not respond to all of their normative appeals. In fact, the libertarian lobbying coalition argued against international countermeasures to both harmful tax practices identified by the OECD: the provision of PTRs for foreign firms and financial secrecy. In the view of the lobbying coalition, forcing tax havens to remove PTRs came down to the creeping harmonization of tax rates, infringed on fiscal sovereignty, and would eventually "hamstring America's competitive advantage in the world economy" (Mitchell 2001c, 24). Likewise, the coalition framed the attempt to lift financial secrecy as an attack on the right to privacy, inviting high-tax European nations to use the OECD to impose additional reporting requirements also on the United

States, which was itself allowing foreigners to invest confidentially (Task Force on Information Exchange and Financial Privacy 2002). Paul O'Neill, the Bush administration's secretary of the Treasury, embraced the first argument. After several meetings with libertarian lobbyists, he explained to his OECD colleagues that the United States was in favor of tax competition, as it forced governments to become more efficient. Therefore, obliging tax havens to remove tax regimes designed to encourage foreign investment ran counter to the Bush administration's tax policy priorities (O'Neill 2001c). In contrast, O'Neill discarded libertarian concerns over restrictions to privacy, and welcomed "the priority placed on transparency and cooperation to facilitate effective tax information exchange" (O'Neill 2001a, 82).

In accordance with O'Neill's stance, the Bush administration linked its further participation in the OECD initiative to the removal of all recommendations interfering with national tax codes, thereby forcing the remaining member states to adopt the US position. At the same time, the Bush administration did not oppose the blacklisting of countries based on transparency and exchange of information criteria, and maintained the Clinton administration's QI program, which the Treasury could have repealed by regulation. As I will further elaborate in chapter 4, this ambivalent response to normative arguments from libertarian lobbyists had two main reasons. First, information exchange did not interfere with national tax codes, and therefore did not oblige tax havens to remove regimes enabling multinationals to avoid taxes elsewhere. From the perspective of Secretary O'Neill this meant that information exchange did not interfere with international tax competition, which he and the libertarian opponents to tax harmonization interpreted as a desirable constraint on government profligacy. Second, tax evasion, the activity to be tackled by information exchange, was a criminal offense. Providing law enforcement agencies with additional information to prosecute such offenses matched the law-and-order instincts of many Republicans.[8] Hence, O'Neill underlined, he had taken an oath obliging him to execute US tax laws as written, which implied going after those "who illegally evade taxes by hiding income in offshore accounts" (O'Neill 2001a, 82).

Against this background, we can conclude that the importance of normative constraints to the use of coercion against tax havens has been highly contingent on the US government's political orientation and the legality of the tax minimization strategy targeted by regulation. Instead of normative change, the change of power from the Bush to the Obama administration and a strong focus on criminal tax evasion were decisive for the adoption of FATCA in 2010. As I will argue later, a Democratic government and legal constraints on the discursive power of otherwise influential interest groups are, indeed, the main preconditions for the use of coercion against tax havens by the US government. In their absence, multinationals and wealthy individuals prevent effective action.

When Does a Great Power Enforce Change?

Secrecy jurisdictions have not voluntarily agreed to participate in the AEI, nor have norms consistently prevented the US government from interfering with these jurisdictions' legal systems. The main lesson from the unexpected end of bank secrecy is thus that a great power like the United States can effect fundamental change in international tax policy and the domestic tax policies of less powerful countries, if necessary, through coercion. A government reaches great power status if it controls an internal market large enough to reduce its dependence on international trade and investment relative to the government's negotiating partners and uses its regulatory capacity to effectively restrict market access for foreign firms or investors (Simmons 2001; Bach and Newman 2010). When both elements are in place, a great power can issue credible sanction threats, linking noncompliance with its tax policy demands to exclusion from its domestic market. Small countries have to play along, since their firms earn a substantial share of their profits in the great power's market and therefore depend on access (Drezner 2008; Krasner 1976). The foreign portfolio investment placed through financial institutions in major secrecy jurisdictions is, for instance, highly concentrated in a few major markets, particularly the United States (see chapter 2). If private banks in secrecy jurisdictions lost access, their business model would be at risk. After all, they mainly serve as conduits through which a foreign investor can relieve the return she earns on an investment in a third country of its tax burden. Without access to major financial markets, her investment opportunities decrease, her return shrinks, and the advantages of her offshore arrangement disappear. Accordingly, private banks in secrecy jurisdictions depend even more on access to major markets than they depend on their promise of confidentiality.

If the United States can unilaterally effect fundamental change in international tax policy, however, a second puzzle emerges. Whereas FATCA significantly increases financial transparency in countries other than the United States and thereby goes a long way toward curbing tax evasion by US households, a series of data leaks, investigative reports, and academic studies show that tax avoidance by US multinationals has continued unabatedly over the past decade (Day 2015; Gamperl, Obermaier, and Obermayer 2017; Levin and McCain 2013). According to the latest estimates, the US fisc loses at least twice as much annual tax revenue to corporate profit-shifting as to tax evasion by households with offshore accounts (Clausing 2016; Zucman 2014; Tørsløv, Wier, and Zucman 2018).[9] This situation persists, even though the Obama administration, which initiated FATCA in response to the UBS scandal of 2008, was equally committed to curbing corporate tax avoidance at the outset of the administration's term. In fact, President Obama and Secretary of the Treasury Timothy Geithner announced a two-pronged strategy for "leveling the playing field" for US taxpayers when presenting their first budget and revenue proposals in May 2009. In addition to a "[crackdown] on the abuse of tax havens by individuals," which eventually evolved into FATCA, this strategy included countermeasures to the indefinite deferral of tax payments on foreign profits and the circumvention of controlled foreign company (CFC) rules by US multinationals (Office of the Press Secretary 2009).

To pressure legislators and business into the adoption of these measures, the Obama administration initially supported a British-German initiative for an OECD project against corporate tax base erosion and profit-shifting (BEPS) in the G20. The original intent behind the BEPS project was "to ensure that profits are taxed where economic activities occur and value is created" (G20 Leaders 2013, 4). The emphasis on a realignment of taxation and real economic activity was a response to a series of investigative reports showing that US multinationals such as Amazon, Apple, Google, and Starbucks did not pay taxes on their foreign profits either in the European source countries where they made a large share of their turnover or at their place of residence in the United States where they developed most of their intellectual property. Instead, they manipulated royalty and interest payments between their foreign subsidiaries so as to divert taxable income to corporate tax havens such as Bermuda, Ireland, or the Netherlands where no or only limited economic activity took place (Bergin 2012; Griffiths 2012; Levin and McCain 2013; Murphy 2009). As countermeasures, the draft reports on BEPS released by the OECD's committee on fiscal affairs (CFA) proposed three crucial changes. First, the transfer pricing guidelines should be revised so as to give tax examiners greater leeway in the reassessment of transactions between related firms (OECD 2014b). Second, the definition of permanent establishment (PE) in the OECD's model tax treaty should be expanded to prevent firms from artificially avoiding a taxable presence in a source country (OECD 2014f). Third, multinationals should be obliged to deliver annual reports, breaking down their profits, sales, payroll, and internal payments on a country-by-country basis, thus facilitating the detection of mismatches (OECD 2014c).

In the context of the BEPS project, however, the Obama administration did not foster change through the enforcement of a regulatory template, as it did with FATCA in parallel negotiations over multilateral AEI. Instead, the administration ended up defending the regulatory status quo, thereby perpetuating an orthodox interpretation of the fundamental principles of international tax law, which allow multinationals to geographically separate taxable income from underlying economic activity. First, US negotiators made sure that tax examiners can only adjust the price of a transaction between related firms under exceptional circumstances: the transaction has to have taken place less than five years ago and involve an intangible asset, whose ex post value does not match the firms' ex ante projections for clearly foreseeable reasons (Finley 2016; OECD 2015a). That is, multinationals merely have to adjust their projections to their profit-shifting objectives to avoid any risk of reassessment. Second, the CFA made proposed changes to the PE definition optional after the US representative threatened to reserve against their inclusion in the model tax treaty (Martin 2015; OECD 2015e). Accordingly, both parties to an existing bilateral tax treaty have to endorse the new definition to make it effective. Third, the United States—along with other governments—greatly reduced the transparency created through country-by-country reports by insisting on their confidentiality and removing royalty, interest, and service fee payments from the list of reportable items (Stewart 2014; OECD 2015d).

Why did the Obama administration use US power to curb tax evasion by US households but not to limit tax avoidance by US multinationals? In this book, I argue that a Democratic administration is, indeed, a necessary condition for the enforcement of countermeasures to tax evasion and avoidance by the United States. Democratic party ideology—mainly defined by affluent egalitarians—has traditionally endorsed progressive tax reform in accordance with the ability-to-pay principle: that is, the tax rate should rise with the taxpayer's income to ensure that the strongest shoulders carry the largest fiscal burden (Bartels 2009). For a progressive tax system to work, however, the most potent taxpayers—wealthy individuals and profitable corporations—also have to be taxed on their global income. Otherwise, their effective tax rate falls and the revenue necessary to relieve the middle and lower classes disappears. Therefore, Democratic tax reform depends on the deterrence of both: tax evasion by wealthy individuals with offshore accounts and tax avoidance by multinationals with large foreign profits. In contrast, Republican party ideology—mainly defined by affluent libertarians—has traditionally favored flat taxes on capital income and corporate profits. From this perspective, saving and investment by wealthy individuals is decisive for economic growth. Hence, the tax system should encourage corresponding decisions. Otherwise—so the Laffer curve suggests—capital flight is the likely result (Bartels 2009). Instead of posing a challenge, tax evasion and avoidance thus provide an important justification for Republican tax reform. Here, the objective is to outplay rather than subdue competition from tax havens.

Yet a Democratic administration is insufficient for the enforcement of countermeasures to tax evasion and avoidance by the United States. Affected domestic interest groups may wield enough power in the political process to block proposals increasing the tax burden on their foreign income. This power depends on their ability to access policymakers, credibly threaten them with divestment, and convince them of the legitimacy of the affected groups' tax minimization strategies (Fairfield 2010; Fuchs and Lederer 2008). A multinational corporation could, for instance, threaten to cut jobs in a policymaker's electoral district if she supports higher taxes on its foreign income. Alternatively, the corporation could stress the legality of its tax planning strategy, shifting the blame for tax avoidance toward legislators writing incoherent tax codes. In contrast, wealthy individuals who evade taxes by underreporting their foreign income break the law. Despite their access to policymakers, they will thus find it difficult to openly state their case, since the public rarely considers crime legitimate and policymakers usually avoid lenience when debates over law enforcement become politically salient (Kirchler, Maciejovsky, and Schneider 2003; Stuntz 2001). Tax-evading individuals thus wield less power in the political process than tax-avoiding multinationals. Accordingly, only the combination of a Democratic administration and an illegal tax minimization strategy awaiting regulation is sufficient for the United States to enforce countermeasures.

When we look at international tax policy from this perspective, we understand why FATCA creates new reporting requirements for foreign banks but none for US financial institutions. The Obama administration wanted to curb tax evasion by US households with offshore accounts. Simultaneously keeping US wealth managers from abetting tax evasion by foreign taxpayers, however, would have provoked resistance from the financial sector, endangering the survival of the entire legislative project. Hence, the US forced all other governments to deliver data but spared domestic banks from a meaningful increase in financial transparency (see chapter 5). Likewise, we understand better why the Obama administration eventually defended the international tax system's status quo in negotiations over the BEPS project's final recommendations. Because of business opposition, Democratic attempts at ending the deferral of tax payments on foreign profits had failed, depriving the administration of a domestic regulatory model. Reforms proposed by European governments could have attributed a larger share of US multinationals' foreign profits to their own coffers. Hence, the Obama administration decided that minimizing the foreign tax burden of US multinationals was still better than having European governments increase their tax take at the expense of the US (see chapter 6). As a result, US multinationals started to pay taxes on their foreign profits only once the Trump administration provided tax haven conditions itself, reducing the tax rate on repatriated income from 35 to 10.5 percent (Drucker 2018).

My emphasis on the interaction between party ideology and business power in American politics runs counter to two alternative explanations for the emergence and different outcomes of bargaining over multilateral AEI and the BEPS project. According to the first explanation, the financial crisis provided exceptionally permissive conditions for multilateral initiatives against tax evasion and avoidance by creating the need for bank bailouts and stimulus packages, which exacerbated the budget constraints of many governments (Eccleston 2012); by weakening the lobbying position of finance both in secrecy jurisdictions and the United States (Emmenegger 2017; Eccleston and Gray 2014); and by imposing fiscal austerity on voters, thus increasing the political salience of revelations showing that corporations and wealthy individuals were not paying their fair share of tax (Seabrooke and Wigan 2016). While these mechanisms certainly influenced the timing and speed of negotiations, none of them has proved decisive for the proposal and eventual (non-)adoption of countermeasures to tax evasion and avoidance at the international level.

In fact, Barack Obama (2007), motivated by the redistributive goal of restoring tax fairness for the middle class, had already turned the enforcement of new information exchange standards and the strengthening of CFC rules into important campaign pledges in September 2007—that is, half a year before the failure of Bear Stearns, the first crisis-related collapse of a major bank, in March 2008, and more than a year before the adoption of the Troubled Assets Relief Program (TARP), the US government's first bailout package, in October 2008. Accordingly, the Obama administration's proposal of FATCA in 2009 corresponded to tax policy priorities defined before the budgetary fallout from the financial crisis became clear. These priorities rather resulted from revelations orchestrated by Carl Levin, the Democratic chairman of the Senate Permanent Subcommittee on Investigations (PSI). Under his leadership, the body's reports and hearings exposed that Liechtenstein Global Trust (LGT) and UBS had conspired to circumvent the reporting of US clients to the IRS, a legal obligation flowing from their participation in the US Treasury's QI program (Levin and Coleman 2006, 2008). This program, in turn, had been introduced by the Clinton administration in 2000 when the federal budget was balanced. Still, one of its main purposes was to increase compliance from US taxpayers with foreign accounts (see chapter 3).

Moreover, the US financial industry did not have to be on the defensive to let the QI program and FATCA pass. The industry simply was not negatively affected by the programs, which created new reporting requirements for foreign banks but none for US financial institutions. Instead, the QI program reduced the regulatory burden related to US banks' role as withholding agents by shifting responsibility for the correct identification of foreign recipients of US-source income to foreign banks. By obliging foreign banks to disclose the identities of US account holders to their US withholding agents, the program moreover provided US banks with an opportunity to lure away their foreign competitors' wealthy clients (see chapter 3). Likewise, FATCA only obliges foreign banks to report their US clients' capital income to the IRS. The US government's bilateral FATCA agreements with foreign countries do not grant reciprocity, and the United States does not participate in the multilateral AEI agreement (see chapter 5). According to a former US Treasury official, the Obama administration spared US banks from new reporting requirements because their regulatory burden had already increased in the aftermath of the financial crisis.[10] Hence, if the US financial industry was weakened, this weakness created lenience rather than severity among tax officials in the Obama administration.

Finally, the crisis certainly increased the political salience of scandals revealing that wealthy individuals and corporations shirked their fiscal obligations at a time of budgetary stress. The PSI's 2006 report on the circumvention of the QI program, for instance, received much less media coverage than the 2008 follow-up although the first report essentially contained the same information.[11] Also the British and German governments would not have proposed the BEPS project without the steady stream of investigative reports between 2009 and 2012, exposing tax avoidance by US multinationals (see chapter 6). Yet the Clinton administration's adoption of the QI program demonstrates that Democrats also introduced new reporting requirements for foreign banks in the absence of a tax scandal breaking in the aftermath of a financial crisis (see chapter 3). Likewise, unprecedented public awareness of the shortcomings of the international tax system after the crisis was not enough to break business opposition to meaningful changes. The key request of civil society organizations, for instance—the publication of country-by-country reports—was included in the BEPS project's final recommendations, but the US and other governments severely reduced the reports' effectiveness by insisting on their confidentiality and removing information on intrafirm transactions from the list of reportable items (see chapter 6). As one of the main advocates for country-by-country reporting concluded, "the greatest multinational corporate transparency measure to be agreed by international policymakers in recent decades, has been strangled at birth" (Cobham 2015b).[12]

According to the second alternative explanation, different balances of power in international bargaining over countermeasures to tax evasion and tax avoidance were decisive for the Obama administration's success in enforcing multilateral AEI and its parallel failure to focus the BEPS project on the adoption of CFC rules. From this perspective, the global dominance of the US capital market, indeed, provides the US government with unmatched power in bargaining over the regulation of financial institutions, including their tax-related reporting obligations. In contrast, the foreign tax credit—a provision in US tax law reducing US corporate tax by the amount of foreign taxes paid—makes the US government's tax revenue contingent on the foreign tax burden of US multinationals, over which the US government allegedly has no control. Hence, foreign governments can check US power in bargaining over countermeasures to tax avoidance by threatening to increase taxes on US multinationals at source, thereby effectively reducing the tax revenue of the United States (Grinberg 2015; Lips 2019).

This explanation departs from the erroneous assumption that the resistance of foreign governments prevented the Obama administration from pushing for the adoption of stronger GFC rules during the BEPS project. Instead, the administration had already failed to implement corresponding measures domestically because of opposition from US multinationals. Therefore, the US government lacked a domestic regulatory template during negotiations over the BEPS project, initially opening agenda space for governments seeking to expand the taxation of multinationals at source. Between the publication of the project's draft reports and the adoption of final recommendations, however, the Obama administration defended the international tax system's status quo against all attempts at a significant expansion of source countries' right to tax (see chapter 6). Thereby, the administration acted in accordance with the traditional international tax policy of US governments, which have since the adoption of the foreign tax credit in 1918 forged an international tax regime that reduces source country taxation to an absolute minimum (Avi-Yonah 2007; Picciotto 1992).[13] Rather than being vulnerable to tax increases at source, the United States has for a century used its market power to enforce international standards and bilateral tax treaties that prevent source countries from such increases.

How the Argument Unfolds

Whether international rules against tax evasion and avoidance are tightened or not, essentially depends on the domestically defined preferences of the United States. The US government enforces tighter rules when a Democratic administration is in power and proposed regulation targets a clearly illegal tax minimization strategy like tax evasion by individuals with offshore accounts. The status quo prevails under a Republican administration or when proposed changes affect legal tax avoidance strategies by powerful interest groups such as US multinationals. To show that this dynamic applied not only in the aftermath of the financial crisis of 2008 but shaped all OECD attempts at curbing tax evasion and avoidance since the abolition of capital controls in the 1980s, this book's empirical part extends beyond the emergence of multilateral AEI and the BEPS project.

In addition, the book also provides historical narratives on the Clinton and Bush administration's different approaches toward tax evasion and avoidance. Hence, the book covers the following historical episodes: (1) the OECD's HTC project launched by the G7 in 1996, (2) the development of a largely ineffective OECD standard for TIEAs between 2002 and 2008, (3) the emergence of AEI as a global standard for administrative assistance in tax matters since 2009, and (4) the OECD's most recent project on countermeasures to corporate BEPS launched in 2012. Each narrative provides a thick description of the respective US government's tax policy preferences, linking the US position to the OECD initiative's eventual success or failure in reaching its regulatory objectives. The narratives draw on forty-two interviews I conducted with decision makers and tax policy experts in six countries, as well as on official documents, legal commentaries, and coverage in the specialized press.

I fully develop and test my argument as follows: in chapter 2, I devise a theory of power in international tax politics. This theory rejects the contractualist idea according to which joint gains for all parties are a necessary precondition for international agreements. Instead, I argue that great powers can impose their preferred international tax policy on less powerful countries even if this policy leaves them worse off relative to the status quo ante. To this effect, the great power issues a credible threat of sanctions, linking compliance with its tax policy demands to market access for foreign firms. Since small countries are more dependent on access to the great power's market than the great power is on access to their markets, they are highly responsive to a corresponding threat. Yet the great power uses coercion in international tax matters only under restrictive conditions. Domestic politics need to prevent the government from passing regressive tax reform, and legal constraints need to keep the discursive power of affected interest groups in check. Finally, I determine which jurisdictions attain great power status in international tax politics. Although the EU's market power matches that of the United States, internal divisions and European law create a level of regulatory dispersion that prevents the bloc from finding and enforcing a common position. As a result, the United States is currently the only great power in international tax politics.

In chapters 3 and 4, I apply this theory to bargaining episodes before the 2008 financial crisis. Chapter 3 discusses the Clinton administration's tax policy preferences and its resulting stance vis-à-vis the anti–tax evasion and anti–tax avoidance elements of the HTC project. Like the Obama administration a decade later, the Clinton administration unilaterally introduced new reporting requirements for foreign banks through the QI program and backed the adoption of tighter information exchange standards at the OECD level. Because of business opposition, however, the administration failed to close loopholes in US CFC rules enabling US multinationals to indefinitely defer tax payments on foreign income and helped to dilute the HTC project's proposed countermeasures to corporate tax avoidance. Chapter 4 then discusses the Bush administration's regressive tax policy agenda, which led to the withdrawal of US support from the HTC project in 2001. At the request of the Bush administration, the OECD first had to abandon all recommendations interfering with international competition for corporate investment. Second, the OECD had to postpone collective sanctions against secrecy jurisdictions until secretive member states like Luxembourg and Switzerland also complied with OECD standards. Yet the Bush administration did nothing to increase pressure on the respective governments. From a theoretical perspective, chapters 3 and 4 moreover reveal that the US Treasury's responsiveness to normative claims advanced by libertarian lobbyists against international tax cooperation has been contingent on the respective administration's tax policy agenda.

Chapters 5 and 6 then discuss the OECD's post-crisis initiatives against tax evasion and avoidance. Chapter 5 explains how the Obama administration's preference for a progressive income tax system and new information on the circumvention of the Clinton administration's QI program led to the adoption of FATCA. By breaking the principled opposition of secrecy jurisdictions to the automatic reporting of account information to foreign governments, the act enabled the emergence of a multilateral AEI regime modeled on US policy. However, the Obama administration eventually refused to fully cooperate itself, because of financial sector opposition to new reporting requirements allegedly undermining business with foreign clients. As a result of this hypocrisy, US banks currently enjoy a competitive advantage over foreign banks in the attraction of hidden wealth. Subsequently, chapter 6 shows how the Obama administration's tax policy agenda also led to the proposal of countermeasures to corporate tax avoidance. Because of business opposition, however, the Obama administration was unable to implement its preferred countermeasure to corporate profit-shifting—more stringent CFC rules—domestically. The administration therefore lacked a template for international regulation in bargaining over the BEPS project's final recommendations. As a result, and to limit the foreign tax burden of US multinationals, the US government defended the international tax system's status quo against unorthodox reform proposals by other governments, aiming at the expansion of taxation at source.

In chapter 7, I discuss the most recent developments in international tax policy, focusing on the question whether EU member states can overcome their internal division and centralize some regulatory authority over taxation at the supranational level. The European Commission has made several proposals in this regard, including a consolidated tax haven blacklist, a digital services tax, and a common consolidated corporate tax base (CCCTB). Yet their adoption is far from certain, as member state preferences continue to diverge. Interestingly, however, progress is not always blocked by small capital-importing EU countries. Eager to protect its export industry from retaliation, Germany has recently prevented the EU from blacklisting the United States for its hypocritical implementation of the AEI and from introducing a 3 percent tax on revenue from the provision of digital services. The chapter's final section summarizes the key findings of the historical narratives and explains their relevance for political science debates on US hegemony, international norms, party ideology, and business power.

POWER IN INTERNATIONAL TAX POLITICS

The unexpected end of bank secrecy in traditional secrecy jurisdictions and the parallel survival of the status quo in bargaining over countermeasures to base erosion and profit shifting (BEPS) teach us three important lessons about the international politics of taxation. First, smaller countries make costly concessions when faced with a credible threat of sanctions from the United States. Accordingly, the US government can force smaller countries to adopt a regulatory standard like the automatic exchange of information (AEI) even if compliance worsens their lot relative to the status quo. Second, the US government can afford to ignore the same standard it imposes on smaller countries, thereby shifting adjustment costs onto foreign firms and creating a competitive advantage for US businesses. Although the resulting regime redistributes wealth from the rest of the world to the United States, other major economies, including the European Union (EU), have not been capable of countering US hypocrisy. As the Obama administration's defense of the status quo in negotiations over BEPS also suggests, global tax policy cannot currently be shaped against the will of the US government. Yet—and this is the third lesson—the US develops a preference for international action against tax dodging only if restrictive domestic conditions apply. Ideological constraints have to prevent the administration from regressive tax reform, whereas legal constraints have to keep in check the power of interest groups, which are affected by countermeasures to tax evasion or avoidance.

Against this background, I devote the present chapter to the development of a theory of power in international tax politics. This theory identifies market size and regulatory capacity as the decisive resources enabling governments to issue credible threats and inducements with a view toward making other governments do what they would not otherwise do. A lack of regulatory capacity explains why the EU has not wielded the same power in negotiations over global tax policy as the United States despite the EU's similarly sized internal market. In fact, taxation remains an exclusive member state competence. Therefore, the European Commission has no administrative authority to impose penalties on third states or foreign firms not complying with tax good governance standards applicable within the union. At the same time, the principle of nondiscrimination enshrined in EU law prevents individual EU countries from passing sanctions against other member states abetting tax evasion and avoidance. Because of the lack of regulatory centralization in the EU, the US can act as a hegemon in international tax politics. Accordingly, US preferences determined by domestic politics decisively shape the content of global tax policy. The preferences of other governments merely affect the US administration's enforcement strategy.

The Material and Institutional Sources of Power

Market Size and State Power

Scholarship seeking to explain governments' relative power in international bargaining over financial and economic affairs has traditionally focused on the size of a country's internal market. From this perspective, sway over global policy depends on the relative number of foreign firms ready to abide by a regulator's decisions to gain access to customers or suppliers. The larger a market's share in global demand or supply, the greater the financial incentive for foreign firms to secure entry. On the one hand, relative market size thus determines the extent to which a country's market regulation has extraterritorial reach. A company whose profits are highly dependent on sales in a foreign market will, for instance, adapt the company's products or services to local requirements rather than divest. If the rules governing its small home market differ or prevent the company from complying with the rules applicable in the large foreign market, the company will, moreover, lobby its home government for regulatory changes mirroring foreign rules. The gravitational effect of a dominant market may thus lead to the spontaneous diffusion of a powerful government's regulatory model (Simmons 2001; Vogel 1997).

On the other hand, market size also determines whether a government can credibly threaten other governments with market closure to enforce its preferences in international negotiations. The credibility of threats depends on the difference between the costs coercive measures impose on the sender and the costs they impose on the target. If a large country were to close its market to firms from a small country, for instance, the large country would lose a negligible share of its overall imports of goods, services, or investment. In contrast, the small country would lose a substantial share of its corresponding exports. Even if the small country closed its market in return, the large country would lose only a negligible share of its overall exports. The small country, however, would lose a substantial share of its imports. Because the large country is thus less vulnerable to market closure than the small country, the large country can wrestle concessions from the small country by conditioning market access on compliance with the large country's demands. Inversely, the small country has no means to ensure the large country's compliance with global rules (Drezner 2008; Krasner 1976; Legro and Moravcsik 1999).

If we accept the crucial importance of market size for state power, the outcome of international bargaining over countermeasures to tax evasion should depend on the preferences of countries with large financial markets. After all, tax evasion happens when a taxpayer hides wealth or income in a foreign account instead of declaring it in her tax return. Accordingly, countermeasures to tax evasion have to oblige banks and other financial institutions—the most likely custodians of hidden funds—to correctly identify their customers and report information about their assets and income to foreign tax authorities. Banks are, however, unlikely to comply voluntarily with data requests from foreign governments, because the after-tax return banks can offer their wealth management clients depends on financial secrecy as much as it depends on access to lucrative investment opportunities.[1] Therefore, a regulator's ability to obtain account information from foreign banks is conditional on the share of global capital demand to which the regulator can refuse access. If the share is small, a foreign bank may simply choose divestment over compliance. If the share is large, however, the foreign bank will not be able to find equivalent investment opportunities elsewhere. As a result, it has no choice but to abandon secrecy in return for continued market access.

In contrast, the outcome of bargaining over countermeasures to tax avoidance should depend on the preferences of countries with large consumer markets. Here, the regulatory goal is to prevent multinationals, which sell their products or services to customers around the world, from shifting the corresponding profits to tax havens where no substantial economic activity takes place (cf. OECD 1998, 2013b). According to international tax law, income from cross-border investment should either be taxed where the income source is located (source country) or where its beneficiaries reside (residence country).[2] However, multinationals often channel their profits out of source countries untaxed, and then divert them to a corporate tax haven instead of returning them to the residence country. A government's ability to counter these practices unilaterally should increase with

TABLE 2.1 Measures of Financial Market Size in Developed and Emerging Economies

COUNTRY/YEAR	MARKET CAPITALIZATION OF LISTED DOMESTIC FIRMS (%, WORLD TOTAL)		VALUE OF INTERBANK TRANSACTIONS (%, WORLD TOTAL)		VALUE OF SECURITIES TRANSACTIONS (%, WORLD TOTAL)	
	2007	2017	2007	2016[a]	2007	2016[a]
United States	33	41	30	31	30	19
European Union	24	10	51	32	48	48
China	7	11	2	15	1	5
Japan	7	8	8	10	9	9
Brazil	2	1	2	3	4	10
India	3	3	0	0	0	0
Russia	n.a.	1	0	1	0	0

Note: Market capitalization is the share price times the number of shares outstanding for listed domestic companies. Interbank transactions are processed by interbank funds transfer systems and include transactions banks carry out on their own account and on behalf of their clients. Securities transactions are processed by central securities depositories and include all instructions to move securities between accounts.
[a] The latest year for which data was available at the time of writing. Data sources: World Bank (2018); Committee on Payment and Settlement Systems (2011); Committee on Payments and Market Infrastructures (2017).

the share that its consumer market contributes to a multinational's global revenue. The larger the share, the higher the cost of exiting the market for tax reasons. Accordingly, a large source country could withhold taxes on dividend or royalty payments to corporate tax havens, whereas a large residence country could pass controlled foreign company (CFC) rules, adding profits booked in corporate tax havens to taxable domestic income, without risking divestment from multinationals.

If market size were the sole determinant of great power status, that status in international tax politics would characterize the United States and the EU, as a result of the union's common market.[3] As the data presented in table 2.1 show, firms listed in the United States contributed a third of the worldwide demand for equity financing in 2007 and four times as much as European and Chinese firms in 2017. Although the European financial market appears considerably smaller than the US financial market in terms of firm capitalization, the European financial market contributes a larger share to the value of transactions processed by the world's interbank transfer systems and securities depositories. Between 2007 and 2016, the EU's share of funds transferred among the world's banks declined from more than half to a third. Still, the union continues to contribute about as much to the value of worldwide interbank transactions as the United States and twice as much as China. In addition, securities transactions processed by depositories in the EU consistently accounted for almost half of the value of worldwide

TABLE 2.2 Foreign Portfolio Investment from Major Secrecy Jurisdictions in December 2009

LOCATION OF ASSET HOLDER/ ISSUER	UNITED STATES %, TOTAL FPI (RANK)		EUROPEAN UNION[a] %, TOTAL FPI (RANK)		OTHER MAJOR FOREIGN PORTFOLIO INVESTMENT (FPI) DESTINATIONS[b] COUNTRY	%, TOTAL FPI (RANK)	
Austria	7	(2)	80	(1)	None	-	
Bahamas	23	(2)	4	(4)	Brazil	57	(1)
					Mexico	6	(3)
Bahrain	27	(1)	16	(3)	Turkey	22	(2)
					United Arab Emirates	9	(4)
Belgium	6	(2)	88	(1)	None	—	
Bermuda	63	(1)	15	(2)	Cayman Islands	9	(3)
Cayman Islands	52	(1)	8	(3)	Brazil	29	(2)
Curaçao[c]	11	(4)	36	(1)	Indonesia	15	(2)
					Thailand	13	(3)
Guernsey	16	(2)	53	(1)	Cayman Islands	14	(3)
Hong Kong	11	(4)	22	(1)	Cayman Islands	20	(2)
					China	18	(3)
Isle of Man	5	(3)	76	(1)	Cayman Islands	6	(2)
Jersey	23	(2)	55	(1)	None	—	
Luxembourg	16	(2)	60	(1)	None	—	
Macao	8	(4)	29	(1)	Hong Kong	20	(2)
					China	18	(3)
					Cayman Islands	6	(5)
Panama	59	(1)	3	(4)	Colombia	12	(2)
					Brazil	9	(3)
Singapore[d]	21	(2)	26	(1)	Japan	7	(3)
					China	7	(4)
					Korea	6	(5)
Switzerland	14	(2)	58	(1)	None	—	

Note: Major secrecy jurisdictions include all countries identified as such in table 1.1. Reported FPI data refer to the stock of investment in debt securities, equity and investment fund shares as of December 2009. The entity directly investing in an asset—an interposed shell company for instance—is reported as the asset holder. A beneficial owner investing through this entity is not identified. Likewise, the data does not separate investments households make through banks from banks' proprietary trading. Despite these shortcomings, the International Monetary Fund's FPI data remain the best available data for our purposes. BIS Locational Banking Statistics do not include investment in equity, and Treasury International Capital (TIC) data on foreign ownership of US securities does not enable the analyst to determine the US share in a foreign country's overall portfolio investment.

[a]Includes all twenty-seven countries that were members of the EU in December 2009.

[b]Includes all countries receiving more than 5 percent of a tax haven's total FPI.

[c]With its passage to independence in 2010, the Netherlands Antilles changed its official name to Curaçao & Sint Maarten.

[d]Data refer to December 2008 because Singapore made FPI information confidential for most destinations from 2009.

Data source: International Monetary Fund (2018).

transactions over the course of the past decade. Most important, the United States and the EU have dominated all other countries on the usual measures of financial market size in all but one point in time during the past ten years (cf. Simmons 2001; Singer 2007). Whereas Chinese businesses have, indeed, caught up with European firms in terms of market capitalization, interbank and securities transactions processed in the Unites States and the EU have consistently accounted for 60 to 80 percent of the value of worldwide transactions.

Secrecy jurisdictions' dependence on the US and European financial markets is reflected in the international distribution of secrecy jurisdictions' foreign portfolio investment (FPI). In December 2009, three months before the US Congress adopted the Foreign Account Tax Compliance Act (FATCA), the largest share of overall FPI routed through fifteen out of the sixteen secrecy jurisdictions listed in table 2.2 either went to the United States or the EU. In ten out of sixteen cases, one of the two major financial markets accounted for 50 to 90 percent of all investment in debt securities, equity, and investment fund shares carried out via the respective jurisdiction. Other important destinations for individual secrecy jurisdictions include emerging economies such as Brazil, China, and Turkey or other secrecy jurisdictions such as the Cayman Islands and Hong Kong. The latter phenomenon most likely reflects the use of several conduits for a single investment stream. A private bank located in Hong Kong may, for instance, invest the deposits of a Chinese client in an investment fund registered in the Cayman Islands, which uses the money to buy company shares on the New York Stock Exchange. Owing to such constructs, FPI statistics may actually underestimate secrecy jurisdictions' true dependence on access to major financial markets. In any case, the United States and the EU could destroy the business model of most secrecy jurisdictions by closing their markets unilaterally.

A similar picture emerges when comparing the consumer markets of major developed and emerging economies. Table 2.3 reports data for 2013, the year the Group of 20 (G20) and the Organisation for Economic Co-operation and Development (OECD) launched the BEPS initiative (G20 Leaders 2013; OECD 2013a). Whereas the number of potential customers is greatest in China and India, Americans and Europeans have more income to spend on the products and services offered by multinationals. Accordingly, the United States and the EU still account for larger shares of global imports of goods and services than China and India despite the significantly smaller US and EU populations. Their unmatched share of worldwide inbound foreign direct investment (FDI) moreover suggests that multinationals continue to locate most of their activities in the United States and the EU. This observation is of particular importance because international tax law links a government's right to tax a multinational's local revenue to the presence of a permanent establishment (PE) on the government's territory. In the absence

TABLE 2.3 Measures of Consumer Market Size for Major Economies in 2013

INDICATORS/COUNTRIES	US	EU	CHINA	JAPAN	RUSSIA	INDIA
Population (millions)	316	507	1357	127	144	1252
National income (per adult)	49657	29245	11392	30115	22940	6020
Merchandise trade (%, global imports)	12.33	14.78	10.32	4.41	1.82	2.47
Commercial services (%, global imports)	9.85	19.74	7.52	3.70	2.81	2.84
Foreign direct investment (inbound, % world total)	19.4	33.7	3.8	0.7	2.3	0.9

Note: The selection of indicators for market size is based on Drezner (2008, 36). All EU figures refer to extra-EU trade and investment. Data sources: UNCTAD (2014); WTO (2019a); World Inequality Database (2018).

of a domestic plant, office, or warehouse, local sales alone do not justify the taxation of a foreign corporation.[4] Therefore, inbound FDI should be the most relevant indicator of market size in the context of international tax politics.

The extent to which corporate tax havens specializing in the abetment of tax avoidance depend on access to the US and European markets is reflected in the origin of royalty and license fee payments the tax havens receive from abroad. Multinationals often use such payments to shift profits from their branches in high-tax countries to a subsidiary in a low-tax country. Accordingly, countries that do not tax revenue from the foreign lease of intellectual property—either on the basis of targeted expenditures or advance pricing agreements with individual firms—figure among the world's largest recipients of such payments (WTO 2019b). Dutch firms, for instance, collected almost three times the amount of royalties collected by German firms in 2013, despite having invested only 15 percent of what German firms invested in domestic research and development that year (OECD 2018a). The profits multinational firms book in the Netherlands thus do not match their economic activity in the country—a fact that is indicative of tax-motivated shifts (Cobham and Janský 2017; Tørsløv, Wier, and Zucman 2018).

Against this background, the data presented in table 2.4 suggest that 70 percent of the revenue channeled to the Netherlands through license fee payments in 2013 came either from other EU member states or from the United States. Similarly,

TABLE 2.4 Royalty and License Fee Payments Received by Major Corporate Tax Havens in 2013

DESTINATION/ORIGIN	UNITED STATES (%, TOTAL)	EUROPEAN UNION (%, TOTAL)	OTHER IMPORTANT ORIGIN JURISDICTIONS (%, TOTAL)	
Netherlands	11	61	None	
Switzerland	32	34	None	
Ireland	43	19	None	
Singapore	3	6	Australia	(18)
			ASEAN[a]	(17)
			China	(16)
			Japan	(12)
Luxembourg	n.a.	80	None	
Hong Kong	15	15	China	(28)

Note: The listed destinations include all countries among the world's top twenty-five recipients of royalty and license fee payments that effectively exempt such payments from taxation either through targeted expenditures or advance pricing agreements with individual firms (cf. European Commission 2017c, 2017b, 2017d; Inland Revenue Department 2011; Switzerland Global Enterprise 2014). Destinations are listed in descending order according to their share in global receipts of royalty and license fee payments.
[a]Association of South East Asian Nations (Brunei, Cambodia, Indonesia, Laos, Malaysia, Myanmar, Philippines, Singapore, Thailand, Vietnam).

Ireland, Luxembourg, and Switzerland—where the same mismatches between reported revenue and economic activity can be observed—received between 60 and 80 percent of shifted profits from the US and European markets. Hong Kong—the second largest corporate tax haven for license fee payments in Asia—collected about the same share from the United States and the EU combined as from China, whereas profits were shifted to Singapore from an unusually diverse number of markets within its wider region. Still, these figures show that most corporate tax havens would lose their attractiveness as locations for holding companies if they could no longer grant unhindered access to the US and European markets. Hence, the United States and a coalition of large EU member states, incurring revenue losses from profit shifting, should have the power to impose their tax policy preferences on corporate tax havens. The conversion of market size into an effective projection of power, however, depends on a government's regulatory capacity.

Regulatory Capacity and State Power

Regulatory capacity is "a jurisdiction's ability to formulate, monitor, and enforce a set of market rules . . . . At a minimum [it] consists of regulatory expertise, coherence, and the extent of statutory sanctioning authority" (Bach and Newman 2007, 831). An expert administration consists of well-trained and experienced professionals, who independently identify regulatory challenges, develop targeted policy solutions, and deploy the necessary resources to competently monitor implementation of the solutions by market participants. A coherent administration moreover ensures that the rules it develops apply uniformly across the market the administration regulates. The leeway officials enjoy in granting carve-outs and exemptions should be strictly limited, and the likelihood and intensity of audits should not depend on a company's geographical location and political connections to local policymakers. Accordingly, a jurisdiction's regulatory capacity will be higher when administrative authority is centralized than when it is dispersed (Posner 2009). What matters most for the projection of power in international bargaining, however, is an administration's ability to punish noncompliance. The administration must have legal competence to penalize recalcitrant firms through monetary fines or market exclusion. Otherwise, sanction threats become cheap talk. While a large internal market may therefore be necessary for the projection of power, a jurisdiction can harness its potential only through adequate regulatory capacity (Bach and Newman 2010).

Herein lies the key difference between the United States and the EU. Since the adoption of FATCA, the US Treasury can decide to withhold 30 percent of the payments received from US sources by any foreign bank that does not comply with the act's reporting requirements (Grinberg 2012). Even before FATCA was enacted, the Treasury Department had the statutory authority to define the information on US clients that foreign banks had to divulge when seeking the status of a qualified intermediary (QI), and the department could, in principle, extend the reporting and due diligence obligations of all banks in the United States without prior consultation with Congress (cf. IRS 2000; Mordi 2011). When the Department of Justice (DoJ) suspects a breach of reporting obligations defined in QI or FATCA regulations, the DoJ may even threaten to seek the criminal indictment of a foreign bank from a grand jury. Since an indicted bank loses access to the clearing infrastructure for dollar-denominated transactions, such a threat from the DoJ is usually enough to force the targeted institution into a costly nonprosecution agreement. After all, no bank can participate in the international financial system without access to the currency in which the large majority of international transactions are processed. Hence, the dollar's status as the world's key currency significantly increases the US government's regulatory authority over foreign banks irrespective of their exposure to the US capital market (Emmenegger 2015; Helleiner 2002).[5]

In contrast, the administration of direct taxation remains an exclusive member state competence in the EU. Accordingly, the European Commission neither has the authority to change the reporting obligations of banks in the common market, nor can decide to impose sanctions against banks outside the common market that refuse to disclose information on European account holders.[6] Instead, member states have to agree unanimously on new reporting standards as well as on mandates for Commission negotiations on information exchange agreements with third countries. Therefore, Austria and Luxembourg were able to block the introduction of comprehensive AEI as well as the launch of corresponding negotiations with Switzerland for almost a decade (Hakelberg 2015b; Rixen and Schwarz 2012). But also since the transposition of the OECD common reporting standard (CRS) into European law, member states have not been able to develop meaningful sanctions mechanisms against third countries not complying with the new AEI standard. The only measure to date is an integrated blacklist of countries not complying with the EU's tax good governance standards, including participation in multilateral AEI. Yet the corresponding Council conclusions merely propose defensive measures member states could apply against listed jurisdictions as they see fit and subject modifications of the list to unanimous approval by member states even when a country matches the agreed-upon criteria (Council of the European Union 2017). Owing to this lack of regulatory centralization, inclusion does not have direct material consequences for listed countries and can be vetoed by a single EU member. Instead of harnessing the power of the common market, the EU thus leaves responsibility for sanctions and vulnerability to po-tential retaliation with individual member states.

Likewise, tax-avoiding multinationals have, in principle, more to fear from the US Treasury and its enforcing authorities than from the European Commission. For instance, the Internal Revenue Service (IRS) has the statutory authority to remove loopholes in US CFC rules that currently enable domestically headquar-tered corporations to defer tax payments on foreign profits reported in tax ha-vens (cf. IRS 1997, 1998b). Without any additional acts of delegation from con-gress, the service can amend domestic transfer pricing and thin capitalization rules when abuse becomes apparent and introduce entirely new reporting obligations for multinational groups (cf. IRS 2016; US Treasury 2010). Subject to final ap-proval by a Senate majority, the Treasury can moreover renegotiate tax treaties with foreign governments, granting or withdrawing exemptions from withhold-ing taxes on payments from US sources. Within the EU, all of these competences remain with member states. They can each grant foreign companies access to the entire common market, while applying domestic tax law and the provisions of bilateral tax treaties. Over the last decades, tax competition has therefore been more intense in the EU than in the rest of the world (Genschel, Kemmerling, and Seils 2011). The European Commission can merely prevent the most harmful practices by ordering member states to claw back foregone tax payments from companies that have benefitted from selective fiscal privileges. Governments granting tax exemptions unequivocally to all EU firms, however, act within the bounds of their exclusive competence in direct taxation (Mazzoni and Avi-Yonah 2016).

Owing to their respective fiscal sovereignty, member states would thus have to find consensus if they wanted to overcome regulatory dispersion in tax matters. Instead of adopting a common stance with their European partners, however, Ire-land, Luxembourg, and the Netherlands tailor their tax codes to the needs of US multinationals seeking to shift their profits out of the common market untaxed (Pinkernell 2012, 2014). In return, they benefit from high levels of foreign direct investment (FDI) from the United States. In 2013, 60 percent of the US FDI stock in the EU was located in these three countries, 80 percent of which was bound in holding companies. Accordingly, three quarters of the United States' direct in-vestment income from the EU was also channeled through Ireland, Luxembourg and the Netherlands that year (US Bureau of Economic Analysis 2018b, 2018a). Other member states would have to apply pressure to bring corporate tax havens in the EU into line. Their corresponding options are, however, severely con-strained. The freedom of establishment enshrined in EU law posits that multina-tionals running their business from Ireland, Luxembourg, or the Netherlands enjoy unconstrained access to the entire common market. The remaining member states have to treat them as if they were domestic companies. Accordingly, European governments can neither impose withholding taxes on payments to EU corporate tax havens, nor apply CFC rules against multinationals shifting their profits there (Genschel 2002; ECJ 2006). Because of the dispersion of regulatory authority among member states, the EU is thus unable to convert market size into power. As a result, US hegemony in international tax politics currently remains unchallenged.

Great Power Preferences in International Tax Politics

If the US Treasury has the authority to tackle tax evasion and avoidance unilaterally by regulation, why does the department make only sporadic use of its power? In this section, I submit that restrictive circumstances have to be met in domestic tax politics for the US administration to enforce countermeasures to tax dodging. In contrast to popular comment, however, I argue that budget constraints are not at the origin of increased great power activism. Instead, whether the United States supports new international tax rules depends on the feasibility of regressive tax reform and the power of affected domestic interest groups. Democratic administrations are more concerned about the tax system's effective progressivity than their Republican opponents, whereas redistributive regulation at the international level allows the US government to appease powerful domestic interest groups by shifting adjustment costs onto foreign companies and governments.

Barriers to Regressive Tax Reform

Welfare economists assume that governments facing international tax competition seek to maximize the sum of tax revenue and domestic production (Chisik and Davies 2004; Keen and Konrad 2014). Yet how governments weigh these elements and which strategies they apply to attain their goal depends on a range of material and ideational factors. The easiest unilateral strategy to address budget constraints in a tax-competitive environment is regressive tax reform. By shifting the tax burden away from internationally mobile capital and toward immobile labor and consumption, this strategy reduces the risk of losing production to capital flight and generates additional revenue from increased payroll and value-added taxes (VAT). Accordingly, regressive tax reform has been popular among OECD governments from the 1980s throughout the first decade of the

2000s (Beramendi and Rueda 2007; Genschel and Schwarz 2013). At the same time, however, this strategy also violates a fairness norm underpinning most modern tax systems. According to the ability-to-pay principle, high-income earners should contribute relatively more to the financing of the state than low-income earners, since those with high incomes find it easier "to bear the sacrifice of material well-being a tax burden entails" (Slemrod and Bakija 2008, 64). Given that the capital share increases while the share devoted to consumption decreases with the level of income, however, regressive tax reform shifts the tax burden from high-income to low-income taxpayers. Hence, high-income earners and their representatives are likely to support such a reform, whereas low-income earners and their representatives are likely to resist it.

Indeed, students of comparative tax politics consistently find that conservative parties prefer flat taxes on corporate profits and personal capital income. Conservative parties usually justify their preference by citing the larger role of corporations and high-income earners in saving and investment, and the positive correlation between the level of tax and capital flight suggested by the Laffer curve. In contrast, center-left governments prefer progressive taxation of corporate profits and personal capital income, which these governments justify with the ability-to-pay principle (Ganghof 2006). Basinger and Hallerberg (2004) show, for instance, that center-left governments are more hesitant than conservative ones in making competitive cuts to the corporate tax rate. Likewise, Garrett (1995) associates center-left governments with more capital taxation unless an economy is highly integrated in world markets. He explains that left parties favor high taxes on capital but are often constrained by capital mobility. Similarly, Beramendi and Rueda (2007) find that left governments have more progressive tax systems unless they are bound by corporatist commitments. In that case, these governments concede capital relief in exchange for redistribution on the spending side, financed by more indirect taxation. Andersson (2015), in turn, demonstrates that left governments have more progressive tax systems in majoritarian electoral systems, but not in proportional ones. The latter, he argues, allow them to enter into long-term agreements with conservative parties on pairing capital relief with redistributive spending financed, again, by indirect taxes. Since the United States has the power to model international regulation in financial and tax affairs according to its domestic needs and features low levels of corporatism as well as a majoritarian electoral system, Democrats should thus be consistently associated with preserving—or even increasing—the progressivity of the tax system.

In fact, Bartels (2009) demonstrates that Democrats and Republicans implement tax policies consistent with the objective interests of their core political constituencies. Whereas Democratic policymakers develop their positions based on the views of affluent egalitarians and the middle class, Republican policymakers respond to the views of their most affluent constituents only, who want to see their material interests rather than their egalitarian convictions defended. Accordingly, all Democratic administrations between 1948 and 2005 reduced income inequality through increased public investment and spending on employment programs, as well as larger social transfers and more progressive taxation. The former set of policies fostered economic growth and reduced unemployment, disproportionately benefiting the pretax incomes of the lower class. The latter set of policies bolstered the post-tax incomes of the lower class, while limiting the growth of the upper class' post-tax incomes. In contrast, all Republican administrations between 1948 and 2005 increased income inequality through cuts in spending on employment and social programs, inflation containment, and—most important—tax reform. Republican administrations have, in fact, held the common conviction that tax cuts had to benefit the wealthy in particular because of their decisive role in saving and investment. The Reagan and Bush administrations thus reduced tax rates imposed on top incomes and capital gains, with George W. Bush excluding corporate dividends from taxation at the individual level altogether.

Yet party ideology is not the only determinant of government attitudes toward regressive tax reform. Because of its redistributive consequences and impact on the perceived fairness of a given tax system, such reform is politically highly salient. Therefore, corresponding voter attitudes and fairness concerns may also impact government positions. Plümper, Troeger, and Winner (2009) demonstrate, for instance, that conservative governments facing an electorate with predominantly egalitarian convictions are just as unlikely as center-left governments to lower taxes on capital in response to tax competition. Accordingly, both party ideology and voter attitudes may in principle create political barriers to regressive tax reform and force governments to search for an alternative strategy to minimize capital flight. The moral economy of the United States, however, is marked by much higher popular support for market competition and much lower support for redistribution than the moral economies of other developed countries (Koos and Sachweh 2017). It is therefore highly unlikely that a Republican administration would face an electorate with predominantly egalitarian convictions. Even if this were the case, the party's limited responsiveness to tax policy demands from voters other than its most affluent supporters would prevent a modification of its preference for regressive tax reform (Bartels 2009). As a result, Democratic government becomes a necessary condition for US support of an international initiative against tax evasion, tax avoidance, or both. For other governments this role is played by political barriers to regressive tax reform at large.

The Power of Affected Domestic Interest Groups

A government's ideological leaning or electoral strategy is, however, not the only determinant of the government's preferences about global tax policy. The domestic organized interests that are most affected by debated regulation also have significant sway over their government's position (Drezner 2008; Frieden 1991). Anti–tax evasion measures mostly affect resident individuals hiding financial wealth and capital income offshore as well as domestic banks providing offshore services to nonresidents. In contrast, anti–tax avoidance measures mostly affect locally headquartered multinationals that artificially shift their profits to tax havens. Their common objective is to maximize profits by minimizing the tax burden imposed on themselves or their clients. Whether policymakers take the preferences of these groups into account depends on their respective instrumental, structural, and discursive power. Instrumental power refers to an interest group's ability "to exert direct influence on government decision makers through campaign contributions and lobbying efforts" (Hacker and Pierson 2002, 280). Structural power is based on an interest group's ability to make credible threats of disinvestment (Lindblom 1977), and discursive power refers to an interest group's ability to shape the interests and perceptions of policymakers and the general public by linking the interest group's demands to established norms and ideas (Fuchs and Lederer 2008).

Wealthy individuals, including those evading taxes, tend to have the necessary resources and access to exert instrumental power over tax policymakers. As discussed earlier, elected decision makers in the US usually adjust their tax policy agendas to the interests of the wealthiest individuals among their constituents. This tendency may be the result of material incentives such as campaign contributions or more frequent personal interactions with local elites (Bartels 2009). In contrast, tax evaders' structural power is limited by their inability to make credible divestment threats. Since their tax liability is linked to their citizenship or place of residence, tax evaders would have to move their center of vital interests to a tax haven, or obtain a new nationality, to prevent their home country from taxing their uncovered foreign capital income. Yet such a decision implies the cutting of exactly those social ties that may be constitutive of an individual's wealth. Hence, US millionaires rarely migrate for tax or other reasons (Young 2017). In any case, an individual's decision to change her place of residence should have a negligible impact on employment compared with the relocation of company headquarters or factories.[7] Finally, tax evaders also have limited discursive power, as they break the law by concealing foreign capital income from the tax office. While their status as criminals reduces their authority in public discourse, the norm of equality before the law obliges policymakers to distance themselves from any crime to preserve the justice system's perceived legitimacy. As tax evasion is a law-and-order issue as much as a tax policy issue, open support for the perpetrators is likely to be minimal.

The domestic financial sector should have even more instrumental power over tax policy than wealthy individuals. In many countries, financial elites are regularly recruited into senior government positions, while their associations coordinate closely with policymakers over regulatory projects (Fairfield 2010). The revolving door between finance and government is particularly busy in the United States, where previous employment with an investment bank is the norm for secretaries of the Treasury, and financial institutions offer lucrative consultancy positions to retiring senior officials. Hence, the sector is directly involved in financial policymaking over which the sector also exerts substantial structural power. In the US, the financial industry increased its GDP share from 16 percent in 1975 to 24 percent in 2005, whereas the manufacturing sector's share fell from 29 to 16 percent over the same period (Krippner 2005, 178). Finance has thus become a dominant industry sector that can make credible divestment threats, as a result of the abolition of capital controls and the technological ability to manage assets from anywhere in the world (Helleiner 1995). The sector's discursive power is reflected in its ability to establish dominant ideas about how an economy should be organized. Apparently, this ability persists even after the 2008 financial crisis, causing scholars to puzzle over neoliberalism's resilience and the incremental character of post-crisis regulatory reform (Blyth 2013; Thatcher and Schmidt 2013; Moschella and Tsingou 2014). Accordingly, the US position in international bargaining over financial regulation has consistently been shaped by an overarching concern for the competitiveness of US finance. The US government protects its financial institutions from the costs of international regulation by enforcing agreements that mirror domestic regulation and undercutting foreign initiatives promoting divergent rules (Helleiner 2014; Oatley and Nabors 1998; Simmons 2001; Singer 2007; Rixen 2013).

Multinationals other than financial institutions wield similar power over policymakers. Tax officials usually form an epistemic community with tax advisers and chief financial officers of large corporations. Tax officials often seek advice or even collaborate with tax law firms in drafting legislation and move back and forth between the public and private sector in some countries (Seabrooke and Wigan 2016). In the United States, corporate tax lawyers walk through the same revolving door between government service and private practice as their colleagues in finance. Hence, Treasury is well aware of the needs of multinationals headquartered in the United States (cf. IPB Tax 2013; KPMG 2014). In addition, large corporations contribute important sums to the campaigns of elected politicians and sponsor several lobbying groups focusing on tax policy (Center for Responsive Politics 2015). The impact of multinationals, however, does not depend only on access. Multinationals also have the ability to make credible divestment threats. Corporations can, for instance, relocate headquarters and activities to low-tax jurisdictions instead of just shifting the profits, leaving governments a choice between a loss of revenue from corporate taxes and a loss of jobs (Hong and Smart 2010). Finally, multinationals can justify tax avoidance with the legality of tax planning, thereby shifting the blame to legislators who fail to remove loopholes. Alternatively, multinationals can invoke the public good by stressing their obligation to maximize profits on behalf of shareholders and by linking a lower tax burden to more investment and jobs. The number of policymakers considering the demands of tax-avoiding multinationals legitimate should therefore be higher than the number of policymakers sympathetic to tax evaders. Against this background, we can thus conclude that the limited power of affected interest groups is a necessary condition for government support of an international initiative against tax evasion, tax avoidance, or both.

The Interaction of Political Barriers and Business Power

In actual bargaining over international tax policy, decision makers obviously have to adapt to political barriers to regressive tax reform and demands from powerful interest groups at the same time. Decision-makers may, for instance, accommodate public outrage over a tax avoidance scandal by calling for more stringent international rules, while making concessions on their exact content to appease business opposition. Accordingly, different combinations of the two factors of political barriers and business power should produce different government positions toward international tax initiatives. Table 2.5 provides a stylized summary of possible constellations. Its top-left corner displays the combination of high political barriers to regressive tax reform and low adjustment costs for powerful interest groups, which is most conducive to government support for international tax initiatives. A poster example for this situation would be a center-left government that responds to its constituency's fairness concerns by supporting an initiative that increases financial transparency in secrecy jurisdictions to the level already practiced by domestic banks. Such an initiative would increase pressure on resident tax evaders with limited power in the political process and improve the competitive position of domestic banks by leveling the regulatory playing field. The constellation becomes less permissive, however, if adjustment costs are high. This may be the case when standards debated at the international level threaten to increase the foreign tax burden of resident multinationals. As the table's bottom-left corner shows, the government is likely to respond by trying to block rules domestic business considers particularly harmful, as the Obama administration did in the context of the BEPS project. Given the government's ideological

TABLE 2.5 Interaction of Explanatory Factors in Determining
Government Preferences

		POLITICAL BARRIERS TO REGRESSIVE TAX REFORM	
		HIGH	LOW
ADJUSTMENT COSTS FOR POWERFUL INTEREST GROUPS	LOW	Government fully supports international initiative against tax abuse.	Government is indifferent, reduces tax burden on internationally mobile tax bases.
	HIGH	Government supports international initiative in public, but opposes rules affecting domestic business.	Government rejects initiative, reduces tax burden on internationally mobile tax bases.

commitment to—or popular demand for—tax fairness, however, it will not withdraw support from the initiative as a whole.

As shown in the table's bottom-right corner, a government will oppose an initiative altogether only if low political barriers to regressive tax reform combine with high adjustment costs. This will be the case when neither a majority of voters nor a governing party's core constituency demands action against tax dodging, but other governments do. A right-wing government with a flat-tax ideal may, for instance, need capital flight as a justification for competitive tax cuts at home. The government will thus reject international rules that could lead to a reduction of capital flight and a corresponding increase in the effective tax burden of domestic multinationals. Against this background, the conservative government will embrace international tax competition and lower the domestic tax burden on internationally mobile assets. Whereas this most restrictive constellation may also lead a government to question previous agreements, low adjustment costs in combination with low political barriers to regressive tax reform make a government more or less indifferent toward international proposals. This may, for instance, be the case when lenient transparency standards allow a conservative government to appear tough on criminal tax evasion but require additional reporting only from foreign instead of domestic banks, and keep loopholes open for more sophisticated domestic tax evaders. Such a constellation may thus lead a government to pursue international tax "politics without conviction" (Eccleston 2012, 60).

Preference Constellations and Great Power Strategies

The regulatory preferences of the United States—currently the undisputed hegemon in international tax politics—determine the outcome of initiatives against tax evasion and avoidance. The preferences of smaller governments still matter, however, in that they determine which strategy the US government applies to im-

TABLE 2.6 Combinations of Government Preferences and US Strategic Choice

		GREAT POWER PREFERENCE	
		PRO	**CONTRA**
SMALL-COUNTRY PREFERENCE	**PRO**	Great power strikes voluntary agreements with foreign governments.	Great power unilaterally defects. Undermines international initiative.
	CONTRA	Great power uses coercion to impose its preferred rules on foreign governments.	No initiative.

plement its preferred international rules. If the administration expects considerable resistance from other governments, for instance, it will deploy measures to "change the choices of other . . . regulators at reasonable cost" (Simmons 2001, 597). Accordingly, foreign opposition to the US government's preferred international rules merely "affects the means of regulatory coordination, not the ultimate end" (Drezner 2008, 88). If a small-country coalition were, for instance, to agree on a higher level of financial transparency than practiced in the United States, the US administration could unilaterally defect and undermine the coalition's scheme by attracting hidden capital to US shores. If, in contrast, the small-country coalition practices a lower level of financial transparency, the United States could force these countries to apply stricter standards by linking compliance to financial market access. Table 2.6 summarizes the US government's strategic options in international tax politics.

The stylized overview of preference constellations pits the great power's stance toward a given international tax initiative against the position of smaller governments. This analysis can be applied to bilateral as well as multilateral bargaining. The most permissive constellation is, of course, when smaller governments agree with the great power's preferred international rules, as they provide the smaller governments with similar domestic benefits. This constellation is summarized in the top-left corner of table 2.6 and results in voluntary agreements between the great power and foreign governments. If the great power meets or expects resistance from foreign governments, however, it will use coercion to impose its preferred rules nonetheless. If neither the great power nor a smaller government is in favor of new international tax rules, there will be no corresponding initiative, because an actor capable of putting the issue on the agenda of an international organization is missing. If small countries promote such an initiative and meet the support of the great power, we end up in the bottom-left corner again. Yet if the great power is satisfied with the status quo, while smaller governments launch an initiative for new rules, the great power will undermine this initiative by defecting unilaterally, as already described earlier. In more formal terms, we can thus conclude that the preferences of other governments determine the strategy a great power deploys to implement its preferred international tax rules.

Analytical Strategy: Testing a Theoretical Model with Historical Narratives

My aim in this book is to explain transformative change in the fight against tax evasion and avoidance. Transformative change occurs when a paradigm governing the taxation of cross-border investment and economic activity at a given point in time is superseded by a new paradigm. As the previous sections make clear, I posit that regulatory stasis will be overcome only if the United States—the hegemon in international tax politics—decides to turn from veto player to change agent. This decision, in turn, depends on the feasibility of regressive tax reform and the adjustment costs a departure from the status quo entails for powerful domestic interest groups. Once the United States has become a change agent, the position of foreign governments determines whether the US administration implements change through voluntary agreements or coercion. The relevant forum for initiatives against tax evasion and avoidance has traditionally been the OECD (Eccleston 2012; Rixen 2008). However, since my approach is based on theories of tax competition, which assume perfect capital mobility, I consider only anti–tax haven initiatives the OECD launched after this precondition had emerged at the international level. International capital mobility is usually associated with the abolition of capital controls, the establishment of the double-tax avoidance regime, and the EU's Single European Act (Genschel 2002; Helleiner 1996; Rixen 2008). As governments had achieved these objectives only by the end of the 1980s, my study seeks to make causal statements on all initiatives against tax evasion and avoidance launched by the OECD after 1990.

In addition to the political process leading toward the multilateral adoption of AEI, these initiatives include the OECD project against harmful tax competition (HTC), the organization's campaign for the adoption of bilateral tax information exchange agreements (TIEAs), and its most recent project against base erosion and profit shifting (BEPS) by multinational firms. The HTC project was launched by the G7 in 1996 in response to growing concerns over the volume of investment routed through tax havens. The project focused on increasing financial transparency as well as removing preferential tax regimes benefiting foreign over domestic firms. The project dissolved into the TIEA campaign in 2001 when the Bush administration withdrew US support from the project's anti–tax avoidance elements. Between 2001 and 2009, the OECD thus focused on the promotion of bilateral information exchange agreements providing for the mutual provision of administrative assistance upon request. Following the UBS scandal and the adoption of FATCA in 2010, the organization's focus shifted toward the development of a global standard for AEI, and its multilateral adoption achieved in 2014. Finally, the G20 tasked the OECD in 2013 with providing a report on BEPS as well as recommendations for its abatement. This mandate resulted in a series of fifteen reports presented in 2015 and an ongoing political struggle over the interpretation and implementation of the included recommendations.

Historical Narratives and Process Verification

Focusing on a small number of initiatives that stand in temporal sequence raises several methodological issues. First, the universe of potential cases contains only four events. Therefore, quantitative analysis based on randomized case selection is unreliable, as a result of the "problem of precision" (Gerring 2007, 87). Second, the initiatives under study tend to build on the given regulatory context. They are most often responses to the perception that previous attempts at curbing tax evasion and avoidance have failed. Past experience thus informs the preferences of domestic actors as to the need for new initiatives against tax evasion and avoidance. Instead of seeing initiatives against tax evasion and avoidance as independent cases, which is a prerequisite for making causal claims based on their systematic comparison, they must thus be interpreted as episodes in a more long-term historical process. Accordingly, the following empirical chapters will not provide case studies in the classical sense. They will rather present several analytical narratives probing the plausibility of the theoretical model and thereby increasing our confidence "that it has captured the central, generalizable dynamics rather than unique elements of a particular case" (Büthe 2002, 489). The narratives are analytical in that they draw a common structure from the theoretical model and focus on those elements of the historical record considered most salient for explaining the outcome of OECD tax initiatives. Within each narrative, process verification is applied to connect this outcome to the causal conditions emphasized in this chapter.

Process verification denotes the application of process tracing in theory testing. According to Bennett and George, "the general method of process tracing is to generate and analyze data on the causal mechanisms . . . that link putative causes to observed effects" (1997, 5). Proponents argue that a causal explanation is insufficient if it relies merely on the establishment of a causal effect based on observed covariance in independent and dependent variables. Instead, it is necessary to study the process linking causes to effects to ascertain that a cause really matters for the reasons assumed by the researcher. Given that my theory provides for several causal steps building on one another to produce the outcome,[8] the method is most suitable for subjecting the theory to a rigorous test. In doing so, I rely on data drawn from official documents and statistics, previous academic research, coverage in the specialized press, and forty-two interviews with experts in international tax policy from international organizations, national governments, and the private sector. I conducted semistructured face-to-face interviews over the course of one and a half years in five different countries, and also had conversations by phone with experts located in a sixth country. My goal was to obtain a balanced ratio of testimony from interlocutors of all professional backgrounds and political leanings, as well as from small and large countries. Moreover, I gave priority to speaking to actual decision makers rather than informed bystanders. As a result, I am usually able to triangulate obtained data on a specific event from several sources. As most interlocutors agreed to provide information, including on international negotiations, only under the condition of anonymity, I will use a general description of the interviewee's function (for example, "OECD tax official") when citing testimony, along with the date of the interview.

Operationalization of the Theoretical Model

The theory developed in this chapter shall explain transformative change in anti–tax evasion and avoidance regulation. Transformative change implies a shift from an established to a new underlying paradigm that alters the logic of action in the regulated field (Hall 1993; Streeck and Thelen 2005). Tax evasion occurs when a household conceals financial wealth and related capital income from the tax office. The crucial prerequisite for tax evasion is the ability of secrecy jurisdictions to hide the identities of foreign investors, as local tax offices could otherwise obtain information on their residents' offshore capital income and augment their tax base accordingly. Therefore, we will observe transformative change in the fight against tax evasion only when regulation replaces the norm of financial secrecy with financial transparency. Financial transparency implies that national tax authorities can readily obtain information on their residents' foreign capital income through official channels. In contrast, tax avoidance refers to accounting schemes enabling multinational corporations to inflate profits in low-tax countries while deflating them in high-tax countries. These practices are enabled by the arm's-length principle in international tax law that obliges tax authorities to treat subsidiaries of a group as separate entities. Accordingly, we will observe transformative change in the fight against tax avoidance only when regulation ends the artificial separation of group subsidiaries and treats multinational firms as unitary entities instead. Unitary taxation implies that the profits of a multinational group are consolidated at the headquarters and then apportioned to individual jurisdictions based on a certain formula.

Whether or not transformative change has occurred at a given point in time subsequently informs the preferences of domestic actors about the need for new international tax initiatives. Center-left governments or voters with egalitarian convictions should, for instance, be even more likely to oppose regressive tax reform if they have the impression that the present regulatory context already allows capital owners to evade their fair share of tax. Therefore, we should expect these groups to voice their demand for international action against tax dodging once they obtain information on the deficiencies of the present regulatory context. Such information may, for instance, be provided by tax authorities, which realize that their foreign counterparts usually turn down requests for administrative assistance. Such information may also be provided through data leaks from foreign banks or law firms revealing that domestic actors evade or avoid taxes offshore despite existing regulation. To accommodate the causal feedback loop created by the impact of past regulation on the current preferences of voters and governments, I will begin every analytical narrative by describing how public scandals or administrative action made actors who are generally in favor of progressive taxation aware of tax dodging and caused them to demand political action. Accordingly, I will assess the importance of barriers to regressive tax reform based on the public availability of information on tax abuse and the government participation of left parties enabling the conversion of information into executive action at the international level.

Similarly, past regulation should also impact to what extent a new initiative against tax dodging affects domestic interest groups. As discussed above, multinationals are, for instance, generally interested in maximizing their earnings per share. A comparatively cheap strategy in this regard is investment in tax law expertise, enabling tax burden minimization in a given regulatory context. Once a multinational has understood how to reach its goal within the present system, however, the investment turns into a sunk cost, causing the firm to prefer legal certainty provided by the status quo to uncertainty created by new initiatives. Adjustment costs should therefore be higher when rules established at the international level depart significantly from the previous regulatory approach and thus oblige affected domestic interest groups to invest in new expertise, compliance procedures, and organizational structures. Accordingly, the analytical narratives will not only trace interest group preferences back to the impact of international tax initiatives on the interest groups' effective tax burden or business model, but also emphasize the extent of administrative adjustment international tax initiatives are likely to precipitate. The yardstick in this regard is whether new rules require affected actors to change their compliance procedures and organizational form.

To connect these domestic factors to the final outcome at the international level, the analytical narratives will first clarify the extent to which government preferences revealed in interviews and speeches by decision makers, as well as official documents, match the position expected for a given combination of domestic conditions in table 2.5. Once government preferences have been empirically determined, the narrative will identify the constellation in table 2.6 that best matches observed bargaining and check whether the great power chooses its strategy as expected. We observe coercion when the US administration explicitly links other countries' access to its internal market to compliance with US demands. At a minimum, such a threat has to be articulated in an official government declaration. Yet it may also be included in legislation, regulation, or court orders. In contrast, we observe voluntary compliance when other governments adopt the great power's preferred rules in the absence of a sanctions threat. This requires that the other governments endorse the relevant international agreements and implement them domestically. Hence, unilateral defection occurs when the great power does not transpose international rules into domestic law. In sum, transformative change will occur only if (1) revelations of tax dodging lead a Democratic US administration to demand more effective rules, (2) and these rules are reconcilable with the interests of powerful domestic veto players. Legal constraints may, however, significantly depress the discursive power of an otherwise influential interest group. The analytical narratives presented in the following chapters will show how the presence and absence of these factors determined the outcome of all OECD initiatives against tax evasion and avoidance after 1990.

COUNTERING HARMFUL TAX PRACTICES

Analysts agree on the Clinton administration's decisive role in putting the issues of tax evasion and avoidance on the agenda of the Group of Seven (G7), and subsequently the Organisation for Economic Co-operation and Development (OECD) (Eccleston 2012; Kudrle 2003; Rixen 2008). Yet disagreement remains as to the reasons for its failure to lead the harmful tax competition (HTC) initiative to success. While some authors refer to timing, arguing that the Clinton administration was simply unable to finish its work on the issue before the end of its term in 2000 (Palan, Murphy, and Chavagneux 2010), others claim that tax havens successfully exploited the regulative norm of nonintervention to defend themselves against OECD requests for more cooperation in tax matters (Sharman 2006a). This chapter shows that the Clinton administration was, indeed, concerned about the impact of tax havens on the perceived fairness of the US tax system, international financial stability, and the US sanctions regime, and thus promoted an international campaign against underregulated financial centers. The OECD, however, made the strategic mistake to tackle tax evasion by individuals and tax avoidance by multinationals in a single project, creating opposition from business associations in the United States and elsewhere. Instead of credibly linking noncompliance with OECD recommendations to economic sanctions, the Clinton administration thus accepted the severe dilution of the HTC initiative's anti-avoidance elements even before the Bush administration took office in 2001. A nested comparison of two unilateral tax initiatives moreover reveals that the Clinton administration generally failed to pass regulations curbing tax avoidance but succeeded in passing regulations against tax evasion.

The Clinton Administration's Tax Policy Agenda

William J. Clinton's election as president of the United States in 1992 ended 12 years of Republican government. Under Presidents Ronald Reagan and George H.W. Bush, income inequality and public debt had dramatically increased because of regressive tax reforms, cuts to public investment in job training and wage subsidies, and a massive surge in military spending (Bartels 2009; Danziger and Gottschalk 1997). Catering to widespread public disenchantment with inequality and an "unfair" tax system perceived as "benefiting the rich," Clinton had thus promised an income tax cut for the middle class during the electoral campaign (Steinmo 1994, 13). After the election, however, Lloyd Bentsen, secretary of the Treasury, and Robert Rubin, chairman of the National Economic Council, argued that priority should be given to deficit reduction, as this might impress financial market analysts, trigger more private saving and investment, and reduce interest rates. Bentsen and Rubin's idea of restoring business confidence defeated proposals for Keynesian stimulus in internal debate (Steuerle 2008). Hence, the Clinton administration removed the middle-class tax cut from its first budget proposal for 1994. Instead, it proposed an expansion of earned income tax credits (EITC) for the working poor, financed by higher taxes for upper-income individuals and corporations (Graetz 1993). As President Clinton explained in his first State of the Union speech, the goal of EITC expansion was to "reward the work of millions of working poor Americans by realizing the principle that if you work forty hours a week and you've got a child in the house, you will no longer be in poverty" (cited in Hotz 2003, 146).

The measure was indeed retained in the Omnibus Budget Reconciliation Act of 1993, which was supposed to cut the deficit by $500 billion over five years, and also introduced new tax brackets and higher rates for top personal and corporate incomes, as well as slightly higher taxes on motor fuel consumption. Because of large Democratic majorities in both chambers of Congress, the act passed in summer 1993 despite forty-one Democratic representatives and six Democratic senators voting against the bill (Sabo 1993). These members of Congress justified their opposition with concerns over the electoral impact of supporting increased taxes on income and energy consumption (Rosenbaum 1993; Sullivan 1993). On balance, however, "the net effect in 1993 was to give more to low-income families, leave the middle class more or less untouched, and zap the rich" (Steuerle 2008, 166). By passing the Omnibus Budget Reconciliation Act, the Clinton administration thus managed to reconcile deficit reduction with increased tax progressivity, which some even interpreted as a reversal of Reaganomics (Fram 1993). Still, the political cost of increasing taxes was enormous, as 50 percent of survey respondents, even those with low incomes, felt affected (Steuerle 2008). According to Robert Rubin, "the mischaracterization of our deficit reduction as a tax increase on the middle class" was a major reason for Democratic defeat in congressional elections of 1994 (Robert Rubin and Weisberg 2003, 153). As a result, Republicans regained full control of Congress for the first time since 1951, subsequently preventing the Clinton administration from pursuing major legislative initiatives. Its focus therefore shifted to the international level where the Treasury, in particular, aimed to foster projects that could support deficit reduction by creating additional revenue and growth. As Brad DeLong and Barry Eichengreen (2001, 2) explain:

> Following the loss of Democratic control of the Congress in 1994, all ambitious domestic initiatives were obviously dead in the water. If this didn't exactly create a political vacuum and a demand for newspaper headlines that could only be filled by international events, it at least facilitated the efforts of Treasury and other economic agencies to bring these issues to the attention of the president and his core political advisors.

Among the international issues raising concerns within Treasury was the proliferation of tax havens and their increasing use by US investors. This concern was based on a number of economic studies questioning the survival of capital taxation in open economies (cf. Gordon 1992; Frenkel, Razin, and Sadka 1991), which were taken up by international bureaucracies like the OECD, the International Monetary Fund (IMF), and the European Commission, and empirically supported by massive capital flight from Germany to Luxembourg following the introduction of a withholding tax on interest in 1988 (cf. Cassard 1994; Owens 1993; Ruding 1992; Tanzi 1995). At the time, the increasing role of tax havens in financial intermediation had become apparent following the removal of barriers to capital mobility over the course of the 1980s. As a result of the "tax cut cum base-broadening strategy" OECD governments had devised in response to tax competition (Ganghof 2000, 611), however, increased capital mobility had not yet impacted their revenue from the taxation of corporate profits and capital income (Webb 2004; Zucman 2014). Still, proponents of the welfare state bought into economic projections of declining capital taxation, anticipating the near "end of redistribution" (Steinmo 1994, 9). Against this background, the Treasury's international tax counsel, Joseph Guttentag, as well as his deputy, Philip West, argued for enhanced cooperation in tax matters within the OECD, citing the abuse of transfer pricing, hybrid entities, and lack of information exchange as major areas of concern (Guttentag 1995; West 1996). According to Reuven Avi-Yonah (2005, 314), Guttentag and West were the main players behind a transition in US international tax policy from the "age of competition" to the "age of cooperation."

The potentially erosive impact of tax havens on the US tax base was, however, not the only reason for the Clinton administration's preoccupation with them. From its perspective, the financial opacity they provided to investors also abetted money-laundering and corruption and undermined the stability of the financial system as well as the US sanctions regime (Wechsler 2001). At the time, cases had multiplied involving drug cartels using Caribbean secrecy jurisdictions to launder their proceeds from narcotics sales in the United States. Financial institutions and law firms in the secrecy jurisdictions not only helped to hide the true origin of funds through the provision of bank secrecy or shell corporations; they also invested illicit funds in financial, real estate, and arts markets on behalf of criminal organizations. In parallel, the belief spread among senior law enforcement officials that draining the money supply of criminal organizations was the most effective way to reach their senior figures. Accordingly, legislation enabling tougher prosecution of the placement of illicit funds in US banks was passed throughout the 1980s, leading to an increasing number of cases and convictions. Ultimately, however, this legislation led only to a shift in transfer strategies from simple bank transfers to physical smuggling and the use of nonbank financial institutions. The prevention of money laundering in secrecy jurisdictions after illicit funds had been successfully transferred out of the United States thus required international action. A fortiori this was the case because the laundering of funds that had never been in the United States could still affect US interests. For instance, financial sanctions against particular individuals or governments could easily be circumvented by setting up shell corporations and nominee accounts in secrecy jurisdictions (Sultzer 1995; Williams 1997).

Based on these tax and law enforcement concerns, the Clinton Treasury came to the conclusion that a new strategy against tax havens was needed. Moreover, "any strategy had to be global and multilateral, since unilateral actions would only drive dirty money to the world's other major financial centers" (Wechsler 2001, 49). However, it was believed that such an anti–tax haven initiative should not be pursued via the United Nations, where countries with underregulated financial markets were a majority. Instead, the Clinton administration preferred working with the G7 and OECD to first establish consensus among large industrialized countries. Once international standards had been developed in these more exclusive formats, noncompliant jurisdictions would be pressured into cooperation through naming and shaming as well as collective sanction threats (Wechsler 2001, 49). In the area of taxation, this strategy led to and was pursued via the OECD's harmful tax competition initiative, the genesis of which is the subject of the next subsection.

International Politics: Countering Tax Abuse via the OECD

Based on the reasoning described previously, the Clinton administration initiated discussions on an international initiative against tax evasion and avoidance in the G7 in 1995 (Eccleston 2012; Rixen 2008). The idea was welcomed by European G7 members, which were at the time struggling to contain tax evasion and avoidance within the European Union (EU). Following the liberalization of capital flows through the Single European Act and the capital markets directive of 1987, EU member states witnessed an increased volume of cross-border transactions and investments. However, because of the unanimity requirement in matters of direct taxation and fears that tax harmonization within the EU would lead to capital flight from the common market, EU member states were unable to reach consensus on tax cooperation despite several proposals from the European Commission to this effect (Genschel 2002; Radaelli 1999). An initiative binding governments beyond the EU, however, had the potential to alleviate the risk of capital flight to third countries. The interests of France, Germany, Italy, and the United Kingdom were thus largely aligned with those of the United States. As a result, G7 leaders issued a joint call on the OECD to "establish a multilateral approach under which countries could operate individually and collectively to limit the extent of [harmful tax] practices" (G7 Leaders 1996, para. 16).

As requested, the OECD established "Special Sessions on Tax Competition," which were tasked with elaborating a report on "harmful tax competition," eventually published in January 1998. In that report, the organization identified tax havens providing financial secrecy, preferential tax regimes (PTRs), or both as potentially harmful—that is, tending to "erode the tax bases of other countries, distort trade and investment patterns and undermine the fairness, neutrality and broad social acceptance of tax systems generally" (OECD 1998, 8). Tax havens were associated with "no or only nominal taxation" of capital income or corporate profits, a lack of transparency and administrative assistance, and an absent link between tax residency and substantial economic activity. From the OECD's perspective these factors were indicative of a jurisdiction "attempting to attract investment or transactions that are purely tax driven" (OECD 1998, 22). PTRs essentially referred to tax breaks granted only to foreign corporations, ring-fencing the domestic tax base from their impact. Examples cited by the OECD included the exemption of foreign profits from residence taxation, "deductions for deemed expenses that are not actually incurred," and the acceptance of transfer-pricing arrangements that do not reflect the arm's-length principle, thereby overstating a subsidiary's local profits (OECD 1998, 30–32). The OECD made nineteen recommendations for fighting these practices, focusing on the collective application by member states of unilateral defense measures and the toughening of administrative assistance clauses in bilateral tax treaties. In addition, the OECD threatened secrecy jurisdictions with blacklisting and sanctions should they not respond to requests for administrative assistance from foreign tax authorities. In contrast, no such threat was issued toward corporate tax havens offering PTRs, most likely because most large OECD members also had such regimes in place (Rixen 2008).

With the exception of Luxembourg and Switzerland, which abstained from the vote, all OECD member states approved the HTC report at the 1998 Ministerial Council. The Clinton administration also expressed its support, pledging to transpose OECD recommendations into national law by 2000. To that effect, the administration announced reporting requirements for all payments going to tax havens identified by the OECD as well as the "termination of credits for taxes paid at source in these countries" (Palan, Murphy, and Chavagneux 2010, 217). Subsequently, Treasury also included these measures in its Green Book of Revenue Proposals for fiscal year 2001 (cf. US Treasury 2000). In contrast, the forty-one jurisdictions identified as tax havens by the OECD for providing secrecy, PTRs, or both tried to attack the HTC project on normative grounds, as a result of their lack of material power resources. Their aim was to convince OECD governments to abandon the campaign by stressing its inconsistency with norms these governments generally promoted. For instance, the jurisdictions argued the project was undermining their fiscal sovereignty and depriving them of an IMF-approved development strategy. Moreover, they claimed that the project's top-down approach—excluding them from negotiations, while making them subject to its provisions—violated the principle of multilateralism. Last but not least, the jurisdictions also accused the OECD of applying double standards, as it cracked down on non-OECD tax havens but ignored the practices of Luxembourg and Switzerland as well as the PTRs established by larger member states (Sharman 2006a; Webb 2004).

Although these arguments gained traction with the multinational business community and the financial and tax service industries in particular, the OECD still identified forty-one jurisdictions as tax havens in June 2000 and threatened them with the collective application of defense measures. Again, the Clinton administration was supportive of OECD efforts, with Secretary of the Treasury Lawrence Summers declaring the United States "would fully cooperate in preparing sanctions for tax havens that fail to reform" (Associated Press 2000b). In response, six out of the forty-one identified tax havens, including some major players like Bermuda and the Cayman Islands, signed agreements with the OECD in which they pledged to abolish harmful provisions in their tax codes in exchange for being removed from the draft list of uncooperative tax havens that could be hit with countermeasures (cf. Government of Bermuda 2000; Governor of the Cayman Islands 2000). Accordingly, these six jurisdictions were missing from the final tax haven blacklist included in the OECD's 2000 progress report, whereas the remaining thirty-five jurisdictions were threatened with collective defense measures if they did not sign a memorandum of understanding (MOU) by July 31, 2001, obliging them to abandon their harmful tax practices (cf. OECD 2000). By the end of 2000 the HTC initiative thus seemed to be fostering good progress toward the goal of eliminating the most harmful features of tax haven business models.

Effectively, however, submission to the OECD came at relatively low cost for the targeted jurisdictions, as multinationals organized in the Business Industry Advisory Council (BIAC) had successfully lobbied for a removal of the substantial economic activity criterion from the OECD's tax haven definition. By removing corporate tax planning from the scope of the HTC project, business gave Bermuda, the Cayman Islands, and other relatively sophisticated countries, acting both as secrecy jurisdictions and corporate tax havens, the opportunity to polish their reputations by renouncing parts of their tax evasion business while at the same time expanding their tax avoidance business with multinationals (Eccleston 2012; Webb 2004). Tax havens were thus provided an opportunity to avoid blacklisting and the risk of sanctions without making fundamental changes to their business models. Still, these jurisdictions failed to halt the HTC initiative altogether by turning dominant norms against their key proponents. Instead, the following subsections will show that differences in material power resources were decisive in this episode of bargaining over international tax cooperation. Rather than tax havens, the domestically defined preferences of the United States, which has traditionally dominated tax policymaking in the OECD, largely shaped the content of the HTC initiative at this stage (Avi-Yonah 2005; Farquet and Leimgruber 2014; Graetz 2000).

Implementing Anti–Tax Evasion and Avoidance Measures Domestically

As demonstrated previously, the Clinton administration was fully supportive of the OECD's HTC initiative and prepared to deploy sanctions against noncooperative tax havens. The administration's support was based on economic projections of declining revenue from capital taxation in open economies and a general concern over the relevance of secrecy jurisdictions for organized crime, corruption, and financial instability. Moreover, support was driven by a concern for the publicly perceived fairness of the US income tax system. As Lawrence Summers explained in an interview in 2000, "[the US] tax system is based on voluntary compliance. That compliance depends on people having the sense that others, particularly those who are more fortunate, pay the taxes they are required to pay" (Associated Press 2000a). However, the Clinton administration faced strong opposition to its international tax agenda whenever it affected the tax-planning practices of US multinationals. Therefore, Treasury accepted the dilution of the substantial economic activity criterion in the OECD's 2000 progress report, extended check-the-box rules to US multinationals' foreign subsidiaries despite prior doubts as to potential exploitation of the rules through the setup of hybrid entities, and later backed down from withdrawing corresponding regulations. When neither the interests of US multinationals nor those of US financial institutions were adversely affected, however, Treasury was able to pass regulations—for instance, when creating the qualified intermediary (QI) program.

Adjusting the HTC Initiative to Business Preferences

With the approval of the United States, the OECD's Committee on Fiscal Affairs (CFA) had adopted an HTC report aiming both at tax evasion by individuals and tax avoidance by multinationals. Yet dealing with both elements in a single project turned out to be a strategic mistake. One of the elements meant to counter avoidance was the substantial economic activity criterion included in the report's tax haven definition. From the OECD's perspective, granting a corporation tax residence in "the absence of a requirement that [its] activity be substantial . . . suggests that a jurisdiction may be attempting to attract investment and transactions that are purely tax driven" (OECD 1998, 24). This practice was considered harmful and thus ought to be ended by governments wishing to comply with OECD recommendations. Yet making a corporation's tax residence conditional on substantial economic activity in the respective country posed a fundamental threat to corporate tax-planning strategies, which usually hinge on the ability of multinationals to shift profits to low-tax jurisdictions where no production takes place and no value is added (Pinkernell 2014). Accordingly, business lobbyists in the United States and elsewhere staged a campaign against the criterion, trying to convince OECD governments of its incompatibility with basic liberal norms (Webb 2004).

BIAC's initial response to the HTC report was drafted by Richard Hammer, who also served as chief tax counsel for the United States Council for International Business (USCIB) (Ralph 2000). USCIB, in turn, is the main lobbying group for US multinationals at the OECD, its membership including many corporations reputed for their tax-planning savvy. Following consultations with multinationals and their tax advisers, Hammer criticized the OECD for not having met with representatives of businesses prior to the release of the HTC report (Ralph 1999). Moreover, Hammer framed tax competition as a means to impose fiscal discipline on governments, forcing them "to make more efficient use of tax revenues" (BIAC 1998, cited in Webb 2004, 811), a variant of the traditional liberal interpretation of tax competition as "the taming of Leviathan" (Sinn 1992, 177). Against this background, he went on to argue "that it was legitimate for businesses to consider tax differentials in planning and structuring their investments" (Webb 2004, 811). These two arguments subsequently became the basis for corporate criticism of the HTC project, frequently employed by representatives of multinationals and corporate tax advisers (cf. Couzin 2000; Katsushima 1999).

Yet corporate critics of the OECD did not object to all forms of international tax cooperation. In fact, they were supportive of efforts to combat tax evasion by means of greater financial transparency and in favor of removing regulations ring-fencing tax breaks for foreign-owned corporations from domestic firms. As Webb (2004) suggests, business associations were more conciliatory toward these measures because they either did not directly affect their members or were conducive to expanding targeted expenditures to the entire economy. Regarding information exchange, banks from wealth management hubs such as Florida or Texas were of course opposed to reporting additional client data. Accordingly, the Clinton administration put corresponding proposals on the back burner (Freedberg 2002). Yet the banks were indifferent toward new reporting requirements for foreign financial institutions (FFIs) and corresponding sanction threats against secrecy jurisdictions. Hence, the banks did not back the anti-OECD campaign launched in parallel by the Center for Freedom and Prosperity (CFP) (Sharman 2006a).[1]

At any rate, the OECD Secretariat was swift to accommodate corporate criticism, as it feared opposition from national business associations could cause individual member states to defect from the initiative, thereby endangering the project's survival. In cooperation with BIAC the OECD thus created a liaison group "to ensure that the views of the business community are heard," acknowledging "a need for better communication between business and government, and, in particular, a more inclusive attitude on the part of governments toward the views of the business community" (Hammer and Owens 2001, 1305). Moreover, Jeffrey Owens, the OECD's head of fiscal affairs, explicitly accepted the legitimacy of corporate tax planning, conceding in a joint article with Richard Hammer that "multinational enterprises should be permitted access to certain corporate organizational and structural vehicles, such as co-ordination centres and holding companies" (Hammer and Owens 2001, 1303). Under the chairmanship of Joseph Guttentag, previously international tax counsel in the Clinton Treasury Department, and with the consent of the United States, the CFA therefore adopted some subtle changes to the HTC report's substantial economic activity criterion during the second half of 2000.

As Kudrle (2008, 7) explains, the CFA first "grafted [ring-fencing] on to insubstantiality as an alternative source of concern" by redrafting the criterion as follows in the 2000 progress report: "the jurisdiction facilitates the establishment of foreign owned entities without the need for a local substantive presence or prohibits these entities from having a commercial impact on the economy" (OECD 2000, 10). On this basis, the CFA then shifted the blame for insubstantiality onto jurisdictions that were denying firms benefiting from preferential tax treatment the opportunity to operate in the domestic market. In the MOU offered to tax havens willing to comply with OECD demands, the requirement for being exonerated from the charge of providing tax residence in the absence of substantial economic activity was thus formulated in a rather twisted way:

> For any preferential tax treatment accorded to other service activities, each Party will remove any restrictions that deny the benefits of that preferential tax treatment to resident taxpayers, to entities owned by resident taxpayers, or to income derived from doing the same type of business in the domestic market. (OECD 2000b, 4 cited in Kudrle 2008, 7)

Effectively, this meant that tax havens were allowed to provide tax residence to firms without a substantive presence in these jurisdictions' territory if they stopped ring-fencing preferential tax treatment of foreign companies from the domestic economy. By November 2000 the CFA had thus neutralized the fundamental threat to corporations' "legitimate" tax-planning strategies that the original formulation of the substantial economic activity criterion had posed. While Lawrence Summers and Philip West reiterated strong US support for the HTC initiative and urged tax havens to comply with OECD demands, in their capacities as secretary of the Treasury and international tax counsel they had also allowed the CFA to dilute important terms and definitions when they interfered with the interests of US multinationals (Associated Press 2000c; Burgess 2000). As a result, corporate tax havens could enter into MOUs with the OECD to avoid sanctions without risking their stake in tax avoidance schemes. Only those secrecy jurisdictions that refused to make limited adjustments to their administrative assistance practices eventually faced a risk of sanctions from the United States and other OECD members.[2]

Poking Loopholes into Controlled Foreign Company Rules

The Clinton administration's inability to implement measures limiting the extent of tax avoidance by US multinationals is even better illustrated in the parallel debate over check-the-box regulations. These regulations, proposed by the Internal Revenue Service (IRS) in 1995, were meant to simplify entity classification for tax purposes. Until then, taxpayers and the IRS had used the so-called Kintner test to determine whether an entity was a corporation or a partnership, the latter being disregarded for tax purposes because partners—who also assumed full liability for the partnership's debt—were taxed on its profits at the personal level. With the multiplication of corporate legal forms at the state and international levels, however, determining whether or not a certain company passed the criteria of the Kintner test became increasingly cumbersome for tax authorities. At the same time, well-advised taxpayers were increasingly able to tailor their company's legal form so as to obtain their desired classification for tax purposes (IRS 1995). Against this background, some IRS officials as well as business associations began to argue for a simplification of entity classification through an elective approach. That is, taxpayers should be allowed to choose their desired classification by simply checking a box on an IRS form. According to the proponents of this approach, this change would reduce the administrative burden for the IRS, which would no longer have to analyze foreign law to determine entity status, and remove inequities between sophisticated and unsophisticated taxpayers, as the former were de facto already able to choose their desired classification under the Kintner regulations (Mullis 2011).

After public hearings on the issue had yielded almost unanimous support for check-the-box regulations from the business and tax services community, the IRS adopted the regulations in 1996 despite internal warnings as to their potential abuse through the setup of hybrid entities (Dean 2006; IRS and Treasury 1996). Contrary to contemporary wisdom, the proliferation of hybrid entities was not an unintended consequence of check-the-box regulations. In fact, some officials within Treasury and the IRS were fully aware that allowing taxpayers to choose the classification of foreign entities could abet tax avoidance by multinational corporations.[3] Joseph Guttentag (1995, 449), for instance, told tax professionals at a conference in 1996 that "the major concerns with respect to the check-the-box proposal center on the international area, specifically the problems presented by organizations treated as taxable by one jurisdiction and as transparent by another, the so-called hybrids." Likewise, Robert Culbertson, IRS associate chief counsel (international), told members of the American Bar Association in 1995 he expected an extension of check-the-box regulations to foreign entities to increase the number of hybrids (Mullis 2011). Yet proponents from the tax service community managed to allay these fears, arguing that a move from de facto electivity to formal electivity would lead to merely an incremental increase, if any, in the number of hybrids, which would be more than made up for by the increase in simplicity, efficiency, and fairness provided by check-the-box regulations (cf. NYSBA

1995). In acknowledgment of internal concerns over hybrids, final regulations still indicated that

> Treasury and the IRS will continue to monitor carefully the uses of partnerships in the international context and will take appropriate action when partnerships are used to achieve results that are inconsistent with the policies and rules of particular Code provisions or of US tax treaties. (IRS 1997, 216)

In accordance with expectations from internal critics, a large number of US multinationals subsequently began to bring about inconsistencies between the classification of their foreign subsidiaries in the United States and the host country by simply checking the box. This enabled them to circumvent US controlled foreign company (CFC) regulations, as well as taxation at source (IRS 1998b; Office of Tax Policy 2000).

CFC regulations, included in the Internal Revenue Code as subpart F by the Kennedy administration, were intended to curb the ability of US taxpayers to defer tax payments on profits earned by foreign corporations under their control. Until then, such profits were taxed in the United States only once they were redistributed as dividends to US shareholders. Profits retained abroad remained tax-free. The Kennedy administration considered deferral inequitable and distorting, as it disadvantaged taxpayers without foreign income vis-à-vis taxpayers with foreign income, and therefore created an incentive to invest abroad rather than in the United States. In its original CFC proposal the administration therefore suggested that all foreign income of US-controlled foreign corporations be taxed currently. Because of concerns over the competitiveness of US multinationals, however, Congress eventually reduced the scope of subpart F to passive income earned by foreign subsidiaries in low-tax jurisdictions (Office of Tax Policy 2000).

The setup of hybrid entities simplified by check-the-box regulations does, however, enable deferral even for this income category. A US multinational may, for instance, own a CFC in a high-tax jurisdiction ("High Tax Co"). To avoid having High Tax Co's income taxed at source, the multinational could instruct High Tax Co to create a branch in a low-tax jurisdiction ("Low Tax Br") and opt for disregarded entity status under check-the-box regulations. Low Tax Br could then offer High Tax Co a loan repayable with interest. As High Tax Co's host country classifies Low Tax Br as a foreign corporation, High Tax Co can deduct interest payments as business expenses from its local tax bill. As the IRS classifies Low Tax Br as a disregarded entity subsumed under High Tax Co, the loan and interest payments cancel each other out from the US perspective. There is thus no passive income to be taxed currently under subpart F. As a result of this "earnings stripping with a disregarded loan" strategy, the US multinational may thus significantly reduce its tax bill both in the United States and abroad (Mullis 2011).[4]

Based on their monitoring effort, Treasury and the IRS concluded in 1998 "that the use of certain hybrid arrangements . . . is contrary to the policies and rules of subpart F," and that "the recent entity classification regulations . . . (the 'check-the-box' regulations) have facilitated the creation of the hybrid branches used in these arrangements" (IRS 1998a, 18). Accordingly, the IRS released temporary "regulations to address such arrangements, and [requested] public comments with respect to these subpart F issues" (IRS 1998a, 18). The response from the business and tax service communities was devastating. Tax practitioners argued that temporary regulations were equivalent to an extension of subpart F, for which the IRS lacked the necessary authority (Cooper and Torgersen 1998). Moreover, they claimed "that much of the planning had the effect of reducing foreign taxes, an objective that historically has been viewed as a good business objective from a US perspective" (DeCarlo, Granwell, and Suringa 1998, 21). Accordingly, curbing the abuse of check-the-box rules was interpreted as a blow to the competitiveness of US multinationals (Carson, Cinnamon, and Kronbergs 1998).

US multinationals in response formed several lobbying coalitions with their tax advisers and accountants to convince Congress of their arguments. Eventually, the chairmen of the Senate Finance Committee and the House Ways and Means Committee fell into line, expressing their belief "that Congress, not the Department of the Treasury or the IRS, should determine policy issues relating to the treatment of hybrid transactions under subpart F" (Cooper and Torgersen 1998, 68). Accordingly, they threatened the IRS with a moratorium on its temporary regulations if it did not withdraw them "until a complete analysis of subpart F could be undertaken and laws passed through the proper legislative process" (Cooper and Torgersen 1998, 68). Only six months after the IRS had issued regulations to curb the abuse of check-the-box rules it thus revoked them in June 1998 (IRS 1998b).[5] Hence, the Clinton administration was unable to prevent abuse of its CFC regime under subpart F, while the OECD recommended the collective adoption of CFC legislation as a defensive measure against harmful tax competition (cf. OECD 1998).

Enforcing the Qualified Intermediary Program

The Clinton administration's attempts to curb international tax avoidance by US multinationals were defeated by business opposition. However, Treasury and the IRS managed to introduce some withholding and reporting requirements for foreign banks to limit tax evasion by US taxpayers with foreign accounts. The QI program and its accompanying regulations were developed from 1997 and finalized in 2000. They entered into force on January 1, 2001 (IRS 1999, 2000). The program encouraged FFIs to become QIs by signing a contract with the IRS. As QIs they are required to report US-source income received by their clients and withhold the corresponding US taxes. In exchange, FFIs are allowed to report income earned by non-US clients on a pooled basis instead of reporting every client individually. This provision enabled FFIs to shield client data from the IRS and US banks acting as withholding agents, which were potential competitors. Nonetheless, US-source income earned by US taxpayers still had to be reported on an individual basis (Government Accountability Office 2007).

The QI program was supposed to ensure the efficiency of the US withholding regime against the background of increased investment in US securities by non-institutional investors. In 1913, Congress had taken the fundamental decision to withhold tax on income from investments in the United States before this income leaves the country. This included dividends and certain bond yields that were to be taxed at 30 percent. However, other forms of capital income, including interest from bank deposits, Treasury bonds, and corporate debt obligations, were exempt from withholding to attract foreign investment. In addition, the US government offered lower withholding tax rates to foreign countries in bilateral tax treaties. US financial institutions, acting as withholding agents for the IRS, thus had the formal obligation to identify the income source and the beneficial owner's nationality, withhold accordingly, and transfer resulting tax revenue to the IRS. Exempt income still had to be aggregated by source and destination and then reported to the service (Government Accountability Office 2007). Identification of beneficial owners relied exclusively on so-called "statements of eligibility" provided by nonresident aliens to US withholding agents. There was, however, no system in place that would enable the withholding agent to verify the accuracy of obtained information through documentation provided by FFIs actually servicing the beneficial owner. This lack of verification created uncertainty as to whether US-source income was correctly reported and withheld upon (Shay, Fleming, and Peroni 2002, 123–24).

The growing number of small foreign investors in the United States exacerbated the problem and increased the administrative burden for US withholding agents. Through the QI program, the IRS tried to improve the situation by shifting "the burden of investigating beneficial ownership on foreign financial institutions rather than on US custodians, and . . . providing clear rules requiring withholding in the absence of documentation" (Shay, Fleming, and Peroni 2002, 123–24). Under the new regulations, FFIs had to forward client information obtained through know-your-customer (KYC) due-diligence procedures for every client wishing to be exempt from US withholding tax to the withholding agent managing their correspondent account. By providing this type of data to a US bank, an FFI basically invited a competitor to lure away its wealthy clients. Therefore, the IRS granted FFIs registering as QIs an exemption from individual reporting of their non-US clients. Instead, they were allowed to report pooled income and obliged to directly withhold and transfer corresponding US tax to the IRS. Income earned by US taxpayers still had to be reported and withheld on an individual basis. But in accordance with general US tax law, IRS regulations did not require FFIs to look through foreign corporations. As a result, US taxpayers could hide behind interposed entities to evade US income tax and, after the QI program had been established, also illegitimately obtain tax exemptions or treaty benefits on their investment in US securities (Government Accountability Office 2007).

The program was very successful with FFIs, as it enabled them to avoid the 30 percent withholding tax on US investments for their clients, while protecting their anonymity from US banks and the IRS. As some tax professionals concluded at the time: "Because of the relative secrecy benefits provided to non-US citizens or residents, the failure of a private bank to qualify as a QI would put that bank in a competitive disadvantage in the marketplace" (O'Donnell, Marcovici, and Michaels 2000, 33). Inside the United States, the program received very little commentary during its elaboration phase because it actually shifted responsibility for the identification of beneficial owners to FFIs, thereby reducing the administrative burden for US withholding agents. In fact, in setting up the QI program, the IRS also responded to "years of requests from US banks and brokers to consolidate, clarify, and reduce documentation rules" (Kentouris 1997, 18). At the same time, those US persons whose interests were most affected—US investors evading tax by operating through foreign banks—could not publicly defend their position and were not considered a legitimate lobbying group by any influential political force.[6] Although the program had many loopholes and was thus easy for US taxpayers to circumvent, it still provided "some level of deterrence against tax fraud and evasion" (Shay, Fleming, and Peroni 2002, 128). Moreover, the IRS had "effectively created the first major operational precedent for the concept of a cross-border anonymous withholding regime" (Grinberg 2012, 17).

Theoretical Implications

The Clinton administration entered office with the goal of restoring the tax system's progressivity. Because of internal concerns over the budget deficit, however, a promised tax cut for the middle class was replaced by a more targeted EITC for the working poor, financed by higher taxes on high incomes and fuel consumption. Although this package did not have a meaningful impact on the after-tax incomes of the middle class, its regressive element was interpreted as a tax raise for this income group, leading to Democratic defeat in the congressional elections of 1993. Faced with a Republican Congress, the Clinton administration's focus subsequently shifted from legislative projects to international initiatives with the potential to increase growth and tax revenue. Within the area of taxation, the administration thus consulted with other developed countries organized in the G7 and OECD to set up an international initiative against harmful tax competition.

A corresponding report elaborated by the OECD Secretariat concluded that tax havens offering financial secrecy and PTRs were abetting tax evasion by individuals and tax avoidance by corporations. The OECD made nineteen recommendations for ending harmful practices and threatened tax havens with blacklisting and sanctions should they not comply with OECD demands. As a result of business opposition, however, the report soon lost much of its corporate dimension, enabling sophisticated tax havens to submit to the OECD while defending their stake in the tax-planning schemes of multinationals. Although the Clinton administration publicly backed the OECD's sanctions threat, the administration had not leaned against this shift in the HTC project's underlying focus. At the same time, the administration also failed to defend the US CFC regime against abuse through hybrid entities, the collective adoption of which was one of the defensive measures against harmful tax competition recommended by the OECD. In contrast, some regulatory progress was achieved when multinationals were unaffected and administrative costs could be shifted from domestic to foreign entities. Through the QI program, the Clinton administration introduced new reporting and withholding duties for FFIs, which at least deterred some less sophisticated investors from evading US income taxes on their foreign capital income. This progress happened while the US budget was balanced and in the absence of a financial crisis.

We thus observed a Democratic administration that put tax cooperation on the international agenda as a result of concerns over the perceived fairness of the US tax system, financial stability, and the effectiveness of the US sanctions regime. However, the multilateral HTC initiative soon lost momentum, as it also affected the tax-planning schemes of multinational corporations. From their perspective, the corresponding OECD recommendations created additional costs instead of competitive advantages. Hence, they organized opposition against the initiative's avoidance-related elements. In reaction, the Clinton administration allowed the dilution of the substantial economic activity criterion, while continuing to strongly support the HTC initiative in public. The administration's positioning thus fits well into the bottom-left corner of table 2.5, summarizing the expected stance of a government faced with political barriers to regressive tax reform and high adjustment costs for powerful interest groups. At the international level, the Clinton administration made credible sanction threats to force initially reluctant tax havens to the negotiating table. Once important definitions had been diluted, however, tax havens could enter into virtually costless agreements with the OECD to avoid the risk of being sanctioned. Over time, and largely as a result of domestic business opposition, the US strategy thus shifted from coercion to enabling voluntary agreements with tax havens.

The reference to regulative norms played a major role in the communication strategy of tax havens. Yet it did not prevent the OECD or the United States from requesting greater administrative assistance and more financial transparency from these tax havens. In late 2000, six major secrecy jurisdictions even formally committed to respect OECD standards for information exchange in order to be removed from a blacklist. This measure should not have been necessary if normative arguments against foreign interference and extraterritoriality had really turned the decision of tax-haven governments to remain noncooperative into a legitimate policy option. Rather than fending off OECD interference on normative grounds, tax haven governments seized the opportunity to avoid the reputational cost of being included in a blacklist once the OECD had watered down its requests in accordance with demands from domestic business associations in the United States. Likewise, the Clinton administration was not prevented from cracking down on tax avoidance by its electoral defeat. Rather, it bowed to pressure from US multinationals and thus reduced the HTC initiative's scope even before the Bush administration came into office.

4

THE SWIFT RETURN OF
TAX COMPETITION

Students of international tax politics agree that the lack of support from the Bush administration eventually killed the Organisation for Economic Co-operation and Development's (OECD) harmful tax competition (HTC) initiative. Accordingly, there is broad acknowledgment of the US government's ability to determine the direction of the OECD's tax work (cf. Eccleston 2012; Palan, Murphy, and Chavagneux 2010; Rixen 2010; Sharman 2006b). Yet analysts disagree over the reasons for its hostile attitude. Whereas some claim that the Bush administration was indifferent toward the project when it entered office and adopted a negative stance only after intense lobbying from libertarian activists (Sharman 2006b), others refer to an intrinsic motivation based on the apparent mismatch between the administration's supply-side tax cut agenda and international efforts to increase the effective tax burden on capital as well as the administration's general skepticism toward multilateral cooperation (Eccleston 2012).

This chapter will demonstrate that the Bush administration was critical of the project from the outset of the administration's first term and therefore had an open ear for the anti-OECD narrative proposed by libertarian advocacy groups. Despite recurrent exchanges between senior Bush appointees and these lobbyists, however, the US Treasury did not fully embrace their requests. Much to their chagrin, it merely removed the anti–tax avoidance elements from the project, while still providing nominal support to its anti–tax evasion measures. The Bush administration's policy was thus more in line with the position of US multinationals represented by the United States Council for International Business (USCIB) than with the fundamental libertarian critique of tax cooperation in general. The administration's ability to transform this position into actual OECD policy despite being isolated within the Group of Seven (G7) is testimony to US power in international bargaining over tax matters.

The Bush Administration's Tax Policy Agenda

During the 2000 presidential campaign, his electoral platform presented George W. Bush as a "compassionate conservative," who favored both tax cuts and increased spending on health care and education. This strategy was, of course, credible only against the background of the budget surplus achieved under Clinton (Steuerle 2008, 199). The cornerstone of the strategy was the Bush tax plan, which provided for an across-the-board reduction in marginal income tax rates, an expansion of the child tax credit, and the abolition of the estate tax on inheritance. Bush and his advisers claimed that "the Bush tax cuts benefit all Americans but reserve the greatest percentage reduction for the lowest income families." Moreover, Bush and his advisers stated cuts would not lead the budget into deficit but leave room for debt reduction instead (Bush Campaign 2000). However, analyses soon revealed the supply-side tax cut agenda behind the plan. According to a widely cited study by Citizens for Tax Justice (2000), the Bush proposals actually provided the top 1 percent of the income distribution with a 13.6 percent tax cut, whereas the bottom 20 percent received only a 5.5 percent cut. Expressed as a share of the proposed tax cut's overall value, the top 1 percent could expect 43 percent of the benefits, whereas the bottom 20 percent would receive less than 1 percent. In addition, the study found that, everything else being equal, this exoneration of the rich would completely eat up the projected budget surplus over the course of the ten-year fiscal period for which the tax cuts were devised.[1]

Despite the Bush team's rhetoric, these numbers suggested that the plan provided for a strongly regressive outcome, matching the traditional Republican conviction that "in order to be successful, tax cuts had to be directed primarily to the wealthy because of their larger role in saving and investment" (Karier 1997, 76). In fact, Lawrence Lindsey, the plan's main author and Bush's chief economic adviser, had built his Washington career in the 1980s on "an academic defense of tax cuts as a spur to economic growth [that] endeared him to the Republican Party's supply-side wing" (Stevenson 1999). Accordingly, Democrats criticized the Bush tax proposals for their lack of fairness. Vice President Al Gore, Bush's main electoral opponent, called the plan "a risky scheme to reward the wealthy" (Stevenson 2000), whereas the Democratic Party's spokeswoman, Jenny Backus, warned the plan would "jeopardize the future of Social Security and Medicare" (Fournier 1999). On the conservative side, commentators were split. Grover Norquist, president of Americans For Tax Reform, praised the plan for "[putting] serious reductions in marginal tax rates, Ronald-Reagan style, back on the table" (Dionne 1999). Likewise, a group of reputed economists known for their neoliberal convictions endorsed the plan in a newspaper ad (Coy 2000).[2] Martin Feldstein, a member of the group, also wrote two op-eds for the Wall Street Journal praising the proposals (Feldstein 1999, 2000). Skeptical voices from among the supply-siders merely criticized the plan as "too timid," and George W. Bush countered with an announcement that he was open to additional tax cuts. "It's the beginning. It's not the end," he told critics, according to the *Washington Post* (Dionne 1999). In contrast, several moderate Republicans, including Alan Greenspan and John McCain, considered the extent of the cuts "fiscally irresponsible," given the uncertainty linked to projections of future growth in gross domestic product (GDP) (Steuerle 2008, 200). McCain, Bush's main opponent in the Republican primaries, even embraced the analysis by Citizens for Tax Justice during a TV debate, stating, "Gov. Bush's tax plan has 60 percent of the tax cuts for the wealthiest 10 percent of America" (Dionne 2000).

Despite opposition from Democrats and moderate Republicans in Congress, deep tax cuts remained the Bush administration's priority after entering office in January 2001. By February 8, the president was already presenting his tax package to Congress as part of the annual congressional budget resolution. Including the package in this type of bill had several procedural advantages. Budget resolutions prevent filibusters and limit the time for debate as well as the number of amendments. As one commentator wrote at the time, "in the evenly split Senate, these advantages will be essential to enact anything like the [proposed] tax package" (Taylor 2000). Despite widespread skepticism as to its chances of adoption, Chairman Chuck Grassley and Ranking Member Max Baucus got the bill past the Senate Finance Committee by extending phase-ins for certain measures, slightly limiting the scope of others, and including some pet projects of skeptical members to secure their support. After similar maneuvering on the Senate floor, the bill eventually passed by a 62–38 margin. Twelve Democrats, all of them either involved in drafting the bill in the Finance Committee, facing reelection the same year, or multimillionaires themselves, voted with the Republicans (Bartels 2009). As a result, President Bush signed one of the biggest tax cuts in history into law on June 7, 2001. Its supply-side orientation was once more underlined in a Treasury companion paper to the bill. Justifying the phaseout of the estate tax, the authors argued that it "impedes economic growth because it levies yet another layer of taxes on capital. More capital investment means higher incomes for all workers" (US Treasury 2001, 8). While critics still lamented the act's unfairness and its adverse impact on the budget, Republican deputies and corporate lobby-ists were just warming up. The US Chamber of Commerce announced further requests for business tax breaks, while Glenn Hubbard, the White House's chief economist, prepared a proposal for a reduction of the dividend tax (Bartels 2009).

President Bush and his advisers continued to be sympathetic to these requests, despite projections of a growing deficit. In addition, the modest downturn fol-lowing the September 11 attacks gave the administration another pretext for aban-doning fiscal discipline in favor of what it sold as a boost to the economy. In ac-cordance with their supply-side convictions, the president and his economic advisers thus put together another tax package giving major relief to capital, while leaving the tax bill of the middle and lower classes virtually unchanged (Steuerle 2008). In addition, September 11 also convinced law enforcement services within the Bush administration of the need to prevent terrorist financing. This convic-tion gave a boost to international anti-money-laundering activities at the Finan-cial Action Task Force (FATF), and provided a backstop against efforts from the Center for Freedom and Prosperity (CFP) and congressional Republicans to com-pletely unravel the OECD's transparency and information exchange work (Pa-lan, Murphy, and Chavagneux 2010; Eden and Kudrle 2005).

The Bush administration's first post-2001 tax initiative was the Job Creation and Worker Assistance Act of 2002. Among other things, it provided US corpo-rations with more generous depreciation allowances for purchases of certain as-sets and tax refunds on business losses incurred as far as five years back. That is, companies were allowed to deduct 50 percent of an asset's value from their tax bill in the year of purchase, instead of deducting only the depreciated value of the asset in every year it is utilized. As Slemrod and Bakija (2008, 49) explain, "spreading the deduction out over time is generally less favorable to the firm than allowing a full deduction at the time of purchase because the tax savings from an immediate deduction can be invested and accumulate interest." In general, mak-ing depreciation allowances more generous and extending the period during which past business losses are eligible for tax refunds are ways to reduce the ef-fective tax rate on corporate income. Still, both parties in Congress were in favor of the measures because they not only provided supply-siders with lower mar-ginal tax rates on capital but could also be sold to Keynesians as a government stimulus, freeing up a large sum for additional investment over a relatively short period of time (Steuerle 2008).

In contrast, the Bush administration's second proposal for a major tax pack-age after 2001 was highly contentious. Its main elements were the exemption of dividends from taxation as personal income and the reduction of capital gains taxes on sales of corporate stock. Moreover, the package provided for the accel-eration of cuts to marginal tax rates imposed on upper income brackets, which would have been phased in over a longer time period under the 2001 package. Given that it is usually upper-income people who earn dividends and capital gains, the overall proposal provided for a $700 billion loss in tax revenue almost exclusively to the benefit of the richest members of society (Bartels 2009). The sheer size of the tax cuts even led several moderate Republican senators to oppose the package, which made them the subject of aspersive campaigns by the Club for Growth, a conservative lobby group financed by unnamed wealthy individuals (Hacker and Pierson 2005). Still, they joined Democratic members of the Senate Finance Committee in requesting a $350 billion ceiling for the proposed cuts. In view of reconciling these concerns with massive pressure from Republicans in the House,[3] the committee leadership decided to tweak the bill through the heavy use of sunsets and phase-ins. By having the most expensive provisions expire after a few years, the leadership reduced the bill's immediate cost below the ceiling requested by the Senate Finance Committee. However, the changes also provided Congress with the ability to extend the cuts beyond their initial date of expiry, with a cost at the time projected to be $736 billion (Hacker and Pierson 2005).[4]

Because of this design, the bill easily passed the Republican-controlled House. In the Senate, however, Vice President Cheney had to cast his tie-breaking vote to enable the adoption of the tax package against opposition from forty-six Democrats, three Republicans, and one Independent (Bartels 2009). Whereas critics outdid one another in the use of pejorative rhetoric in their commentary on the final act, conservative lobby groups and most Republicans rejoiced. As Hacker and Pierson (2005, 48) recount,

> Senate Republican leaders gathered at a press conference to celebrate passage of a cut that was formally far smaller than the one they had originally sought but anticipated to cost far more. When a reporter skeptically inquired as to whether the tax cut just passed was "smoke and mirrors" designed to make a large tax cut smaller, Senator George Allen of Virginia said, "I hope so." All the senators laughed.

Another observer described general optimism among Republicans as to future tax cuts and extensions as follows:

> To conservative groups, who have every intention of pushing for an annual tax cut, arguments over the size of each one are hardly worth worrying about in the long run. "We're going to be negotiating over the size of the tax cut every year for 10 years," said Grover Norquist, president of Americans for Tax Reform. "At the end of 10 years, you're going to see how much progress 'not getting everything you want' gets you." House Majority Leader Tom DeLay called the shrunken . . . cuts "awe-

some," adding, "And it's only the beginning." Senate Majority Whip Mitch McConnell echoed DeLay's assessment: "All I can tell you is, we keep on winning, and we expect to win again." (Ota 2003, 1245)

Despite projections of a ballooning deficit and the modest economic slowdown after September 11, the Bush administration's supply-side tax cut agenda was thus in full swing. Congressional Republicans were eager to extend sunset provisions built into tax packages, while conservative lobby groups with substantial sway over Republican representatives were even seeking additional cuts. The entire Republican establishment was thus geared toward reducing the tax burden and limiting government. Accordingly, the committed pursuit of international cooperation against tax dodging would have been rather inconsistent. As the next sections make clear, this is why the Bush administration withdrew support from the HTC initiative and resorted to a "politics without conviction" strategy at the OECD during the following years (Eccleston 2012, 60).

In Praise of International Tax Competition

Owing to its supply-side tax cut agenda, the Bush administration was "ideologically predisposed to accept the critiques of the right-wing coalition that had formed in the US to oppose the HTC project" (Webb 2004, 813). Accordingly, associations like the Center for Freedom and Prosperity (CFP), the USCIB, and the US Chamber of Commerce intensified their lobbying of Treasury and Congress, produced alarmist newspaper op-eds, and rounded up support from the same group of neoliberal economists that publicly backed the Bush tax package (Levin and Lieberman 2001; Shaxson 2012). In his publications, Daniel Mitchell, the CFP chief lobbyist, incessantly warned against OECD attempts to establish "a cartel for the benefit of high-tax nations" that would "emasculate financial privacy and undermine fiscal sovereignty . . . , impoverish less-developed nations and hamstring America's competitive advantage in the world economy." "Fortunately," he reminded his readers, "President Bush can pull the plug on this misguided initiative simply by telling high-tax European nations that America will not impose financial protectionism against low-tax countries" (Mitchell 2001c, 24). Whereas Mitchell pushed a die-hard libertarian agenda, vilifying any form of international tax cooperation as a socialist plot against flat taxes and small government, Richard Hammer, USCIB's chief tax counsel, chose a more moderate approach. Representing the interests of US multinationals, he continued to argue against the OECD's interference with "legitimate tax-planning opportunities" in his communication to Treasury. Yet he acknowledged "the need for responsible and legitimate information exchanges, . . . [counseling] Treasury to use its best efforts to change the focus of the [HTC] project to deal solely with transparency" (Hammer 2001, 164–65).

The lobbying soon bore fruit. The media discovered the issue, with the *Washington Post* even adopting the CFP characterization of the OECD as "global tax police" (Novak 2001). Likewise, eighty-six members of Congress applied CFP rhetoric in a joint letter to Secretary of the Treasury Paul O'Neill, characterizing the HTC initiative as an infringement on fiscal sovereignty and urging him to withdraw US support. In addition, "Nobel prize-winning economists Milton Friedman and James Buchanan came out in support of the CFP and against the OECD campaign" (Sharman 2006a, 62). Most important, however, the buzz that had been created earned the CFP and US Chamber of Congress a "sympathetic hearing" by virtually every competent political appointee within the Bush administration (Webb 2004, 813). In February 2001, Mitchell and several other CFP lobbyists were given the opportunity to "[make] their pitch to a half-dozen Treasury officials in the office of Mark Weinberger, the department's chief tax official and a new Bush appointee" (Giridharadas 2001). In addition to a score of follow-up appointments with senior Treasury officials, another meeting between Weinberger and the CFP was held in March. Moreover, Mitchell and his colleague Andrew Quinlan met with Lawrence Lindsey, Glenn Hubbard, and Cesar Conda, a senior adviser to Vice President Dick Cheney. Eventually, these consultations culminated in a meeting in mid-April between Ed Feulner, the president of the Heritage Foundation, which is the CFP's main sponsor, and Secretary O'Neill (Sharman 2006a).

The intensification of the lobbying effort is, indeed, reflected in the evolution of O'Neill's attitude toward the HTC project. Following a meeting of G7 ministers of finance in February, he still announced quite nebulously that certain aspects of the initiative were "under review by the new Administration." He claimed to support "the priority placed on transparency and cooperation to facilitate effective tax information exchange," but underlined that it was "critical to clarify that this project [was] not about dictating to any country what should be the appropriate level of tax rates" (O'Neill 2001a, 82). The secretary further elaborated this position over the course of the following months, arguing in May that "in its current form, the project [was] too broad and . . . not in line with this Administration's tax and economic priorities" (O'Neill 2001c, 84). Questioned at a Senate hearing in July, he then clarified that the US had argued for a removal of the substantial economic activity criterion from the OECD's tax-haven definition and against the use of ring-fencing as an indicator for PTRs, given that "it [did] not provide an adequate basis to distinguish regimes that facilitate tax evasion from regimes that are designed to encourage foreign investment but that have nothing to do with the evasion of any other country's tax law" (O'Neill 2001b, 51).

After the OECD had already diluted the substantial economic activities criterion with the acquiescence of the Clinton administration and in response to lobbying from the USCIB, the Bush administration now further refocused the OECD initiative according to the counseling it had received from US multinationals in the guise of Richard Hammer. Using its weight in the OECD's Committee on Fiscal Affairs (CFA), Treasury removed virtually all elements interfering with corporate tax planning from the HTC project, including conditionality of tax residency on substantial economic activity and critical reviews of PTRs. As a result, the initiative soon dealt exclusively with increased transparency and information exchange, just as Hammer had requested in his communication with Treasury (Palan, Murphy, and Chavagneux 2010; Eden and Kudrle 2005). The CFP's concerns were most visibly taken into account in O'Neill's rhetoric and the timing of his withdrawal from the HTC project. By refocusing the OECD's tax work on information exchange and the fight against tax evasion, however, Treasury did not comply with the more extreme requests from Mitchell and his colleagues. Accordingly, the CFP showed an ambivalent reaction to O'Neill's turnaround. Although Quinlan and Mitchell celebrated the end of the OECD's tax harmonization agenda, which was their wording for measures against tax avoidance, they complained in June "that it is still not clear whether we have stopped the assault on financial privacy." Still, they assured their sponsors and supporters that "in the coming months, we will be fighting to ensure the correct outcome" (Quinlan and Mitchell 2001, 105).

The Demise of the OECD's HTC Initiative

As part of its progress report, the OECD had published a blacklist of thirty-five tax havens in June 2000. With the public backing of the Clinton administration, the OECD threatened these tax havens with sanctions should they not remove the harmful features of their tax codes by July 2001. In the following months several of the listed jurisdictions sat down with the OECD to find an agreement, be removed from the blacklist, and avoid sanctions (Adams, Mallet, and Peel 2001). While the Bahamas announced it would prohibit the anonymous registration of international business companies (IBCs) and withdrew banking licenses from seven suspicious institutions, Grenada shut down seventeen banks in March 2001 to clean up its financial sector (Canute 2001a). At the same time, the prime minister of St. Vincent complained about a 20 percent reduction in IBC registrations over the course of 2000, while the number of banks registered in Antigua fell from seventy-eight in 1998 to eighteen by 2001 (Canute 2001b). From the perspective of the OECD, things were developing in the right direction at the beginning of that year. Yet the optimism soon faded. The Bush administration's foot-dragging, along with outreach from the CFP encouraging tax haven governments to stand firm while the libertarian lobbyists were working Treasury (Mitchell 2001b), brought negotiations with the OECD to a halt. Instead of making overhasty commitments, many tax havens now preferred to wait and see, hoping that the United States would eventually withdraw its support from the HTC initiative. As a senior OECD official told the *Financial Times* in April: "There is a hiatus. Nothing is happening because the US position is unclear" (Adams, Alden, and Peel 2001, 6).

Indeed, the OECD's Secretariat and its large European members grew increasingly nervous, sensing that without unambiguous US support the HTC initiative could fail. Accordingly, the OECD sent a delegation to Washington to persuade Treasury of the project's merit and to make sure Treasury would back the OECD's tax work in the conclusions to an upcoming meeting of G7 ministers of finance (Adams, Alden, and Peel 2001). But neither the OECD, nor the secretary's European counterparts, could convince O'Neill to support the initiative. Accordingly, the April communiqué of G7 ministers of finance expressed support for the FATF's anti-money-laundering work but made no mention at all of the OECD's tax initiative (cf. G7 Ministers of Finance 2001). Instead of seeking consensus with European partners, O'Neill (2001c, 83–84) announced the withdrawal of US support two weeks later in an official statement. "Following up on the thoughts I shared with my G7 counterparts at recent meetings," he began, "I want to make clear what is important to the United States and what is not." He then explained that the United States was in favor of tax competition because it forced governments to become more efficient. In fact, it provided his government with an additional incentive to reduce the tax burden for all Americans and simplify the tax system. Nonetheless, tax cheats were breaking the law and had to be caught. But the United States would use bilateral information exchange agreements for that purpose. When the US government shared common goals, it would continue to work with G7 partners. "In its current form," however, the HTC project was "too broad and . . . not in line with this Administration's tax and economic priorities" (O'Neill 2001c, 83–84).

While the USCIB and the CFP were celebrating, European G7 members tried to pick up the pieces. The UK exchequer stated, "Our position is absolutely clear. We support the initiative. The US concerns will be discussed in the OECD." Along the same lines, Bruno Gibert, the French chairman of the harmful tax practices working group, confirmed, "Member countries would consider how to respond 'in a constructive way'" (Adams and Peel 2001, 14). However, these diplomatic reactions only masked the major discontent in European capitals that became apparent at the OECD's Ministerial Meeting a week later. In the absence of O'Neill, who was represented by Glenn Hubbard, European ministers tried to put pressure on the United States, which was isolated on the issue. But Hubbard stuck to his position, reaffirming that the US government would participate only in a stripped-down version of the project that focused on information exchange. This time, the Europeans responded angrily. Laurent Fabius, then French minister of finance, told his colleagues: "Whether it concerns the struggle against the greenhouse effect, or against money laundering and tax havens, the largest power in the world cannot disengage from the planet's problems" (Beattie 2001, 10). A European OECD official concurred: "How far can it go? Do we scrap all attempts to make people pay taxes?" (Alden and Peel 2001, 12). But their enragement did not help. After several rounds of negotiations in the CFA, OECD ambassadors agreed in July that the HTC's tax avoidance elements should be scrapped and no sanctions imposed on blacklisted tax havens at least until 2003 (Peel 2001a, 2001b). In order to save some elements of the HTC initiative, the Europeans had thus agreed to a reform of the OECD's tax work that fully matched the Bush administration's priorities.

Their surrender was eventually enshrined in the OECD's 2001 Progress Report. It defined the fight against "anti-competitive . . . practices designed to encourage noncompliance with the tax laws of other countries" as the HTC initiative's new goal and made clear that the OECD would only rely on "the transparency and effective exchange of information criteria" when blacklisting noncooperative jurisdictions (OECD 2001, 4). Most important, it withdrew the collective sanctions threat by acknowledging that "each OECD member country retains the sovereign right to apply or not to apply any defensive measures as appropriate" (OECD 2001, 10). Although the Bush administration's anti-tax ideology found little support among other OECD members, the organization had still minimized the regulatory burden for multinationals and corporate tax havens accordingly. As Webb (2004, 815) observes, "no other country has the power to single-handedly alter the course of the OECD."

Implementing the "Politics without Conviction" Strategy

Treasury had acceded to most of the demands from the right-wing lobbying coalition when removing the "tax harmonization" elements from the HTC initiative. Yet the department had continued to support the initiative's transparency and information exchange dimension for several reasons. First, information exchange did not interfere with national tax codes and therefore did not oblige corporate tax havens to remove provisions that enabled multinationals to avoid taxes elsewhere. From the perspective of Secretary O'Neill this lack of interference meant that information exchange did not affect international tax competition, which he and the libertarian opponents of tax cooperation interpreted as a desirable constraint on government profligacy. Second, tax evasion, the activity to be tackled by information exchange, was a criminal offense. Providing law enforcement agencies with additional information to prosecute such offenses matched the law-and-order instincts of many Republicans.[5] In fact, O'Neill underlined that he had taken an oath obliging him to execute US tax laws as written, which implied going after those "who illegally evade taxes by hiding income in offshore accounts" (O'Neill 2001c, 83).[6] Third, the September 11 attacks and the ability of Al-Qaeda to finance both their perpetrators and their preparation gave law enforcement agencies another reason for wanting to pierce the veil provided by secrecy jurisdictions (Eccleston 2012; Shaxson 2012).

In contrast, the libertarian lobbying coalition and many Republicans under its influence were still seeing their ultimate goal of minimal taxes and a minimal state endangered by international information exchange. As their wealthy sponsors' desire to reduce their tax burden to zero was difficult to communicate, however, they argued instead that information transfers from banks to tax authorities were an infringement of citizens' right to privacy. Daniel Mitchell of the CFP reminded his followers that "information exchange for tax purposes, even when limited to specific cases, is inconsistent with sound tax policy, respect for privacy, and international comity" (Mitchell 2001a, 108). Along the same lines, the Prosperity Institute accused Treasury of ignoring "the important balance between due process and privacy concerns on the one hand, and law enforcement or tax administration efficiency on the other" (Mastromarco 2001, 104). Most important, several libertarian lobby groups teamed up to form the "Task Force on Information Exchange and Financial Privacy." The group was chaired by former Republican senator Mack Mattingly and included former appointees in the Reagan and George H. W. Bush administrations, members of the Mont Pèlerin Society, and senior figures from George Mason University (cf. Task Force on Information Exchange and Financial Privacy 2002).[7] In its final report, the task force observed that the US government was itself "[allowing] foreigners to invest confidentially in the US" and thus engaged in the same behavior the OECD criticized in secrecy jurisdictions. Hence, if the US government continued to support the OECD's efforts, it would only motivate high-tax European nations to use the OECD to impose reporting requirements on the United States also. These requirements would hurt the United States' attractiveness for foreign investment, lead to massive capital outflows, and sacrifice the privacy of US taxpayers. Accordingly, the US government should prevent the OECD from "the total abolition of any financial privacy in the 41 targeted countries" (Task Force on Information Exchange and Financial Privacy 2002, 35–36).

These arguments were taken up by the business press and several senior Republicans such as House Majority Whip Tom DeLay. In a letter to Secretary O'Neill he criticized information exchange initiatives as "assaults on financial privacy and due process legal protection . . . driven by a desire to thwart international tax competition." "But since the United States is the world's biggest beneficiary of tax competition," he added, "it makes no sense for America to participate in an endeavor that will undermine our competitive advantage in the global economy" (DeLay 2001, 101). Interestingly, however, arguments stressing the risk that reporting requirements imposed on secrecy jurisdictions could eventually also be imposed on the United States apparently did not gain currency with the potentially affected financial sector. Of course, US banks were still opposed to providing additional data on their foreign clients. They were, however, indifferent toward new reporting requirements for foreign banks, and corresponding sanction threats against secrecy jurisdictions. The most likely reason is that US banks—in contrast to libertarian lobbyists—were aware of the established US practice of seeking additional reporting from foreign banks while shielding the US financial sector and its clients from similar requirements (Eccleston 2012). This approach was reflected in the QI program. Moreover, Treasury often negotiated tax information exchange agreements (TIEAs) providing for unilateral information reporting from the treaty partner, whereas the IRS did not per se respond to requests for administrative assistance from foreign governments. As a former Treasury official explains, Latin American countries, which provide the largest client base for wealth managers in Florida and Texas, cannot usually count on cooperation from the United States:

> The truth is, half of Latin America we don't have information exchange agreements with. There are other countries where it is clear that the US would act very slowly. So in theory we should exchange information with Venezuela, but we are not going to, it's not actually going to happen.[8]

Given this configuration of domestic interests, the Bush administration wanted to avoid being perceived as lenient on law enforcement issues, while also taking the criticism of die-hard libertarians among its core constituency into account. The result of its strategic deliberations was the pursuit of "politics without conviction" (Eccleston 2012, 60). In accordance with demands from libertarian lobby groups, the administration made sure that the criminal (money-laundering, terrorist-financing) and civil (tax evasion) aspects of financial opacity were dealt with separately. The FATF continued to be responsible for the former and the OECD for the latter. In addition, domestic efforts to combat terrorist financing were linked to the FATF's money-laundering work, instead of the OECD's transparency and information exchange efforts (Palan, Murphy, and Chavagneux 2010). More important, however, the United States advocated for information exchange upon request at the OECD, instead of the automatic information exchange that had just been established within the EU for interest payments to nonresidents (Shaxson 2012). The upon-request standard was, however, known to be ineffective because it conditioned requests for administrative assistance on substantiated suspicions against particular individuals. That is, tax authorities had to present prior evidence of tax evasion before they could ask their foreign counterparts for information. Yet prior evidence was hard to come by in the absence of information from their foreign counterparts about a taxpayer's foreign accounts (Genschel and Rixen 2015). A potential workaround would have been the permission of group requests. Such requests would have enabled tax authorities to demand information on a particular category of individuals, for instance investors in a particular fund associated with tax evasion. However, Secretary O'Neill denounced such requests as "fishing expeditions" irreconcilable with citizens' right to financial privacy (O'Neill 2001b, 53). Therefore, the OECD's information exchange and transparency work did not increase pressure on tax evaders to repatriate their hidden funds (Johannesen and Zucman 2014).

The first element of the Bush administration's "politics without conviction" strategy was the endorsement of a toothless standard for international information exchange to address concerns over "financial privacy." The second element of the strategy was the deferral of sanctions against uncooperative secrecy jurisdictions until OECD members Switzerland and Luxembourg had also agreed to grant greater administrative assistance in tax matters. This was a direct response to criticism from libertarian lobbyists and tax haven governments concerning the "hypocrisy and double standards between the OECD's treatment of nonmember havens as opposed to abstaining members" (Sharman 2006a, 91). By abstaining from the vote on the HTC report and its progeny, Switzerland and Luxembourg had made clear from the beginning of the project that they would not consider themselves bound by its recommendations. Of course, this stance invited other tax havens and their libertarian advisers to decry the initiative's discriminatory character. Such arguments had not kept the Clinton administration from backing the OECD's sanction threat. For reasons described earlier, however, the Bush administration endorsed these concerns and distanced itself from countermeasures proposed by the OECD. At a Senate hearing in July 2001 Secretary O'Neill made the following confession:

> I do not have any trouble with the idea of sanctions properly applied and
> fairly applied at all, but I did have trouble—now, I must tell you I found

it pretty compelling to listen to the finance ministers of people from countries as small as 4,500 people say, "Well, if you are going to do this to us, is Switzerland going to comply?" I thought that was not a bad argument: "Well, if you are going to do this to us and you are going to use the power of the 30, are you going to do it to yourself or not?" I thought that was a pretty good question. (O'Neill 2001b, 21)

Of course, the credibility of any sanctions threat from the OECD is greatly reduced without the United States on board. Accordingly, the organization reframed its discussion of countermeasures based on the Bush administration's position. The OECD's 2001 progress report, released in November, stated "that a potential framework of coordinated defensive measures would not apply to uncooperative tax havens any earlier than it would apply to OECD member states with harmful preferential regimes" (OECD 2001, 10). Instead of using coercion, the OECD now had to revert back to its traditional "method of dialogue and persuasion" (Palan, Murphy, and Chavagneux 2010, 218). In the words of Jeffrey Owens, the OECD's chief tax official, the organization abandoned "the Al Capone approach and replaced it with the Martin Luther King approach" (Easson 2004, 1066). First, this shift implied rhetorical de-escalation. Senior OECD officials now expressed their understanding for tax haven concerns over the establishment of a level playing field. Accordingly, they pledged to pursue common principles applicable to both OECD members and nonmembers (Sharman 2006a). In addition, the OECD established the Global Forum on Transparency and Information Exchange. Instead of fixing standards and imposing them on nonmembers, the Global Forum invited secrecy jurisdictions and other third countries to join OECD members in the elaboration and monitoring of information exchange standards. The first result of this more inclusive approach was the Model Agreement on Information Exchange published in 2002 (Rixen 2008).

In accordance with the Bush administration's general suspicion of multilateral agreements and Secretary O'Neill's announcement that the United States would implement greater information exchange by means of bilateral treaties, the Model Agreement was essentially a template for bilateral TIEAs. It also provided for a multilateral mechanism, which, however, allowed a country acceding to the agreement to select the other signatories with which the country was willing to exchange information. Otherwise, the Model Agreement effectively made information exchange upon request the international standard for international cooperation in tax matters (Rixen 2008). The Model Agreement even included some incremental improvements over the pre-HTC period in that it prohibited compliant countries from refusing to transfer information on the grounds that they (1) did not collect requested data domestically or (2) had bank secrecy provisions in place that outlawed such transfers. Yet when the CFA also included these provisions in the OECD's Model Tax Convention, the template for double-tax agreements, Switzerland and Luxembourg (subsequently joined by Austria and Belgium), upheld reservations against the relevant articles 23–26 (Webb 2004). Previously, they had already vetoed a CFA decision obliging OECD member states to provide domestic tax authorities access to banking information, marking the first time a veto had been used in that body (Parker and Burton 2003). Once more, these countries made clear that they did not consider themselves bound by OECD recommendations. Since their cooperation was the crucial prerequisite for countermeasures against noncompliant jurisdictions outside the OECD, these countries' sustained opposition took the sanction threat off the table for good.

At this point, what had started as a dynamic anti–tax haven initiative "[slowed] to the speed of the last ship in the convoy" (Parker and Burton 2003, 17). John Snow, O'Neill's successor as secretary of the Treasury, urged Switzerland, the most important opponent to financial transparency, to be more forthcoming in its replies to requests for administrative assistance. Yet this came in the form of appeals rather than requests backed up by credible sanction threats (Parker and Burton 2003). At the same time, the Global Forum set out to review the implementation of the "upon-request standard" in its eighty-two member countries. In a report published in 2006, the Global Forum concluded that most national tax authorities were able to access bank data. However, only fifty countries also exchanged such information for tax purposes (Rixen 2008). In addition, members of the Global Forum had also begun to sign TIEAs. The situation was, however, far from sufficient for putting a meaningful constraint on tax evasion. The United States, for instance, had pledged to strike agreements with 50 percent of the thirty-five tax havens originally blacklisted by the OECD by 2002 (Levin and Lieberman 2001). By 2008, however, the United States had concluded only eleven such agreements (Global Forum 2014). Along with industry champions Switzerland and Luxembourg, there were thus plenty of jurisdictions left that did not even grant administrative assistance under the restrictive conditions of the upon-request standard.

Theoretical Implications

The Bush administration's main goal was to reduce the tax burden on corporate profits and capital income. Because of this supply-side tax cut agenda, the administration was skeptical toward the HTC initiative from the outset of its first term and gave libertarian critics of the OECD's tax work a sympathetic hearing. While the Bush Treasury Department bought into these critics' arguments against the removal of PTRs, however, the department could not be convinced to completely abandon the transparency agenda. Hence, the department gave priority to removing those elements from the HTC initiative's scope that interfered with the tax-planning practices of multinational firms, thereby unraveling the project in its original form. In contrast, the administration adopted an ambivalent position concerning the OECD's work on information exchange. Giving in to the Republican Party's law-and-order instincts, the Bush administration formally kept the fight against tax evasion and financial secrecy on the agenda. Yet the administration made sure that the OECD withdrew its sanctions threat against secrecy jurisdictions that refused to become more transparent, thereby reducing the effectiveness of the organization's efforts in this area.

We have thus observed a Republican administration skeptical toward multilateral attempts at curbing tax evasion and avoidance. From its perspective, international tax competition provided a perfect reason for its preferred domestic tax policy of reducing taxes on capital. Against this background, the reduction of competitive pressures by means of international cooperation seemed counterintuitive. Hence, the Bush administration put priority on neutralizing those OECD recommendations that were likely to impose costs on US multinationals. Yet it also withdrew the sanctions threat against secrecy jurisdictions that refused to become more transparent. The Clinton administration had aimed to reduce both tax evasion and avoidance but abandoned the latter goal in response to corporate lobbying. In contrast, the Bush administration was not particularly keen to end either tax evasion or tax avoidance but kept the fight against tax evasion on the agenda to cater to the Republican Party's law-and-order instincts. Yet the administration pursued this agenda without conviction. Finally, the Bush administration's ability to transform its priorities into OECD policy despite being isolated in the G7 reflects the US government's ability to change the direction of the organization's tax work through unilateral defection.

THE EMERGENCE OF
MULTILATERAL AEI

The Obama administration's Foreign Account Tax Compliance Act (FATCA) decisively changed bargaining over more financial transparency (Grinberg 2012; Palan and Wigan 2014). Before the act, secrecy jurisdictions usually refused to provide administrative assistance to foreign tax authorities. Soon after the act's passage, these jurisdictions suddenly agreed to automatically provide data on the accounts of nonresidents on a multilateral basis. Yet analysts still disagree on the factors enabling the act's passage and the mechanisms through which concessions granted to the United States obliged secrecy jurisdictions to also offer greater cooperation to the rest of the world. While some claim that the financial crisis created an important window of opportunity for measures against secrecy jurisdictions (Eccleston and Gray 2014), others point to the UBS scandal as the decisive catalyst for enhanced tax cooperation (Emmenegger 2017). As to the transmission mechanism, some approaches stress the importance of normative pressure exerted by the Group of 20 (G20) and the Organisation for Economic Cooperation and Development (OECD). After the passage of FATCA, these organizations declared automatic exchange of information (AEI) the new global standard for tax cooperation and threatened noncompliant countries with blacklisting (Eggenberger and Emmenegger 2015). Others interpret concessions to the United States as focal points enabling third states to better coordinate their efforts against secrecy jurisdictions (Emmenegger 2017).

This chapter will demonstrate that FATCA has its origins in the longstanding efforts of anti–tax haven activists within the Democratic Party. These activists utilized testimony from a whistleblower and former UBS private banker to prepare a report on the bank's illegal offshore business with US clients. To increase publicity, they held a corresponding Senate hearing, which eventually triggered the UBS scandal. Shortly afterward, Barack Obama entered office. The scandal, his cordial relationship with Democratic anti–tax haven activists, and personal interest in the issue made combating tax evasion and avoidance a top priority for his administration. In contrast to proposed anti-avoidance measures potentially affecting US multinationals, legislation requesting more transparency from foreign banks serving US clients easily passed Congress. The result was FATCA, a law threatening foreign financial institutions (FFI) unwilling to report account data of US clients with a 30 percent withholding tax on payments from US sources. The act changed international bargaining over information exchange via two channels. By forcing secrecy jurisdictions to enter into AEI agreements with the United States, FATCA activated a most-favored-nation clause obliging EU members to grant greater cooperation offered to a third country also to one another. In addition, the principle of AEI contained in FATCA preempted Swiss attempts at promoting anonymity-preserving withholding agreements as the international standard. Faced with the prospect of applying AEI to US clients and different withholding regimes to other nationalities, even Swiss banks eventually realized that a single global standard, although it meant more transparency, was less costly for them. Eventually, the United States exploited widespread compliance with AEI by refusing to participate itself. Therefore, the country currently enjoys an almost exclusive competitive advantage in the attraction of hidden capital.

The Obama Administration's Tax Policy Agenda

The Bush tax cuts of 2001 and 2003, and the resulting spike in income inequality, made tax justice an important theme for Democratic presidential candidates ahead of the 2008 elections. During the Democratic primaries, Hillary Clinton (2007a, 2007b) regularly referred to "the President's reckless tax cuts for those at the top" in her campaign speeches. Likewise, John Edwards (2007) argued "our tax system has been rewritten by George Bush to favor the wealthy and shift the burden to working families." The candidate putting most emphasis on this issue, however, was Barack Obama (2007), who devoted an entire keynote speech to "tax fairness for the middle class" in September 2007. In that speech, he identified "a successful strategy [by special interests] to ride anti-tax sentiment in this country toward tax cuts that favor wealth, not work," linking that strategy to increasing wealth and income inequality and pledging to restore a progressive tax system. To that effect, he promised to "end the preferential treatment that's built into our tax code by eliminating corporate loopholes and tax breaks," announced lower taxes on labor and consumption, and pledged the United States would "lead the international community to new standards of information sharing" in the fight against tax evasion (Obama 2007).

This emphasis was certainly politically opportune, as a large majority of respondents polled by Gallup in April 2007 felt corporations and upper-income people were paying too little tax (Carroll 2007). Yet this sentiment is quite constant over time, and Barack Obama had a history of promoting progressive tax reform. As an Illinois state senator he had sponsored the state's earned income tax credit in 2000, providing low-to-moderate-income earners with a tax break (Irvine 2000). As a US senator he had participated in several attempts at making minimum wage earners eligible for a child tax credit on their income tax (Lincoln 2005; Obama 2006). Moreover, he had co-sponsored Senator Carl Levin's Tax Shelter and Tax Haven Reform Act in 2005, and his Stop Tax Haven Abuse Act in February 2007 (Levin 2005, 2007). The 2005 bill, among other things, proposed penalties for the promoters of tax avoidance schemes qualified as abusive by the IRS, and the abolition of tax credits for taxes paid to tax haven governments. The 2007 bill reintroduced some of these measures. More important, however, the act sought to enable the Treasury secretary to prohibit the opening of correspondent accounts in the United States and the acceptance of credit cards issued by FFIs from a country seen as impeding US tax enforcement. Barack Obama's interest in tax justice had thus clearly developed ahead of the financial crisis. Rather than just a useful campaign topic for the 2008 elections, it seems to have been part of his more fundamental political convictions as a "loyal Democrat" (GovTrack.us 2019).

Nonetheless, the bank bailouts of 2008 provided a breeding ground for public outrage over the concealment schemes used by Union Bank of Switzerland (UBS) and Liechtenstein Global Trust (LGT) to hide their US clients from the IRS. Under the leadership of Carl Levin, the Senate Permanent Subcommittee on Investigations (PSI) had already revealed in a 2006 report that Swiss and Liechtenstein banks helped their US clients to circumvent the qualified intermediary (QI) program (Levin and Coleman 2006). The QI program had been set up by the IRS under Clinton mostly to get an overview over who held US securities offshore. Yet it also obliged FFIs to collect withholding taxes on US-source capital income on behalf of the IRS and report US clients holding US securities directly to the service. As an incentive for signing up, the IRS exempted participating FFIs from withholding taxes on their US investments. Virtually all FFIs doing business in the United States thus registered as QIs. But instead of fulfilling the reporting requirement, they created or purchased interposed legal entities registered in Panama and other secrecy jurisdictions to hide the true residence of their US beneficial owners. As a result, foreign corporations formally received 70 percent of US-source capital income in 2003 (Government Accountability Office 2007). Despite the report and a corresponding hearing before the PSI, however, the issue did not attract much public attention throughout 2006 and 2007.[1]

This changed when the PSI released a second report and held another hearing on the issue in July 2008.[2] The report benefited greatly from the testimony of Bradley Birkenfeld, a former UBS private banker who had participated in an IRS whistleblower program following a 2006 reform guaranteeing informant awards (IRS 2015). Birkenfeld provided the IRS, PSI, and Department of Justice (DoJ) with documents and e-mails proving the setup of a program by senior UBS private bankers for the systematic circumvention of the QI program's reporting requirement (Hässig 2010). Based on this evidence, the DoJ detained Martin Liechti, head of wealth management for North and South America at UBS, in April 2008, while the IRS obtained a first John Doe summons from a US federal judge, obliging UBS to surrender nineteen thousand client files or be subject to civil penalties in the United States (Simonian 2008; Schaub 2011). Under the impression of this concerted action, Mark Branson, the chief financial officer (CFO) of UBS's global wealth management branch, admitted wrongdoing during the PSI hearing in July and announced UBS would end its offshore business with US clients (US Senate 2008b). Against the background of Treasury's recent bailouts of Bear Stearns, Freddie Mac, and Fannie Mae, the PSI report's estimate that circumvention of the QI program cost the US Treasury $100 billion in tax revenue, implying a higher tax burden for honest US taxpayers, created what a senior OECD tax official called "the perfect storm" (Levin and Coleman 2008).[3]

Carl Levin and his cosponsor Barack Obama used increased media attention to call for the swift adoption of their anti–tax haven bill. While Levin spread the message in several televised interviews (Chung 2008; Levin 2008), Obama issued a press statement stating that "Washington must take the recommendations of the Subcommittee's report seriously . . . and enact the Stop Tax Haven Abuse Act that I introduced with Senators Levin and Coleman to combat tax abuse" (States News Service 2008). Although there was no immediate legislative activity ahead of presidential elections, senior IRS and DoJ officials, who had either already been confirmed by the Democratic Senate majority or were positioning themselves for promotion under the incoming Democratic administration, heard the message and intensified their efforts (Hässig 2010; US Senate 2008a). In November 2008, the DoJ indicted Raoul Weil, head of global wealth management at UBS, for "conspiring with other executives, managers, private bankers and clients of the banking firm to defraud the United States" (DoJ 2008). The following month it offered UBS a deferred prosecution agreement (DPA), providing for the suspension of criminal investigations against the bank in exchange for a $780 million fine and the transmission of 250 client files. In parallel, Treasury officials worked with their French and German counterparts to put the issue of financial secrecy on the agenda of the G20.[4] Despite the remote connection of financial secrecy to the outbreak of the financial crisis, heads of state and government thus declared at their first crisis meeting in Washington that "lack of transparency and a failure to exchange tax information should be vigorously addressed" (G20 Leaders 2008). In reaction, the OECD circulated an updated draft blacklist of countries not complying with its upon-request standard for information exchange, prompting Austria, Luxembourg, and Switzerland to drop their reservations against the administrative assistance clause of the OECD's model tax convention in March 2009 (OECD 2009). This was considered a breakthrough at the time but proved to have little effectiveness in curbing tax evasion, as a result of the weakness of the upon-request standard (Johannesen and Zucman 2014). In any event, Treasury officials and congressional staff were already preparing the next step.

Preparing Anti–Tax Haven Legislation

When Barack Obama took office as president of the United States in January 2009, he was committed by his own statements and to his former cosponsor Carl Levin to push for the adoption of the Stop Tax Haven Abuse Act. However, Treasury officials were skeptical toward the bill, as they perceived the proposed exclusion of tax haven FFIs from correspondent accounts in the United States as too disruptive. Instead, they suggested an approach complementary to the QI program, extending its reporting requirements and using a 30 percent withholding tax on the US-source revenue of noncompliant FFIs as sanctions mechanism. During the following months this proposal was further developed in a drafting process led by the chief tax counsel of the House Ways and Means Committee and with representation from the IRS and Senate Finance Committee. According to several interview partners, the most senior people in the room had already drafted the QI program under Clinton.[5] The final product was then part of a long list of anti-evasion and anti-avoidance measures included in Treasury's Green Book on revenue proposals for 2010 and discussed in the president's budget proposal (cf. US Treasury 2009; Office of Management and Budget 2009).

On the occasion of the release of these documents, President Obama and Secretary of the Treasury Timothy Geithner announced a two-pronged strategy for "leveling the playing field" for US taxpayers. The first element of the strategy was the "[removal] of tax incentives for shifting jobs overseas" through reforms of deferral and foreign tax credit rules often exploited by corporations to minimize their tax bill. The strategy's second element, "getting tough on overseas tax ha-

vens," involved the closure of loopholes in check-the-box rules allowing multinationals to set up hybrid entities to avoid taxes, an increase in IRS staff investigating tax evasion, and the extension of the QI program's reporting requirements
and sanctions mechanisms discussed earlier (Office of the Press Secretary
2009). In a concomitant press conference, President Obama (2009) explained,
"we're beginning to restore fairness and balance to our tax code. That's what I
promised I would do during the campaign, that's what I'm committed to doing
as President."

Although Obama threw his full weight behind these measures and could work
with Democratic majorities in both chambers of Congress until 2011, proposals
interfering with corporate tax planning did not go far. As under Clinton, Treasury faced massive opposition from multinationals and their lobbyists against a
reform of check-the-box rules and measures to end the deferral of tax payments
of foreign profits (Rubin and Drucker 2014; Scott 2014). The only items from
the Obama-Geithner plan passed by the Democratic Congress before 2011 were
aimed at loopholes in the QI program. As such, these provisions primarily concerned FFIs circumventing their reporting obligations. Following the drafting process discussed previously, Senator Max Baucus and Representative Charles Rangel, Chairman of the House Ways and Means Committee, introduced these
proposals to Congress as the Foreign Account Tax Compliance Act (Baucus 2009;
Rangel 2009). The act requires FFIs to report accounts held by US individuals
and—to unravel the concealment schemes used to circumvent the QI program—
to legal entities beneficially owned by US individuals. For such accounts, FFIs
"must report the account balance . . . , and the amount of dividends, interest, other
income, and gross proceeds from the sale of property" (Grinberg 2012, 23). The
QI program's reporting requirement was thus expanded from income on US securities to all capital income earned by US residents.

Moreover, FATCA does not use incentives like the QI program to make FFIs
participate but instead relies on coercion. As legislators put it quite explicitly, the
act's objective is to "force foreign financial institutions to disclose their US account holders or pay a steep penalty for nondisclosure" (Grinberg 2012, 24). This
penalty is a 30 percent withholding tax "on the gross amount of certain payments
from US sources and the proceeds from disposing of certain US investments."
These monies include the revenue from an FFI's own investments in the United
States, payments beneficially owned by its clients regardless of their residence, and
so-called "pass-through payments" channeled through a participating FFI to a
nonparticipating FFI (Grinberg 2012, 24). The latter provision is meant to also
force into participation those FFIs that are not investing in the United States directly but are investing in or through participating FFIs. As one of the act's original authors put it,

> FATCA tries to use the combined weight of US financial markets and
> financial institutions that must, as a practical matter, do business in the
> US marketplace as leverage with other [FFIs] to ensure near-
> comprehensive participation in FATCA's cross-border information re-
> porting. (Grinberg 2012, 24–25)

Given the act's focus on reporting requirements for foreign banks, US multinationals were largely unaffected and thus did not submit a position when Chairman Richard Neal held a hearing on FATCA in the Subcommittee on Select Revenue Measures (US House of Representatives 2009). Similarly, the American
Bankers Association (ABA) did not object to any of the act's core provisions, as
the reporting requirements and sanctions mechanism did not apply to its members. The ABA did, however, insist that US banks, which were supposed to act as
withholding agents for the IRS under FATCA, would be given enough time to
build necessary administrative infrastructure as well as accurate information on
the participation status of FFIs to avoid penalties for not fulfilling their withholding duties. Despite the additional compliance burden for US banks, the ABA
expressed support for "legislation that will ensure that all US citizens and residents pay their fair share of taxes, and thus, prevent loss of millions of dollars by
the US because of taxpayers that engage in illegal use of offshore accounts" (US
House of Representatives 2009, 80). The association's positive attitude was of
course grounded in the expectation that FATCA would remove incentives for US
clients to hold accounts with Swiss or Liechtenstein banks and could thus produce net new money for the private wealth management divisions of its members. Owing to FATCA's innocuousness for domestic business, Chairman Neal
could thus conclude his opening statement at the FATCA hearing as follows:

> In terms of the economic confrontation . . . America currently is expe-
> riencing, . . . it makes good sense, before we talk about raising revenue
> elsewhere, that we begin talking about closing down these tax havens and
> these loopholes that the American people have justly come to see as be-
> ing patently unfair. (US House of Representatives 2009, 4)

In other words, he was sympathetic to the idea of addressing the fairness concerns of US citizens through a crackdown on secrecy jurisdictions instead of a
hike in taxes on domestic business. Accordingly, Patrick Tiberi, the subcommittee's ranking minority member, congratulated him on a bill that "does not blur
the issues of tax evasion and legal tax practices, and does not include the most
controversial international tax policy changes proposed by the Administration"
(US House of Representatives 2009, 5). As a result of general agreement on FAT-
CA's ability to send a signal of fairness to voters at virtually no cost for domestic

business, the act passed Congress in March 2010 as a financing mechanism attached to the Obama administration's second stimulus package after the financial crisis (Mollohan 2010).

FATCA's Impact on International Tax Politics

FATCA Becomes Intergovernmental

Congress had conceived FATCA as a domestic law with extraterritorial reach, establishing a direct regulatory link between FFIs and the IRS. When the act passed in March 2010, no intergovernmental approach was envisaged. In fact, FATCA's predecessor, the QI program, had worked in exactly the same way, creating obligations for foreign banks, not foreign governments. As Tanenbaum (2012, 623) puts it, FATCA "was steamrolling down on a unilateral basis without any immediate serious attention being given to the pursuit of bilateral or multilateral alternatives." Questioned about why the United States had not tried to tie FATCA into ongoing work on automatic exchange of information at the OECD level (the TRACE project), a former senior Treasury official replied, "Once FATCA was enacted, everything that went on with TRACE, well that was important and we had a lot of resources committed to it, but the law enacted in the US had to be complied with first. So TRACE was understood as an add-on some time in the future."[6] The focus shifted to the international level only once the IRS had published the first guide to FATCA implementation in August 2011.

At this point, many FFIs realized that the act's reporting requirements would collide with data protection and bank secrecy legislation in their home countries, putting them between a rock and a hard place. Either these FFIs had to break domestic law to comply with FATCA or accept the 30 percent withholding tax due in case of noncompliance (Eccleston and Gray 2014). In addition, many FFIs wanted to avoid entering in a privity of contract with the IRS, as this was a very weak basis for changing terms and conditions for their clients and would have subjected them to direct enforcement action by the United States. Instead, they preferred to fulfill FATCA reporting requirements under national law and toward national authorities, which could then pass account information on to the IRS. Accordingly, the FFIs lobbied their respective governments for the creation of corresponding intergovernmental agreements.[7] At the same time, the US Treasury Department grew increasingly concerned over a Swiss campaign for new comprehensive withholding tax deals with other OECD members, which the department understood as a challenge to the principle of AEI embedded in FATCA.[8]

The Swiss campaign was a reaction to demands from the international community for greater administrative assistance after the UBS and LGT scandals. From 2008, the DoJ had pressed an increasing number of Swiss banks for the transmission of US client files by threatening them with criminal indictment in a US court. In parallel, the IRS had requested such files from the Swiss government through administrative assistance. After some initial resistance, the prospect of losing their US banking licenses prompted several Swiss banks to surrender the requested data in violation of Swiss bank secrecy laws. In addition, the Swiss federal court removed the differentiation between tax fraud and tax evasion from Swiss tax law, which the Swiss government had until then used as an excuse for not complying with information requests. As a consequence of that decision, the Swiss government not only responded to the IRS request, but also dropped its reservation against the OECD Model Tax Convention's administrative assistance clause, which had been the basis for the OECD's decision to put Switzerland on the G20-backed tax haven blacklist in 2009 (Emmenegger 2017; Hässig 2010).

After years of concessions, the Swiss Banking Association (SBA) then tried to regain the upper hand and preserve bank secrecy through its so-called Rubik concept for bilateral tax treaties. The concept foresaw the collection of withholding taxes on the capital income of the treaty partner's residents, the proceeds of which would then be channeled back to the treaty partner. In addition, Switzerland would collect and transfer a one-time tax on the treaty partner's residents' financial wealth to cover past tax liabilities (Grinberg 2012, 27). In exchange, the identity of nonresident investors in Switzerland would be protected and the number of information requests from the treaty partner capped at a certain number.[9] The Swiss government embraced this concept and began to offer Rubik agreements to its key trading partners in December 2009 (Emmenegger 2017). In October of the next year, Rudolf Merz, the Swiss minister of finance, could announce the opening of negotiations on Rubik agreements with Germany and the United Kingdom, which were interested in tapping a new and quickly available revenue stream (Israel, Flütsch, and Nauer 2010).[10] This announcement provided Luxembourg and Austria with another pretext to delay the material and geographic extension of AEI at the EU level. More important, however, the British and German governments' interpretation of Rubik deals as a viable alternative to AEI additionally motivated the US Treasury to intercept the Swiss campaign with its own initiative for intergovernmental FATCA implementation.[11]

It was thus shortly after the United Kingdom and Germany had signed Rubik deals with Switzerland in August and September 2011, that Emily McMahon, assistant secretary of the Treasury, announced that the United States "was committed to entering into bilateral and multilateral agreements that would allow financial institutions to comply with FATCA without violating local law" (Grinberg 2012, 25). To this effect, Treasury opened negotiations on a "common approach to FATCA implementation" with France, Germany, Italy, Spain, and the United Kingdom (EU G5) (US Treasury 2012c, 2). From the US perspective, these countries were crucial trading partners whose tax authorities had the necessary know-how and were engaged in cordial relationships with the IRS.[12] From the perspective of the EU G5, the US initiative provided a response to the reservations these countries' domestic banks had about entering into direct contractual relationships with a US authority and to the difficulty the EU G5 faced in materially and geographically extending AEI within the EU.[13] Moreover, the EU G5 hoped for agreements binding the United States to reciprocate information reporting.[14]

After swift consultations, the US government and EU G5 thus issued a joint statement in February 2012. In that statement, the EU G5 committed to implement legislation requiring their banks to collect account information as requested by FATCA and to transfer the reported information automatically to the IRS. In exchange, the United States pledged to eliminate the requirement for banks from the EU G5 to enter into direct contractual relationships with the IRS and to reciprocate information reporting (US Treasury 2012c, 2–3). Together, the United States and the EU G5 committed "to working with other FATCA partners, the OECD, and where appropriate the EU, on adapting FATCA in the medium term to a common model for automatic exchange of information" (US Treasury 2012c, 3). Moreover, the US Treasury had realized at this point that FATCA treaties would meet less resistance from foreign governments if they were embedded in a multilateral AEI framework. As a former official in the department explained:

> FATCA doesn't really work as a unilateral system. The secret to FATCA is that it needs the multilateral agreement. The level of resistance that you have from foreign institutions and sovereigns just disappears once you have a multilateral process. Because now you can't complain that the US is doing something. Now it's an international standard and the US is just the leading implementer. It makes a huge difference.[15]

Following the joint statement, the United States thus used its agenda-setting capacity at OECD level to lend additional momentum to the emergence of AEI as the new global standard for information reporting. Within the next six months, Treasury drafted a model intergovernmental agreement (IGA) in cooperation with the EU G5. The so-called Model 1 IGA, which later also provided the basis for FATCA treaties with secrecy jurisdictions such as the Cayman Islands or Luxembourg, contains a clause obliging signatories to cooperate with the OECD in the establishment of multilateral AEI. The clause states:

> The parties are committed to working with Partner Jurisdictions and the Organisation for Economic Co-operation and Development, on adapting the terms of this Agreement and other agreements between the United States and Partner Jurisdictions to a common model for automatic exchange of information, including the development of reporting and due diligence standards for financial institutions. (US Treasury 2012a, Art. 6, para. 2)[16]

Given that the United States and EU G5 had committed each other as well as future signatories of FATCA Model 1 agreements to pursuing multilateral AEI, it was only consistent that G20 ministers of finance commissioned the OECD shortly afterward to deliver a report on the matter. G20 leaders approved this report in June 2012, calling on all countries to adopt the AEI standard (G20 Ministers 2012; G20 Leaders 2012). The same month, the United States and Switzerland issued a separate joint statement on FATCA implementation, declaring "their intent to negotiate an agreement providing a framework for cooperation to ensure the effective, efficient, and proper implementation of FATCA by financial institutions located in Switzerland" (US Treasury 2012b, 1–2). The corresponding treaty was based on an alternative model agreement, providing for the direct reporting of account information from FFIs to the IRS. The treaty was finalized in December 2012. Four years after the UBS scandal and following constant pressure from the DoJ and IRS on the Swiss government and financial sector, Switzerland had finally lifted bank secrecy for the United States (Emmenegger 2017). By not transmitting account information to the IRS itself, however, the Swiss government had initially tried to limit the damage, save its Rubik campaign, and avoid demands from other governments for equivalent cooperation (Barandun, Niederberger, and Valda 2012; Niederberger 2012; Rutishauser 2012b).

These efforts were to no avail; although the German ministry of finance had tried to play a double strategy, sticking to the Rubik deal to recover past tax liabilities of German tax evaders in Switzerland while promoting AEI as the new global standard through cooperation with the United States and in the G20,[17] the agreement failed in Bundesrat, the German parliament's upper chamber, in November 2012 (Bundesrat 2012). Social Democrats and Greens, who then held a majority in the chamber, had taken issue with several elements of the Swiss-German Rubik deal. At a most fundamental level, the opposition parties criticized the preservation of anonymity and the post-hoc legalization of hidden wealth as an undue privilege for German tax evaders in Switzerland, who had broken the law by underreporting their capital income (Bundesrat 2012, 500). Moreover, Greens and Social Democrats argued the agreement would undermine the work of German tax investigators because it limited the number of information requests to 1,500 a year and banned the active solicitation of stolen account data,[18] which had proved quite an efficient tool at the time to create media attention, waves of voluntary disclosures, and billions in additional tax revenue (Finanzverwaltung des Landes Nordrhein-Westfalen 2018; Ministerium für Finanzen und Wirtschaft Baden-Württemberg 2014). In addition to these domestic concerns, however, Greens and Social Democrats also embraced arguments put forward by the EU, OECD, and US Treasury, saying a Swiss-German Rubik deal would at least delay the material and geographic extension of AEI via FATCA (Bundestag 2010, 8472, 2012a, 20656). Following a recommendation from the OECD's Centre for Tax Policy, Green members of the Bundestag's Finance Committee had, for instance, invited Itai Grinberg, former Treasury official and one of the authors of FATCA, to explain at a public hearing why a Swiss-German Rubik deal could give other offshore centers a pretext to oppose multilateral AEI (Bundestag 2012b).[19] German opposition had thus bought into the strategic considerations of international AEI proponents before rejecting the Rubik deal in Bundesrat.

The almost simultaneous failure of the Swiss-German Rubik deal and Swiss agreement to a FATCA treaty with the United States finally cleared the way for the ascent of AEI as the new global standard for cooperation against tax evasion. While the United States sped up its efforts to extend the reach of FATCA worldwide, striking corresponding treaties with 112 foreign governments, including all major secrecy jurisdictions (US Treasury 2018a), Eveline Widmer-Schlumpf, Swiss minister of finance, announced shortly after agreeing to the FATCA treaty that she would also enter into a dialogue on AEI with the EU (Valda 2012a). Moreover, she created the Brunetti Group, tasked to develop proposals for the reorientation of Swiss international tax policy (Valda 2012b). These developments broke a deadlock in negotiations among member states on a material and geographic extension of AEI within the EU (Hakelberg 2015b), made the G20 endorse automatic exchange of information as a global standard (G20 Leaders 2013), and led to the creation by the OECD of a "common reporting standard" (CRS) based on FATCA (OECD 2014g), which has since been adopted by more than one hundred governments through the "multilateral competent authority agreement" (OECD 2017a).

FATCA Enables Agreement on AEI at the EU and OECD Level

At the EU level, Luxembourg and Austria, the biggest recipients of nonresident deposits from within the euro area (ECB 2015), were blocking AEI on interest payments to nonresidents since the Commission had proposed a Savings Directive in 1998 (Genschel 2002). The Council of Ministers still adopted the directive in 2003, but to reach consensus its proponents had to concede Luxembourg, Austria, and Belgium the right to levy a withholding tax on interest payments to nonresidents instead of collecting account information on behalf of EU partners. This concession meant some additional tax revenue for the rest of the EU, but account holders in these three countries remained anonymous (Rixen and Schwarz 2012). According to the directive, their opt-out from the AEI should end once Switzerland and several non-EU microstates started to report information on EU account holders upon request (European Community 2003, Art. 10). Yet as Luxembourg and others had expected, Switzerland and the microstates merely accepted the withholding option in their Savings Agreements with the EU, postponing EU-wide AEI into the indefinite future (Council of the European Union 2004).

Following the LGT scandal, Peer Steinbrück, German minister of finance, put a revision of the Savings Directive on the agenda of the March 2008 Council on Economic and Financial Affairs (ECOFIN) (Mussler 2008). With the support of his French and Italian counterparts he encouraged the Commission to speed up review of the directive and called for a "material and geographic extension" of its AEI mechanism (Bundesministerium der Finanzen 2008, 31). The Commission presented a corresponding report in fall 2008, conceding that investors could circumvent the directive by either hiding behind interposed legal entities or investing in equity rather than interest-producing debt securities (European Commission 2008b).[20] As remedies the Commission advocated a look-through approach obliging banks to use information obtained through know-your-customer due diligence when determining account ownership, and an extension of the Savings Directive's scope to securities that investors may consider equivalent to debt in terms of their risk profile. In contrast, the Commission did not propose changes to the AEI opt-out granted to Luxembourg, Austria, and Belgium (European Commission 2008a).

Instead of a swift revision of the Savings Directive, however, Germany, France, and other large EU members experienced what Luxembourgian Prime Minister Jean-Claude Juncker had already forecast at the March 2008 ECOFIN meeting: "many years of fascinating debate" (Mussler 2008). During the next four years, Council presidencies made six attempts at passing a revised draft and a mandate for Commission negotiations with Switzerland on a corresponding Savings Agreement.[21] Every time, Luxembourg and Austria refused to agree, arguing that a level international playing field had to be established ahead of their consent. That is, Switzerland had to first signal its willingness to practice AEI with the EU; otherwise, capital flight from the common market was the likely result.[22] Switzerland, in turn, used the nonparticipation of Luxembourg and Austria in intra-EU AEI to justify Swiss unwillingness to do just that (Naegeli 2010). Interestingly, however, Switzerland offered to update its Savings Agreement with the EU in accordance with the OECD's upon-request standard (Naegeli 2011). Yet Swiss politicians knew that the Savings Directive's transition clause made this the crucial condition for a removal of the transitory withholding option, which gave Luxembourg and Austria an additional reason to block any mandate for commission negotiations on a revised Savings Agreement. Because of the unanimity requirement in tax matters there was little to nothing large EU members could do to break this arrangement (Hakelberg 2015b).

The only item on intra-EU cooperation in direct taxation that passed during this period was a severely stripped-down version of a proposal the Commission had made for an Administrative Cooperation Directive. The proposed directive stipulated that the Commission, assisted by a committee of national tax experts, should define income types subject to AEI, as well as the conditions under which information should be exchanged (European Commission 2009). Thereby, the Commission aimed to circumvent cumbersome Council procedures in the future. Unsurprisingly, however, Luxembourg and Austria opposed such annulment of their de facto veto power in tax matters. As a result, the final version of the directive agreed on in December 2010 left everything as it was. AEI became an option for future administrative assistance, but covered income types had to be agreed on in subsequent Council decisions (European Union 2011, Art. 8). Moreover, the Luxembourgian and Austrian finance ministers could celebrate the codification of the availability principle. That is, even if the Council decided to practice AEI on capital income other than interest, tax authorities needed only to transmit data readily available to them. Data that tax authorities did not collect domestically were thus excluded from EU-internal exchange in any case (European Union 2011, Art. 3; Schweizerische Depeschenagentur 2010). Eventually, the directive served only to transpose the OECD's upon-request standard into EU law, including a customary most-favored-nation (MFN) clause obliging member states to extend any greater cooperation offered to a third country also to one another (European Union 2011, Art. 19). This MFN clause seemed benign in December 2010 and thus passed without debate. But the intergovernmental implementation of FATCA would soon turn it into a Trojan horse, breaking Austrian and Luxembourgian opposition to intra-EU AEI.

The same week that Eveline Widmer-Schlumpf announced agreement on a FATCA treaty with the United States, Luc Frieden, Luxembourg's minister of finance, declared his country would also enter negotiations on a FATCA deal, and extend equivalent cooperation to EU partners (Valda 2012a). A few months before, he had still argued in the ECOFIN that the Swiss-German Rubik deal was the better model for an EU-wide solution than AEI. Yet the Rubik deal's failure in the German Bundesrat had definitively taken that option off the table. Frieden's announcement was thus a major and quite sudden change of tack, the underlying reasoning of which Jean-Claude Juncker, prime minister of Luxembourg, made explicit in his state of the nation speech a few months later:

> If we now modify our position, we do it because the Americans do not leave us a choice. They restrict their financial operations to countries which accept automatic exchange of information. If we do not comply with this condition, there won't be any financial operations with the USA. Yet an international financial center cannot cut itself from the American financial circuit. . . . We cannot refuse to also extend to the Europeans the concessions that we have to make to the Americans within the context of a bilateral treaty. (Juncker 2013, 346)[23]

As Germano Mirabile, head of sector for savings taxation at the Commission, explained in May 2013, the reason Luxembourg could not refuse to grant equivalent cooperation to EU partners was the MFN clause contained in article 19 of the Administrative Cooperation Directive. "This means that member states, having concluded a FATCA agreement with the US, need to decide now on a legal basis for their equivalent cooperation with EU partners."[24] Other interview partners confirmed the importance of Luxembourgian participation in FATCA for its acceptance of AEI within the EU and beyond, and the crucial role of the MFN clause as transmitter of US pressure to the European level.[25]

The clause was equally important in relations between the EU G5 and the Austrian government, which was less forthcoming than Luxembourg despite the launch of negotiations on a FATCA treaty with the United States in January 2013 (*Der Standard* 2013). In fact, the Austrian finance ministry initially argued that a direct transmission of account data from Austrian banks to the United States, as foreseen by the alternative model IGA agreed on between Switzerland and the US government, would not create an obligation to accept AEI within the EU, as Austrian authorities were not directly involved in the reporting. From the legal standpoint of the Austrian finance ministry, Austrian banks were cooperating with the United States as a result of the FATCA agreement, not the Austrian government (Bramerdorfer 2015; Szigetvari 2014).[26] Yet this interpretation was far from compelling, as the FATCA Model Agreement on which it was based states in article two that

> [FATCA Partner] shall direct and enable all Reporting [FATCA Partner] Financial Institutions to . . . register on the IRS FATCA registration website with the IRS by July 1, 2014, and comply with the requirements of an FFI Agreement, including with respect to due diligence, reporting, and withholding. (US Treasury 2014b, 6)

The agreement thus bestows an active role on the Austrian government in facilitating automatic information reporting by Austria's financial institutions to the IRS. Therefore, there may have been a basis for an application of the MFN clause. At any rate, the disputed legal situation enabled the EU G5 to uphold a credible threat of suing Austria before the European Court of Justice for respect of the MFN clause. As a senior German tax official explained:

> We told them explicitly in bilateral conversation: either you participate in AEI or we will apply the MFN clause. And then you can go ahead and take legal action, à la this isn't even a case for the MFN clause, but that will take three to five years and you won't be able to see through that.[27]

To further increase the pressure on Austria, EU G5 finance ministers also sent a joint letter to EU Commissioner for Taxation Algirdas Semeta in April 2013, urging effective application of the MFN clause and calling "on all EU Member States . . . to agree without delay on the amending proposal to the Savings Taxation Directive of 2003" (EU G5 Finance Ministers 2013, 1–2). This concerted action against isolated Austria had the desired effect. At the ECOFIN meeting in May 2013, Austrian Minister of Finance Maria Fekter finally agreed to a mandate for Commission negotiations on a revised Savings Agreement with Switzerland. In addition, EU finance ministers decided the revised Savings Directive should be passed once Switzerland signaled its willingness to practice AEI with the EU in these negotiations (Council of the European Union 2013). The latter point was an easy concession to Austrian and Luxembourgian concerns about a level playing field, as Eveline Widmer-Schlumpf had already announced in December 2012 she would discuss AEI with the EU.

In parallel to the US-induced breakthrough at EU level, the intergovernmental implementation of FATCA also put AEI on the agenda of the G20 and the OECD. After G20 leaders had already called on all countries to adopt this practice in June 2012, and the EU G5 had declared their intention to develop a multilateral tax information exchange agreement based on the FATCA Model IGA they had agreed on with the United States, finance ministers and central bank governors reiterated their support in April 2013, endorsing AEI as "the expected new standard" (OECD 2014g, 9). Under the impression of this renewed momentum, the Brunetti Group created by the Swiss minister of finance recommended in June 2013 that Switzerland should practice AEI with the EU and other countries to avoid parallel standards and thus minimize compliance costs for Swiss banks (Brunetti 2013). Beginning with Pierin Vincenz, CEO of Swiss Raiffeisen Group, an increasing number of Swiss bankers had come to the conclusion over the course of 2012 that the administration of multiple Rubik agreements was more complex than the automatic reporting of account information based on a single global standard (Flubacher 2012). As Vincenz explained in an interview, "if we agree to a withholding tax with all neighboring countries this gets very complex, because every country has a separate method for its calculation. Moreover, there will have to be continuous updates. . . . And there will be automatic exchange of information with the USA anyway" (Rutishauser 2012a).[28] By June 2013, the CEO of UBS, the Swiss Bankers Association, and the Swiss Private Bankers Association had also adopted that position (Flubacher 2012; Schweizerische Depeschenagentur 2013b, 2013a). After publication of the Brunetti Group's report, the Swiss ministry of finance thus acknowledged that AEI would become the new global standard for tax cooperation and pledged active participation in its development (Eidgenössisches Finanzdepartement 2013). Moreover, Eveline Widmer-Schlumpf followed up on her December 2012 statement, declaring Switzerland would apply a global AEI standard negotiated at the OECD in its relations with the EU (Valda 2013).

In September 2013, G20 leaders eventually endorsed AEI as the new global standard, calling on the OECD to develop a framework for coherent worldwide application of AEI by mid-2014 (G20 Leaders 2013). Hence, the OECD modeled its CRS on the FATCA IGA agreed on between the United States and the EU G5 to avoid double regulation and ensure a level international playing field. As an OECD tax official involved in its drafting explained, "This made sense on a pragmatic level. FATCA is quite broad so it is useful for many countries. And why invent the wheel again, when you have a standard with a lot of bite? In the end, it is better to have a single standard than several."[29] With the Swiss vote, the standard passed the OECD Committee on Fiscal Affairs in February 2014.[30] Tax Commissioner Semeta could thus report to EU finance ministers shortly afterward that Switzerland was seeking agreement on AEI based on the new global standard (Semeta 2014). After six years of fascinating debate, ECOFIN could thus reach agreement on the revised Savings Directive in March 2014 (European Union 2014a). Moreover, the subsequent European Council ordered finance ministers to adopt a revised Administrative Cooperation Directive by the end of 2014, now intended as a vehicle to transpose the OECD CRS into EU law. As a result of newly established consensus, work went ahead quickly, and ECOFIN was in a position to adopt the directive in October 2014. It codifies comprehensive intra-EU AEI on all types of capital income starting on January 1, 2017, with Austria joining a year later on January 1, 2018 (European Union 2014b). Beyond the EU, fifty-one countries used the G20's endorsement of the OECD CRS in September 2014 as the occasion to sign a multilateral competent authority agreement (MCAA) in Berlin, committing signatories to begin exchanging bank data among each other based on the CRS from September 1, 2017, or 2018, including Switzerland, Luxembourg, Austria, and the Cayman Islands (OECD 2014e, 2014a). An additional

TABLE 5.1   AEI Adoptions among Major Secrecy Jurisdictions

JURISDICTION	FATCA AGREEMENT (MODEL)	OECD COMMON REPORTING STANDARD	
		SIGNED MULTILATERAL AGREEMENT	PASSED IMPLEMENTING LEGISLATION
Austria	yes (2)	yes	yes
Bahamas	yes (1)	yes	yes
Bahrain	yes (1)	yes	yes
Belgium	yes (1)	yes	yes
Bermuda	yes (2)	yes	yes
Cayman Islands	yes (1)	yes	yes
Curaçao	yes (1)	yes	yes
Guernsey	yes (1)	yes	yes
Hong Kong	yes (2)	yes (China)	yes
Isle of Man	yes (1)	yes	yes
Jersey	yes (1)	yes	yes
Luxembourg	yes (1)	yes	yes
Macao	yes (2)	yes (China)	yes
Panama	yes (1)	yes	yes
Singapore	yes (1)	yes	yes
Switzerland	yes (2)	yes	yes

Note: Major secrecy jurisdictions include countries identified as such in table 1.1.

Sources: OECD (2017a, 2018b); US Treasury (2018a).

fifty countries subsequently adopted the standard, including Hong Kong and Singapore (see table 5.1).

By imposing FATCA on FFIs worldwide, developing an intergovernmental approach to its implementation with the EU G5, and striking bilateral FATCA treaties with 112 jurisdictions, the United States had thus enabled agreement on AEI within the EU and at the global level. Within the EU, Luxembourg and Austria would have risked legal action by the G5 if they had not accepted AEI after entering into negotiations on FATCA agreements with the United States. At the global level, the imposition of AEI through FATCA changed the preferences of banks in secrecy jurisdictions. Before FATCA, these banks were seeking to apply the least stringent form of tax cooperation with foreign governments. When FATCA forced them to build the infrastructure for automatic reporting of account information, the banks became interested in practicing a single global standard to minimize compliance costs. As a result, jurisdictions submitting to FATCA generally also pledged to apply the OECD CRS in their relations with other countries (see table 5.1). This pledge, in turn, reduced the risk of capital flight from Luxembourg and Austria to third countries linked to the acceptance of AEI at EU level. By facilitating a multilateral AEI regime through FATCA, the United States had thus created a level playing field for secrecy jurisdictions inside and outside the EU. However, the AEI regime's architect was itself missing from the list of signatories of the MCAA, as accession to the agreement would have meant adoption of reciprocal AEI (Vasagar and Houlder 2014). As the next section will show, the US financial sector was fiercely opposed to new domestic reporting requirements that would enable reciprocity, while the Obama administration was unwilling to pick a fight with finance over this issue. Hence, what politicians and activists alike celebrated as a historic breakthrough for international tax cooperation suffers from a major equity problem: the lack of reciprocal exchange of information from the United States.

The Lack of US Reciprocity

Neither FATCA agreements nor the MCAA, which the United States has not signed, legally bind the United States to reciprocate the information reporting it requests from other countries. The United States is thus receiving data on US account holders from across the world but is not obliged to disclose equivalent information on nonresidents to treaty partners. In fact, the US government pledges to reciprocate information reporting on nonresident account holders only in one variant of FATCA treaties, the Model 1 IGA agreed on with the EU G5. Yet even this IGA does not provide for full reciprocity, given that the United States lacks the domestic regulations to collect all the data from US financial institutions it requests from FFIs, including nonresidents' account balances, non-US-source dividends, and beneficial ownership of trusts (Christians 2013, 2014). Accordingly, Model 1 IGAs feature the following qualificatory clause:

> The United States acknowledges the need to achieve equivalent levels of reciprocal automatic information exchange with [FATCA Partner]. The United States is committed to further improve transparency and enhance the exchange relationship with [FATCA Partner] by pursuing the adoption of regulations and advocating and supporting relevant legislation to achieve such equivalent levels of reciprocal automatic exchange. (US Treasury 2012a, Art. 6)

The Obama administration, indeed, included requests for full FATCA reciprocity in its 2013 and 2014 budget proposals (Office of Management and Budget 2013; US Treasury 2014a). However, these requests did not appear in corresponding Green Books on revenue proposals, which are the documents US tax experts consult when in doubt over Treasury's intentions. As a former Treasury official explained:

The budget of the United States says a bunch of [stuff] that has to do with the spending side, and occasionally it has some language about tax. But that language is political rhetoric. The real proposals, fledged out at a level of detail that matters, are in the Green Book. Not in the Green Book? There is no proposal for reciprocity! In other words, the document a tax lawyer would read doesn't even have it. . . . And that is something you often see in international economic politics, that you send different messages to national and foreign audiences. And this is an example of that. Any uninformed observer would understand that the US government had put out a politically important message. An observer inside the sub-community would see something different.[31]

The Obama administration was thus sending a double message on reciprocity: reassuring its international partners by including corresponding requests in the budgets, while appeasing domestic interests by not retaining them in the Green Books. The underlying rationale for this strategy was apparently that an early focus on reciprocal AEI and corresponding reporting requirements for US banks might have provoked domestic resistance to FATCA, potentially undermining its full implementation. Treasury thus preferred to "take it in steps." As a former senior Treasury official clarified, "In the long-term reciprocity will make sense. But at the front edge the logic is different. If we try to make this perfect today, it will probably never happen and I would say that about FATCA generally."[32] Apparently, Treasury was dragging its feet to avoid the "entrance of [the] US financial industry into the fight" over reciprocity (Garst 2014).

But even the rather limited regulatory changes the Treasury Department proposed in order to send a signal of willingness to US treaty partners received a good deal of domestic resistance. When the IRS issued a regulation in 2012, extending a requirement for US banks to report interest payments from applying to Canadian account holders only to applying to all nonresident aliens (NRAs), the ABA blasted in response: "these . . . regulations will further strain banks' information technology staff and budgets, *for the sole purpose of providing information to the IRS*, especially when there is the risk that many banks will lose billions of dollars in deposit funds due to the resulting loss of many of their NRA customers" (Mordi 2011, 2). Moreover, the banking associations of Florida and Texas, whose members host a lot of Latin American wealth, took legal action against the IRS, "claiming the regulation was overly burdensome and could lead to massive capital flight because legitimate customers might fear their information would be disclosed to, and misused by, rogue governments" (*The Economist* 2014). Although the regulation eventually took effect after the legal challenge was thrown out of court in 2014, US banks can still circumvent the requirement of reporting foreign clients and their capital income by divesting their portfolios of debt securities or hiding their identities behind a trust.

The reason is that the Financial Crimes Enforcement Network (FinCEN), the US Treasury agency responsible for countermeasures to money-laundering, adopted new customer due diligence (CDD) rules in 2016 that allow US banks to identify as the owner of a reported account the trustee who manages assets on behalf of the actual beneficiaries. In fact, the rules allow this practice even when a trust owns more than 25 percent of a legal entity for which a US bank would otherwise have to obtain beneficial ownership information under the new regulations (FinCEN 2016). Whereas foreign banks thus have to look through trusts when determining account ownership under FATCA, according to FinCEN "identifying a beneficial owner . . . would not be possible" for US banks, owing to the complexity of the contractual arrangement (FinCEN 2016, 29412). Because of this gaping loophole, the new obligation for US banks to identify the beneficial owners of other legal entities, which looks like a major improvement over the status quo ante (cf. FATF 2006), becomes virtually meaningless. In fact, a foreigner who previously invested in the United States through an anonymous shell company simply needs to put her assets in trust to remain invisible from her domestic tax authority. Hence, the new reporting requirements the Obama administration adopted to demonstrate some goodwill to US treaty partners reveal a considerable degree of hypocrisy on closer inspection.

According to several sources, the divergence in reporting standards imposed on foreign and domestic banks results from the US financial sector's intense lobbying, which created internal conflict between different branches of the US Treasury. Whereas FinCEN officials were committed to establishing financial transparency, banking regulators felt that US financial institutions had already been stretched thin as a result of post-crisis reforms. Therefore, the imposition of additional adjustment costs without any direct benefit for the United States did not gain priority with the department's senior decision makers.[33] So FinCEN (2012, 2016) took four years to move from proposed to final CDD regulations and also granted US banks an additional two-year transition before the new but ineffective rules took effect in May 2018. In the meantime, committed foreign tax evaders most likely managed to rearrange their financial affairs so as to ensure their continued anonymity. Despite more restrictive CDD, US banks thus continue to enjoy a competitive advantage over FFIs in the management of hidden wealth, which has resulted in a shift of cross-border deposits from traditional secrecy jurisdictions to the United States.

As Max Schaub and I have shown elsewhere, the adoption of FATCA and the emergence of multilateral AEI that FATCA precipitated led to the desired withdrawal of foreign deposits from traditional secrecy jurisdictions between 2010 and 2015. At the same time, however, cross-border deposits in the United States grew at an above-average rate, which suggests that foreign account holders reacted to the AEI by shifting some of their financial wealth to the last reliable secrecy jurisdiction instead of bringing it home (Hakelberg and Schaub 2018). Our results match statements from Austrian tax advisers, who claim that nonresidents shifted some of their financial wealth from Austrian to US banks after Austria agreed to AEI in the EU.[34] Moreover, these findings are corroborated by reports of US wealth managers and tax advisers, who actively promote the secrecy benefits attached to US trusts among affluent foreign households (Drucker 2016). Registrations of corresponding contractual relationships have, indeed, multiplied in secretive US states such as Nevada and South Dakota, whereas industry projections expect the value of assets under management in the United States to grow faster than in most traditional secrecy jurisdictions over the coming years. Against this background, calling the United States the new Switzerland has lately gained some currency among wealth managers (Scannell and Houlder 2016).

During his first two years in office, President Trump showed no intent to mitigate the lack of US reciprocity under FATCA. After all, it is a deal that puts America first. Instead, he signed an executive order, instructing Treasury to "review all significant tax regulations issued on or after January 1, 2016, and . . . identify . . . all such regulations that: (i) impose an undue financial burden on [US] taxpayers; (ii) add undue complexity to the Federal tax laws; (iii) or exceed the statutory authority of the [IRS]" (The President 2017, 19317). Accordingly, Treasury and the IRS focused on the identification of hundreds of corresponding regulations in several reports to the president, albeit without including the new CDD rules, which would have been within the time frame of the president's order (cf. US Treasury 2017b, 2018b; IRS 2018). The IRS thus seems busy defending existing regulations rather than developing additional ones. Likewise, bipartisan legislation on a federal company register that would require formation agents to identify the beneficial owners of all companies the agents help set up remains stalled in the House Committee on Financial Services because of opposition from the financial sectors in secretive US states and the Chamber of Commerce (Maloney 2017; Rubenfeld 2017).

Since no political actor in the United States is willing and able to work toward FATCA reciprocity, foreign governments would have to put pressure on the US government to obtain this goal. As a former Treasury official put it:

> No one in either party is really eager to anger the financial institutions in Miami for no reason. They'll do it, but Florida is a swing state. So you

will only reach real reciprocity the moment that the political cost of forcing US financial institutions to do something they don't want to do can
be weighed against another cost.[35]

On the other side of the Atlantic, however, senior tax officials do not believe
in their ability to impose corresponding costs on the United States. As a former
undersecretary of state in the German ministry of finance conceded, "We couldn't
get more than partial reciprocity from the United States. For domestic reasons
they claimed. So we said ok, this is still better than nothing and of course these
agreements are always give and take."[36] Another senior German tax official explained his government's acceptance of a nonreciprocal FATCA IGA as follows:

> When the need for such an agreement is not equally strong on both sides
> and the other side has sharper swords—that is, access to the American
> capital market—then you won't necessarily get what you want. Even if
> several European countries negotiate with the US there is still a differ-
> ence in power since we are more interested in market access for our in-
> stitutions in the US than the other way around. The Americans don't
> need the German capital market to prosper.[37]

Owing to its market size and regulatory capacity as well as the apparent prev-
alence of a purely national conception of power among German tax officials, the
United States has thus been able to enforce and stabilize a redistributive AEI regime at the international level. As a partner with a US tax law firm already observed in 2015, "fair is what you can get away with and the United States has the
power to defend this outcome."[38]

Theoretical Implications

In accordance with theoretical expectations, we observed a Democratic administration that put the fight against tax evasion and avoidance high on the legislative
agenda. All Democratic candidates had discussed tax fairness during presidential
primaries. But the UBS scandal and Barack Obama's personal affiliation with key
anti–tax haven activists within the Democratic Party made sure the issue stayed
high on the agenda also after the elections. As expected, however, the Obama administration managed to get only anti-evasion measures through Congress.
Anti-avoidance proposals affected the tax-planning schemes of US multinationals, thus creating powerful domestic opposition. In contrast, anti-evasion measures put the regulatory burden mainly on foreign banks, because the US government does not reciprocate automatic information exchange requested from

the rest of the world. As a result, US wealth managers now enjoy a competitive advantage in attracting hidden wealth instead of facing additional regulatory costs.

The US government's ability to maintain such a strongly redistributive outcome points to the importance of coercion for the emergence of the global AEI regime. In fact, the United States triggered the process by forcing foreign banks to routinely report information on US clients to the IRS. FATCA credibly linked noncompliance to partial exclusion from the US financial market. Accordingly, virtually all internationally active banks submitted to US demands, while governments across the world entered into FATCA agreements to ensure continued market access for their financial institutions. As secrecy jurisdictions became more transparent for the United States, these jurisdictions also created demand for greater cooperation from third states. After Luxembourg and Austria had entered into FATCA agreements, for instance, large EU member states invoked a most-favored-nation clause to impose intra-EU AEI on them as well. Likewise, the G20 and OECD declared AEI the new global standard for tax cooperation after Switzerland had issued a joint statement on FATCA implementation with the United States. Thus, the G20 and OECD quenched the hope of secrecy jurisdictions for an anonymity-preserving solution and harnessed bank preferences for a single set of global rules.

Regulative norms did not prevent the United States either from using coercion against secrecy jurisdictions or from taking unilateral advantage of the emerging AEI regime. In fact, secrecy jurisdictions and libertarian activists invoked national sovereignty in tax policymaking as well as the principle of nonintervention to criticize the extraterritorial reach of FATCA. Still, foreign banks registered as reporting institutions with the IRS, accepting the principle of AEI despite not having been involved in the legislative process. Likewise, Switzerland and other secrecy jurisdictions strongly criticized the US government's refusal to reciprocate AEI either under bilateral FATCA treaties or via the multilateral agreement. The argument was reproduced in the media but failed to have an impact on the eventual shape of the global AEI regime. Despite the obvious unfairness, the United States still practices a double standard when it comes to its own reporting standards, and thus maintains a comparative advantage in financial secrecy. Extraterritoriality, interference with foreign sovereignty, and double standards—the normative arguments that halted the harmful tax competition initiative (according to some accounts) thus did not prevent the use of coercion by the United States or the emergence of the global AEI regime.

THE BEPS PROJECT
Long Live Arm's Length

Numerous commentators suggest that the base erosion and profit shifting (BEPS) project, which was launched by the Organisation for Economic Cooperation and Development (OECD) in 2013 in response to a request from the Group of 20 (G20), was the most far-reaching attempt at rewriting international tax rules since the establishment of the international tax system in the 1920s. Yet commentators' superlatives refer much more to the project's ambition than to its final outcome. Scholars acknowledge the OECD's ability to produce new rules and recommendations on virtually all aspects of international taxation within just two years, particularly since discussions on individual rules had regularly taken up to a decade before the BEPS project (Ault 2013; Grinberg 2015). Scholars are less sure about what impact the final reports on fifteen action items—ranging from transfer pricing and the definition of permanent establishments, to new requirements for country-by-country reporting (CbCR)—will have on the way multinational firms are currently being taxed. In fact, the BEPS recommendations largely preserve the cornerstones of the international tax system, including the arm's-length standard (ALS), separate entity accounting, and the benefits principle (Büttner and Thiemann 2017; Picciotto 2015). Still, some scholars suggest that certain elements in the BEPS reports—like CbCR—represent significant steps in the direction of unitary taxation and formulary apportionment (UT+FA) (Avi-Yonah and Xu 2016; Seabrooke and Wigan 2016). Accordingly, the buzzword informing the current academic debate on BEPS has been "creative ambiguity" (Büttner and Thiemann 2017; Grinberg 2015; Picciotto 2015).

Why the authors of the BEPS reports had to resort to ambiguous and sometimes contradictory language to accommodate diverging interests also remains subject to debate. Most analysts suggest that the increased political salience of international tax, resulting from tax avoidance scandals in the aftermath of the financial crisis, put the established expert consensus under pressure. Whereas some argue that this pressure enabled nongovernmental organizations (NGOs) to insert alternative expertise into the discussion (Seabrooke and Wigan 2016), others claim that pressure from their political masters caused national regulators to emphasize national interest instead of technical soundness during negotiations (Grinberg 2015). As a result, conflicts over the allocation of taxing rights emerged between source and residence countries, pitting several large EU members and the emerging economies in the G20 against the United States (Grinberg 2016a).

Against this background, this chapter will clarify that the US government struggled, indeed, to assume its usual leadership position in OECD initiatives. Yet this happened for entirely domestic reasons: the Obama administration's inability to implement its preferred solution to BEPS—a tightening of controlled foreign company (CFC) rules—in the face of opposition by US multinationals, paired with the administration's strong political commitment to tax fairness, which prevented the administration from abandoning the initiative altogether. The administration's lack of purpose initially opened agenda space for other governments. Between the release of a first set of discussion drafts and the final BEPS reports, however, the United States fought a successful rearguard battle, retrenching attempts at expanding the taxing rights of source countries and essentially preserving the status quo. This success occurred despite the inclusion of G20 emerging economies, which could be expected to shift the power balance away from the United States, and in accordance with the preferences of US multinationals. The diffusion of unilateral initiatives by source countries, which are still subject to political conflict, confirms their frustration with the outcome of the BEPS project.

Points of Departure: Limiting Taxation at Source Through Transfer Pricing

Whereas the US government has enforced international cooperation against tax evasion, the United States has not followed through with proposed domestic and international measures against tax avoidance. The reason is opposition from US multinationals, defending their tax-planning practices, and an underlying dilemma faced by developed countries organized in the OECD. In general, these countries host the headquarters and intellectual property (IP) of multinational corporations. These countries are thus interested in an international tax system that emphasizes residence taxation and allows "their" multinationals to repatriate profits from emerging and developing countries where production and sales take place. To this end, developed countries have created OECD transfer pricing guidelines that link taxable profits to added value and added value to the location of IP. Based on these rules, the Chinese subsidiary producing and selling cars on behalf of a German manufacturer pays license fees to the parent company for the use of its IP. This payment reduces the taxable profit in China and increases it in Germany, as license fees are deemed passive income and as such taxable at residence. If the manufacturer manages to locate its IP in a corporate tax haven, however, the same rules also enable it to shift profits there instead of repatriating them. Developed countries can thus either choose to curb profit shifting and risk more source-based taxation or insist on residence-based taxation and risk more tax avoidance. In any case, these countries lose part of their tax base to foreign governments. In contrast to more tax avoidance, however, more source-based taxation would not only reduce the tax revenue of residence countries but also increase the effective tax burden on multinationals headquartered there. In order to reduce the foreign tax burden for their multinationals, OECD governments have thus generally given priority to limiting source-based taxation (Avi-Yonah 2000; Dharmapala 2014).[1]

With the advent of a digital economy dominated by US corporations and the consolidation of the common market, however, this OECD consensus was put into question. In fact, large EU member states grew increasingly concerned at the ability of US multinationals to channel profits out of the common market untaxed.[2] With the complicity of several small EU member states, these companies had set up tax-planning schemes like the "Double Irish with a Dutch Sandwich" to minimize the taxable profits of their subsidiaries in large EU member states. These companies achieved this result through cost-sharing arrangements allowing them to transfer the rights to the foreign use of their IP from the United States to subsidiaries in Ireland, Luxembourg, or the Netherlands. These subsidiaries were granted special deals minimizing tax payments to the respective government and then started collecting license fees for the use of their parent company's IP from their sister subsidiaries in the rest of the EU. These payments reduced taxable profits in large and high-tax member states and increased them in small and low-tax member states. Because of the loopholes in check-the-box rules discussed in chapter 3, these schemes also enabled US multinationals to avoid being taxed on their foreign profits in the United States (Avi-Yonah 2000; Dharmapala 2014; Pinkernell 2014).

As a result, US-owned coffee chains, book retailers, and computer firms enjoy a massive competitive advantage in the common market relative to their local competitors, which lack access to the same tax-planning techniques. Large EU member states could not implement countermeasures through European cooperation, as the unanimity requirement in tax matters enabled the small capital-importing member states to block the passage of meaningful anti–tax avoidance directives in the Council of the European Union. Large EU member states were also unable to implement unilateral defense measures or issue credible sanction threats because common market legislation and jurisprudence from the European Court of Justice (ECJ) prevent member states from limiting market access for other member states. The ECJ's *Cadbury Schweppes* ruling, for instance, bars large member states from applying CFC rules to subsidiaries of resident groups incorporated within the EU. As a result, European multinationals can shift profits to their subsidiaries in low-tax EU countries without having to fear that the tax authorities in their country of residence include these profits as deemed passive income in the headquarters' tax base. As a result of ECJ jurisprudence and the common market legislation on which it is based, tax competition has thus been more intense inside the European Union than in the rest of the world (Genschel, Kemmerling, and Seils 2011; Hakelberg 2015b).

Setting the Agenda: Starbucks and the Inclusion of Emerging Economies

Against this background, tax experts and administrators in the EU have been looking for remedies to tax avoidance in the common market at least since the early 2000s. In 2001, the European Commission first presented its idea for a common consolidated corporate tax base (CCCTB) to the Council of Ministers. The concept foresees the consolidation of the earnings and losses reported by a group's EU subsidiaries at its European headquarters. Instead of having each member state tax the profit reported by a group's local subsidiary, the group's consolidated profit is to be apportioned to member states based on local workforce, payroll, sales, and fixed assets. Member states can then apply their respective tax rates to their share of the consolidated profit. This application of unitary taxation and formulary apportionment (UT+FA) at the EU level should prevent multinationals from shifting profits from high-tax to low-tax member states, for instance, through license fee payments between sister subsidiaries. After all, the shifted profit would be included in the group's consolidated result in whichever member state the subsidiary receiving the payment is located (European Commission 2001).

In parallel, corporate tax lawyers and officials in the EU engaged in an intense debate over the definition of Internet servers as permanent establishments (PE).

The contentious issue was whether transactions processed via a given server—for instance in the context of online shopping—could be taxed by the country in which the server is located (Pinkernell 2014). Given the redistributive consequences of these proposals, however, member states have since failed to agree on the CCCTB, whereas the United States—home to virtually all Internet giants—insisted on limiting source countries' right to tax Internet transactions at the OECD.[3] As a result of this deadlock, expert officials in large EU member states had a hard time raising interest for the issue of tax avoidance with their political masters. As a German tax official explained in 2015:

> All of these issues have been discussed in the OECD's tax committee for at least fifteen years. They never became more than printed paper. Not because they didn't make sense but because there was no political backing. There was no tailwind. So how did it reach the agenda? I believe that politics is not really projectable but there are opportunities and time slots. When I first told the minister about what we had been discussing among experts, he replied that was a nice topic, but he wouldn't fight a lonely battle against Google, Apple, or whoever. And that was it for the moment. That must have been around March/April 2012. And then—I still remember like it was today—just before the G20 summit in Los Cabos, in November 2012, George Osborne [then the UK's minister of finance] expressed his outrage over tax avoidance by Starbucks. Suddenly our minister had this catchy example and my colleagues mailed me from Los Cabos, asking how one could integrate the tax avoidance issue into the final communiqué.[4]

Hence, the United Kingdom and Germany responded to public outrage over Starbucks' tax avoidance in the common market by involving the G20 in the issue. Compared with the CCCTB, this seemed to be a feasible and system-preserving way of increasing the pressure on multinationals.

The British-German G20 initiative also resonated with the Obama administration. The US government was less concerned with US multinationals avoiding taxes in Europe but criticized US corporations for hoarding their foreign profits in tax havens to defer tax payments in the United States. As discussed in chapter 5, President Obama and Treasury Secretary Geithner had presented a strategy for "leveling the playing field for US taxpayers" shortly after entering office. This strategy foresaw the tightening of CFC legislation through reforms of check-the-box rules and other provisions enabling tax deferral. Just as the Clinton administration did (see chapter 3), however, Treasury faced massive opposition from multinationals against these proposals. Again, business argued that an amendment of check-the-box rules would lead primarily to higher taxation of US corporations in EU countries, as a disjunction of their hybrid subsidiaries in Ireland, Luxembourg, or the Netherlands endangered the schemes set up to channel profits out of the common market. According to a tax expert with the congressional staff, many lawmakers were impressed by that argument, thinking "it [was] better for US companies to make money than for Europe to make money as a result of US tax reform."[5] So instead of repealing check-the-box rules, in 2010 the Democratic Congress extended the provisions that had turned them from regulation into legislation under George W. Bush. Even Carl Levin voted in favor (Drawbaugh and Sullivan 2013). As a result, the reform of check-the-box rules disappeared from the US Treasury's Green Book of revenue proposals for fiscal year 2011 (cf. US Treasury 2010, 2009).

Likewise, reforms of deferral and foreign tax credit rules did not make it beyond consultation phase. In the Green Book for fiscal year 2010, Treasury had proposed to disallow the deduction of "expenses from overseas investments while deferring US tax on the income from the investment." Moreover, the department sought to end corporations' ability to receive foreign tax credits for expenses that are either artificially separated from foreign profits through a hybrid entity or based on investments in high-tax countries made only to shelter profits in low-tax countries from US taxation through "cross-crediting" (US Treasury 2009, 29–31). The measures were supposed to motivate US multinationals to repatriate their foreign profits and limit eligible credits against the corresponding tax bill. Unsurprisingly, however, business lobbyists rallied against the measures, arguing that the result of repatriation and limited credits—taxation of foreign profits at 35 percent—would put US multinationals at a competitive disadvantage relative to corporations from most other OECD countries, which exempted foreign profits from taxation (Javers 2009; Leone 2009; Montgomery and Wilson 2009). Senior Democratic tax writers in Congress heard their arguments. Max Baucus, chairman of the Senate Finance Committee, commented on the Obama-Geithner initiative, saying "further study is needed to assess the impact of this plan on US business" (Calmes and Andrews 2009). Richard Neal, chairman of the Subcommittee on Select Revenue Measures of the House Ways and Means Committee, told reporters he had personally lobbied the president to abandon the characterization of tax deferral on foreign profits as tax avoidance (Cohn 2009). As a result of the chairmen's lack of interest in measures interfering with corporate tax planning, no corresponding legislation made it beyond their committees. The proposals for reforms of deferral and foreign tax credit rules were thus still included in Treasury's Green Book of revenue proposals when in 2013 Democrats also lost their Senate majority (US Treasury 2013).

Although the United States and the EU G5 were thus looking at the issue from quite different angles, tax avoidance remained a problem for both, given the increased public awareness and their inability to implement countermeasures domestically. Accordingly, the G20 leaders declared in Los Cabos, "we reiterate the need to prevent base erosion and profit shifting and we will follow with attention the ongoing work of the OECD in this area" (G20 Leaders 2012). In response, the organization presented a report and an action plan on BEPS at the beginning of 2013. The documents summarized the OECD's past efforts against tax avoidance, identified fifteen pressure areas (actions) in which reforms were needed, and proposed the BEPS project as an "effective and inclusive process" for their elaboration (OECD 2013a, 26; 2013b). As part of the OECD's inclusiveness agenda, the organization proposed to integrate non-OECD G20 members into its tax policy committees during the project. Along with the entire BEPS action plan, G20 leaders endorsed this suggestion at their 2013 summit in St. Petersburg (G20 Leaders 2013). From the perspective of the OECD, opening deliberations to emerging economies should prevent the emergence of an alternative venue and thus secure the organization's position as the central forum for decisions on international tax policy. As a German tax official explained in an article:

> The BEPS project has strengthened the OECD's leading role in international tax policy. From the German perspective, this is a strategic success, since principles developed by the OECD tend to reflect the interests of an industrialized country like Germany. These standards will evolve to take the interests of emerging and developing countries into account. But at the same time, they provide a chance for continued unification of international tax standards, which is in the particular interest of Germany with its globally connected economy. (Fehling 2015, 822)[6]

Also, the German representative in the OECD's fiscal affairs committee expected that "the inclusion of all G20 members in the discussion as opposed to a pure OECD discussion [would lead] to a stronger regard for the interests of source countries" (Kreienbaum 2014, 637). Along with the US government, which wanted to strengthen residence taxation through tighter CFC rules, bargaining over BEPS thus involved two country groups with at least partial preferences for increased source taxation. Large EU member states wanted to prevent US multinationals from channeling profits out of the common market untaxed, but still defended the arm's-length standard as the international tax system's underlying principle. Emerging economies participating as observers without voting rights aimed at a more fundamental redistribution of taxing rights toward source countries (Piltz 2015).

Toward New Rules? International Bargaining over BEPS

The Obama Administration's Lack of Purpose

When entering negotiations over BEPS, the Obama administration faced a dilemma. The administration's aim was to use the project to finally pressure business and legislators at home into the adoption of tighter CFC rules. Robert Stack, then the Treasury's international tax counsel, urged US multinationals to end the deferral of tax payments on foreign profits to prevent source countries from claiming a larger share of this supposedly "stateless income" (Stewart 2014). By enhancing Treasury's ability to tax the passive income US multinationals were hoarding in corporate tax havens, the United States would have enforced the residence principle and strengthened its dysfunctional worldwide taxation system (Grinberg 2015; Stack 2015). Yet US multinationals still had no interest in paying tax on the billions of foreign profits hitherto stashed away offshore. Instead, they advocated for a repatriation tax holiday, providing for a tax-free return of foreign profits to the United States, and a switch to a territorial tax system, exempting future foreign profits from US taxes (National Foreign Trade Council 2015; Silicon Valley Tax Directors Group 2015).[7] The Republican chairmen of the Senate Finance and the House Ways and Means Committee, who were the main targets of business lobbying, soon adopted this approach. Accordingly, Congress continued to oppose government proposals amounting to a repair of the worldwide system (Camp 2015; Camp and Hatch 2014). As the Obama administration was unable to get its preferred approach through Congress, the administration could not go first and forge international consensus around its domestic regulatory model. In the absence of a US template for an emerging international standard—as FATCA had been for the multilateral AEI (see chapter 5)—other countries used the opportunity to fill the agenda space (Grinberg 2015; Herzfeld 2015a).

For large EU member states, strengthening CFC rules made little sense for two reasons. First, the ECJ's *Cadbury Schweppes* ruling prevented them from applying such rules to subsidiaries in low-tax countries inside the EU. Hence, CFC rules could not prevent resident multinationals from shifting profits to Ireland or Luxembourg (ECJ 2006; Ruf and Weichenrieder 2013). Second, the main concern of large EU member states was the ability of US multinationals to channel profits out of the common market untaxed. Yet stronger CFC rules merely enable the residence country—in this case the United States—to include profits booked in corporate tax havens in a resident company's tax base. Stronger CFC rules do not enable EU countries to tax nonresident multinationals. Therefore, large EU member states chose a different and somewhat contradictory approach to the BEPS project. While these countries remained committed to the OECD's existing international tax system based on separate entity accounting and the arm's-length standard, they wanted to tweak the rules so as to allow tax examiners greater discretion in the assessment of intra-firm transactions and the identification of PE status. These measures were supposed to give European tax authorities a stake in the taxation of US multinationals and send a signal to emerging economies that their source country interests could be taken into account within the international tax system developed by the OECD (Grinberg 2015; Kreienbaum 2014).

As nonmembers, emerging economies did not always feel bound by the organization's standards when determining the taxable income of local subsidiaries of European firms. As this possibility could lead to unexpected increases in the firms' tax burden, the second goal of large EU member states in the BEPS project was to improve the acceptance of OECD rules among emerging economies. A senior German tax official described this reasoning as follows:

> For instance, we don't have a double-tax agreement with Brazil. Nothing but trouble, because Brazil says, "We make the rules and profit splits as we think is right and if you don't want that you don't do business in Brazil." Then the German firm tells us, "The Brazilians deceived us, now you have to do the offset so that we're not taxed twice." And when we reply that wouldn't be in line with OECD principles, they tell us that Brazil isn't even an OECD member. And that is correct, too. . . . So if I want the OECD to set global standards, I need to convince nonmembers that the rules developed there are also good for emerging economies. And I believe integrating China in the OECD process is better than China developing its own standards. But that means that the club of industrialized countries needs to depart to a certain degree from its usual reasoning. You will not convince emerging economies by saying "this is the rule, take it or leave it."[8]

In many respects, the initial framing of the BEPS project corresponded to the European priorities. In its first BEPS report, the OECD announced that "the main purpose of [the BEPS action] plan would be to provide countries with instruments, domestic and international, aiming at better aligning rights to tax with real economic activity" (OECD 2013b, 8). At their St. Petersburg summit, G20 leaders confirmed this objective, decreeing that "existing international tax rules on tax treaties, permanent establishment, and transfer pricing will be examined to ensure that profits are taxed where economic activities occur and value is created" (G20 Leaders 2013, 4). Although the emphasis on the link between taxation and real economic activity acknowledged the interests of source countries, the OECD excluded a fundamental switch to UT+FA from the outset. In the BEPS action plan, the organization underlined "consensus among governments that moving to a system of formulary apportionment of profits is not a viable way forward," and argued that "it [was] also unclear that the behavioural changes companies might adopt in response to the use of a formula would lead to investment decisions that are more efficient and tax neutral than under the separate entity approach" (OECD 2013a, 14). Given the short time frame and the familiarity of all involved actors with the existing system, solutions to BEPS should rather be found within the bounds of established principles (Ault 2013).[9] As the OECD explained in its 2013 action plan:

> The importance of concerted action and the practical difficulties associated with agreeing to and implementing the details of a new system consistently across all countries mean that, rather than seeking to replace the current transfer pricing system, the best course is to directly address the flaws in the current system, in particular with respect to returns related to intangible assets, risk and over-capitalisation. Nevertheless, special measures, either within or beyond the arm's length principle, may be required with respect to intangible assets, risk and over-capitalisation to address these flaws. (OECD 2013a, 20)

Accordingly, amendments to the OECD's transfer pricing guidelines summarized in actions 8 to 10 became the centerpiece of the BEPS process, at least when considering the submissions from business and civil society (cf. OECD 2017d).[10]

Defending Orthodox Application of the Arm's-Length Standard

The OECD's initial discussion draft released in December 2014 includes new guidance on how to apply the arm's-length standard (ALS) in transfer pricing analyses. To determine the accuracy of transfer prices fixed by multinationals to value transactions between their branches, tax authorities first need to accurately delineate the transaction and then compare "the conditions of the controlled transaction with the conditions of comparable transactions between independent enterprises" (OECD 2014b, 4). The ALS is respected when the conditions and transfer prices of the controlled and uncontrolled transaction match. Yet, because of the tight integration of multinationals and the importance of intangible assets in their internal transactions, tax authorities often struggle to identify comparable transactions between unrelated firms. Therefore, the draft provides guidance on how to identify the functions and risks assumed by transacting group members based on their contracts and actual conduct. The thorough analysis of the facts and circumstances of every controlled transaction shall enable tax authorities to determine "whether actual arrangements differ from those which would have been adopted by independent parties behaving in a commercially rational manner" (OECD 2014b, 26). A transfer price respecting the ALS should thus become identifiable also in the absence of a comparable transaction between independent firms.

Although the OECD's draft mainly underlines the continued applicability of the ALS, the document also introduces some important qualifications: "In exceptional circumstances the transaction as accurately delineated may be interpreted as lacking the fundamental economic attributes of arrangements between unrelated parties" (OECD 2014b, 25). This is the case when an "arrangement does not enhance or protect the commercial or financial position of [involved branches]," or "the Group benefit is limited to post-tax considerations" (OECD 2014b, 25). According to the draft, such situations arise because multinationals tend to divide the activities, legal ownership, and assumption of risk related to an asset among an increasing number of separate legal entities. Because the transactions between these entities make no commercial sense in the absence of centralized control, tax authorities should be allowed to disregard them in transfer pricing analyses. The nonrecognition of a controlled transaction as described in the draft should thus enable tax authorities to attribute the income derived from the use of an asset to those group branches that actually developed or marketed it, instead of the entity formally holding ownership rights (OECD 2014b, 25–27). From the perspective of the OECD, "the non-recognition of transactions, which lack the fundamental attributes of arrangements between unrelated parties, will go far in aligning where profits are reported and where value is created" (OECD 2014b, 37). Still, the organization identified some residual BEPS risks related to information asymmetries between corporations and tax administrations.

In practice, a multinational may transfer patents or trademarks to a subsidiary in a corporate tax haven before they start to generate revenue. Since these intangibles are often unique and early in their development, tax authorities struggle to verify the assumptions the multinational made in projecting the income the patents or trademarks will generate. As a result, tax authorities cannot assess whether the transfer price the tax haven subsidiary paid for the intangible reflects the price an unrelated party would have paid or is at least economically rational. To make up for the authorities' lack of reliable information, the draft thus proposes special measures tax examiners could apply when faced with excessive uncertainty over the value of an intangible transferred between related parties. One such measure relates to hard-to-value intangibles (HTVI) and would permit tax authorities to adjust ex ante income projections based on actual outcomes. That is, if an internally transferred patent turned out to be successful, the tax examiner could adjust the initial transfer price according to the profits eventually generated (OECD 2014b, 41). In most cases, this adjustment would result in a higher transfer price, reduce the profits of the tax haven subsidiary, and increase the taxable profits of the multinational's headquarters. Another measure introduces the behavior of an independent investor as a yardstick, assuming that lower risk and higher returns would lead her to invest directly in an asset instead of in a company that owns an asset but lacks the capacity to exploit it (OECD 2014b, 42). Such a minimally functional entity (MFE) should thus be disregarded for tax purposes and its profit reallocated to the parent company. To facilitate the identification of an MFE, the draft proposes a short list of easy-to-apply qualitative and quantitative indicators. Instead of performing a comparability analysis respecting the ALS, the tax examiner could simply disregard a controlled transaction based on certain attributes of the involved group branches (OECD 2014b, 44). Like the proposed guidance on nonrecognition, special measures could thus have provided tax authorities with additional discretion in the recharacterization of controlled transactions.

Accordingly, these proposals met considerable opposition from multinationals and their tax advisers. In their view, greater leeway for tax examiners increased uncertainty for taxpayers and the risk of disputes between tax authorities and corporations as well as among tax authorities of different countries. This was the case because the new guidance allowed tax examiners to replace objective contractual arrangements between related parties with subjective alternative views of the facts and circumstances of a controlled transaction. As tax authorities did not necessarily come to the same conclusions in their analyses, inconsistencies and double taxation were the likely result. In an exemplary submission to public consultations on the transfer pricing draft, the National Foreign Trade Council (NFTC), representing US multinationals like Caterpillar, eBay, Google, Microsoft, and Pfizer, expressed the following criticism:

> The guidance on the identification of risk essentially mandates that business risks be allocated to the affiliate with functional control over the risk, without regard to the provisions of a written legal agreement or the observed behavior of parties acting at arm's length. The guidance on non-recognition adopts a "commercial rationality" standard that would disregard transactions that have been actually undertaken based on a subjective determination by a tax authority that the transactions were not expected to enhance the commercial position of the parties. Taken together, these proposals would lead to tremendous uncertainty and a proliferation of disputes in all but the simplest fact patterns, are wholly disproportionate to the concerns identified, and, most importantly, are inconsistent with the arm's length principle. (NFTC 2015, 602)[11]

The big four accounting firm KPMG had essentially the same observations:

> The Discussion Draft actively encourages tax authorities to second-guess the contractual arrangements established by taxpayers by stating that they are ". . . at best . . ." the starting point in determining the "accurately delineated transaction." This is recharacterization in substance, and will remove any common understanding of the relevant business arrangements. An increase in the number and size of disputes can be expected, as well as an increase in the difficulty in finding a principled solution to those disputes. (KPMG 2015, 528)[12]

Therefore, multinationals and tax advisers alike requested tax authorities to give priority to written contracts between related parties in their analyses and resort to nonrecognition only when actual conduct deviates from prior legal arrangements. This approach would provide taxpayers with certainty as to their tax structures and minimize legal disputes (KPMG 2015; NFTC 2015; PwC 2015; USCIB 2015).

The same business representatives also opposed the proposed special measures. According to the NFTC, ex post adjustments of transfer prices paid for HTVI were problematic because they undermined certainty for multinationals. Therefore, adjustments should be applied only when the estimated and actual income generated by an intangible differ as a result of "events that could have been foreseen but were not taken into account in the valuation" (NFTC 2015, 614). Likewise, the Silicon Valley Tax Directors Group (SVTDG) argued that ex post adjustments should be permitted only if the taxpayer cannot show that an HTVI subject to a controlled transaction was also traded with unrelated parties under the same circumstances. Since economic projections are never completely accurate over multiyear periods, adjustments should, moreover, be prohibited after five years (SVTDG 2015, 763). As to the independent investor model and the possibility to disregard MFEs, reactions were even less forthcoming. The NFTC (2015, 614) strongly opposed the measure, as "it would substitute the judgment of tax authorities for capital allocation decisions and business judgments of MNEs." The United States Council on International Business (USCIB 2015, 843) argued that these special measures "could result in significant realignment of taxing rights between source and residence countries and should be rejected." The fear of a reallocation of taxing rights through the backdoor was shared by KPMG (2015), and added a political dimension to US multinationals' technical criticism. According to a narrative popular among lobbyists in the US, the BEPS project "invit[ed] the entire world to impose higher taxes on US multinationals,"[13] and special measures were one instance of this invitation. In the words of a senior lobbyist for US multinationals:

> The special measures were put out there because countries wanted them out there. And the fact that they are out there doesn't mean that the

OECD's Centre for Tax Policy supports those. But what worries me and my members about this is when the OECD comes out with a certain model, even if it has not been approved, yet the fact that it has been published in an OECD document gives it some kind of seal of approval. So it is distracting when you see this kind of stuff coming out, because you don't know whether someone will latch on to that independent investor model, even though it makes zero sense.[14]

US multinationals' opposition to the European approach of sticking with the basic principles of the established system, while expanding the leeway of tax examiners (including in source countries), left the Obama administration with a single option. Because of domestic opposition, the administration could not impose its preferred countermeasure to tax avoidance internationally. At the same time, the administration's strong political commitment to tax fairness prevented it from abandoning the BEPS project altogether (Herzfeld 2015a). Therefore, the Obama administration entered into a rearguard battle, essentially seeking to preserve the status quo of the international tax system, including the ALS, separate entity accounting, and the benefits principle (Finley 2017b, 2017a). After the release of the transfer pricing draft, Robert Stack adopted the lobbyists' narrative, suggesting the BEPS project was pushed forward by Europe and Australia to increase the tax burden of US multinationals (Stack 2015). Against this background, he stressed he was determined to protect the US tax base in negotiations and would make sure "that our taxpayers are being treated fairly around the world, that they have rules that are clear and administrable, and that we as the US government are not opening the door to rules that will create greater and greater tax disputes" (Parillo 2014). On the transfer pricing draft in particular, Stack affirmed, "We don't want transfer pricing reports to become basically anti-abuse rules or CFC rules. We want them to clearly articulate the arm's-length standard" (Parillo 2014), adding on another occasion that "there will be no free pass to recharacterize willy-nilly based on vague notions" (Sheppard 2015). The Obama administration's focus thus shifted to preserving legal certainty for US multinationals. This was to be achieved by paring back discretionary measures in the proposed transfer pricing guidelines and through the establishment of binding arbitration for disputes between tax authorities that may arise from remaining ambiguity (Herzfeld 2015b).

In accordance with Stack's announcement that "the US will also be heavily involved in the articulation, editing, and drafting of the final version of the transfer pricing guideline changes" (Sheppard 2015), the final report reflects the priorities of US multinationals discussed previously. The draft section justifying the need for nonrecognition with moral hazard reflected in the proliferation of contractual arrangements and the artificial separation of functions between related parties disappeared (cf. OECD 2014b, 25–26, 2015a, 38–41). Instead, the final guidance allows nonrecognition only in "exceptional circumstances," that is, when "the transaction viewed in its entirety lacks the commercial rationality of arrangements between unrelated parties" (OECD 2015a, 39). In contrast to the discussion draft, however, the final guidance no longer provides indicators for commercial irrationality, such as a negative pretax return for the group. It rather includes two illustrative examples for extremely irrational arrangements that considerably narrow the term's definition (OECD 2015a, 40). Hence, the scope for recharacterization of contractual arrangements between related parties is a lot smaller in the final guidance, which is also reflected in its new emphasis on the circumstances ruling out any form of nonrecognition (OECD 2015a, 39). Directly addressing US multinationals, one tax policy analyst commented this outcome as follows: "Even though the US BEPS negotiators forced the Europeans to accept your self-serving tax-planned contracts, the problem is that you will have to follow the letter of your tax-planned contracts" (Sheppard 2016). Considering the public comments of US business, it appeared that corporations were prepared and able to do so (NFTC 2015, 811; SVTDG 2015, 724).

Similarly, the US hand in drafting the final transfer pricing guidance became evident in the almost complete disappearance of special measures. In the executive summary of the final report, the OECD proudly announced, "The goals set by the BEPS Action Plan in relation to the development of transfer pricing rules have been achieved without the need to develop special measures outside the arm's length principle" (OECD 2015a, 12). Indeed, the independent investor model and the possibility of disregarding controlled transactions with MFEs are missing in the final guidance (cf. OECD 2015a).[15] Although no longer labeled accordingly, the only remaining special measure is the ex post adjustment of controlled transactions involving HTVI. This is the only option from the discussion draft that received some positive feedback from US business during public consultations (as discussed earlier), most likely because it essentially corresponds to the commensurate-with-income provision in US international tax law (Herzfeld 2015b). Still, US corporations requested several restrictions on the use of ex post adjustments, all of which were adopted in the final transfer pricing report. These restrictions include a deadline for transfer price adjustments five years after an asset's commercialization and a prohibition of adjustments when the information provided by taxpayers on their income projections suggests that differences from the actual outcome are the result of unforeseeable or foreseeable but unlikely events (NFTC 2015, 814; SVTDG 2015, 763; OECD 2015a, 111).

As a result, corporations can generally avoid ex post adjustments by providing tax authorities with the details of their ex ante projections. That is, their compliance burden is once more reduced to following their self-imposed legal and economic fictions. Against this background, Andrew Hickman, head of transfer pricing at the OECD's Centre for Tax Policy, reminded US business representatives, "'It could have been worse' is really the key message, so be grateful for the version you have at the moment" (Finley 2016). On the same occasion, Michael McDonald, transfer pricing specialist with the US Treasury, concluded that the differences between the discussion draft and the final report "illustrated the road not taken" (Finley 2016). In other words, the European approach of providing tax examiners with greater leeway in transfer pricing analyses had been halted by the US Treasury's negotiators.

Preventing Enlargement of the Permanent Establishment Definition

To be sure, the rearguard battle dynamic was not limited to transfer pricing issues. The Obama administration also defused other contentious action items that threatened to enlarge the tax take of source countries. One such item was the enlargement of the permanent establishment (PE) definition in the OECD's Model Tax Treaty, which determines when a nonresident corporation has a sufficient connection to a source country to be taxed by the latter (OECD 2014d, Art. 6). Formerly, this required a physical presence such as a local office or factory. Yet the increasing importance of the Internet for commercial transactions enables corporations to access source country markets without local representation. Therefore, large EU member states had long tried to include Internet servers in the PE definition, but were rebuffed by the United States (Pinkernell 2014). The BEPS project provided a new opportunity to lower the PE threshold. In view of this opportunity, the corresponding discussion draft included two important proposals. First, the existing exemption of certain activities, such as storing and delivery of merchandise, from the PE definition would become effective only if these activities played a preparatory or auxiliary role in a company's business model (OECD 2014f, 15–17). Second, commissionaires selling products in their own name but on behalf of a foreign company that is the owner of the products should be included in the PE definition to avoid the artificial circumvention of PE status (OECD 2014f, 10–11).

Through these proposals, large EU member states hoped to resolve tax-planning schemes popular among e-commerce platforms and reduce the fiscal advantages they enjoy over local distributors (Sheppard 2015).[16] Amazon, for instance, would no longer be able to deliver products to customers in the entire common market while billing their purchases only in Luxembourg (Grinberg 2015).[17] In contrast, the US government interpreted these measures as an attack on US multinationals and the US tax base. From the Obama administration's perspective, the profits US-owned companies made in the common market were first and foremost taxable in the United States, where these companies' IP had been developed. Accordingly, Robert Stack declared himself "extremely disappointed" by the PE discussion draft and urged source countries "to acknowledge the sometimes unpleasant reality that very often there's not much value added in their jurisdictions" (Stack 2015). Against this background, Henry Louie, deputy international tax counsel with the US Treasury, threatened to enter a reservation in the OECD's Fiscal Affairs Committee if proposed changes to the PE definition were to be added to the Model Tax Treaty (Martin 2015). To accommodate US opposition, the committee thus decided to make the adoption of the changes optional (OECD 2015c, 14). Even the signatories of the multilateral instrument (MLI) applying tax-treaty-related BEPS recommendations to existing bilateral tax treaties retain the right to reserve against the new PE definition (OECD 2017c, Art. 12 & 13). As a result, neither the US nor the small EU member states hosting the cash boxes of US multinationals currently accept the revised definition in their bilateral tax treaties (US Treasury 2016, Art. 5; OECD 2017b).[18]

Paring Back Country-by-Country Reporting

Likewise, the Obama administration—this time supported by the German government—pared back the proposal for comprehensive country-by-country reporting (CbCR) contained in BEPS action 13. The concept of CbCR was originally developed by the Tax Justice Network (TJN), a group of expert activists fighting corporate tax avoidance and financial secrecy. The concept gained prominence through subsequent endorsements by the European Parliament and the European Commission. The basic idea is to have multinationals report tax payments, profits, and activities on a country-by-country basis, thus enabling tax authorities and civil society to identify mismatches that could be the result of tax avoidance (Seabrooke and Wigan 2016). To this end, the OECD's initial discussion draft proposed a CbCR template, requiring multinationals to annually report for each of their constituent entities pretax and posttax earnings, income and withholding taxes paid, payroll, and number of employees. To facilitate the detection of profit shifting, royalties, interest, and service fees paid among related entities would also be included (OECD 2014c, 15). As to the implementation of CbCR, the draft recommended that the parent company complete the report and then share it with each country hosting a related entity. If the parent company or its local affiliate does not promptly comply, tax authorities would receive the report from their foreign counterparts through an information exchange mechanism (OECD 2014c, 10).

In response to these proposals, business associations from the US and Europe submitted three main points of criticism. First, they argued that many items included in the CbCR template were not normally reported on an entity basis and therefore significantly increased the compliance burden for corporations. Second, the associations warned that tax authorities might misuse information on payroll and intragroup payments for formulary apportionment purposes or to question transfer pricing analyses. Third, business feared that a direct submission of country-by-country reports to source countries would threaten the confidentiality of business secrets. Accordingly, business requested that contentious items be dropped from the CbCR template and reports be shared only among tax authorities on a treaty basis, thus enabling residence countries to withhold information from source countries when the latter do not have sufficient confidentiality safeguards in place (BDI 2014; NFTC 2014; MEDEF 2014; USCIB 2014). The United States and Germany had an open ear for these concerns. Manfred Naumann, the head of division responsible for CbCR in the German finance ministry, argued that to preserve confidentiality and prevent misuse, parent companies should report only to their country of residence, which could then decide whether to relay information to source countries based on a bilateral treaty. In any case, information should never be made public (Naumann and Groß 2014). Along the same lines, Robert Stack affirmed that the US government's goals were to protect proprietary information, reduce the compliance burden, and ensure that information is shared only between tax administrations to preserve confidentiality (Stewart 2014).

Accordingly, the CbCR template contained in the final report on BEPS action 13 no longer obliged corporations to report payroll or intragroup royalty, interest, and service fee payments (OECD 2015d, 29). That is, all items unanimously opposed by US and European business were dropped. In addition, the final report states that "jurisdictions should have in place and enforce legal protections of the confidentiality of the reported information" and "should not propose adjustments to the income of any taxpayer on the basis of an income allocation formula based on the data from the Country-by-Country Report" (OECD 2015d, 22). Again, key business concerns over the misuse of reported data were addressed. Most important, however, the final guidance provides for CbCR from parent companies to residence countries only, whereas the annexed multilateral agreement for CbCR implementation enables governments to choose the other signatories with which they intend to share the reports (OECD 2015d, 23, 50). That is, residence countries can cherry-pick the source countries receiving information on "their" multinationals, either by not signing the multilateral agreement or by selecting among the other parties to the treaty. As a result, the original intent behind CbCR—to enable tax authorities and civil society to identify mismatches between corporate profits, taxes paid, and economic activity—is unlikely to be realized based on the final report on BEPS action 13. Commenting on this outcome, Alex Cobham (2015a), the TJN's current director, concluded, "the [CbCR] standard has been strangled at birth."

The BEPS Project's Implementation
The Proliferation of Unilateral Fixes

To become effective, the BEPS project's final recommendations need to be transposed into national administrative practice. To this end, the OECD uses two soft law instruments, the Transfer Pricing Guidelines and the Model Tax Convention, which member states generally use as templates for their national administrative rules and bilateral tax treaties. In accordance with the Model Tax Convention, article 9 of these treaties usually obliges tax administrations to apply the arm's-length standard in their transfer pricing analyses and ensure that both signatories consistently apply any price adjustment. In these contexts, the Transfer Pricing Guidelines are the key reference, including when disputes end in court (Genschel and Rixen 2015; Rixen 2008). Hence, the OECD's soft law also becomes binding for nonmembers when they enter into a bilateral tax treaty with a member state or base tax treaties with other nonmembers on the OECD template. Over time, nonmembers have, indeed, developed the same propensity as OECD members to strike bilateral tax treaties following the Model Tax Convention. As a result, 3,200 such agreements are currently in place, underlining the global reach of the OECD's tax standards (Arel-Bundock 2017). Yet the swift implementation of updates is difficult in such a system of decentralized multilateralism, as governments normally have to renegotiate their treaties one by one. To speed up the process, the OECD has begun to sponsor MLIs committing signatories to apply certain BEPS recommendations in their mutual relations. Although these agreements are open to all countries, they are voluntary and allow signatories to opt out of contentious provisions (OECD 2017b). Hence, governments can still deviate from many BEPS recommendations, as will be further discussed later.

Since the OECD's Transfer Pricing Guidelines inform the day-to-day practice of tax administrations, a swift application of the changes introduced through the BEPS process could be expected. Yet the language on the analyses of new facts and circumstances for regular transactions and transactions involving HTVI is extensive and challenging to implement even for highly capable tax administrations in developed economies (Avi-Yonah and Xu 2016). In addition, from the perspective of some tax administrations, the guidance's emphasis on the application of the arm's-length standard remains at odds with the BEPS project's promulgated goal of aligning taxation with production and value creation. Although the scope for price adjustments has been significantly reduced in the final report, some divergence in the interpretation of the new language is likely. Accordingly, multinationals and practitioners deplore uncertainty over the exact implementation of BEPS recommendations (Büttner and Thiemann 2017). In response, the OECD continues to publish supplementary documents on the implementation of contentious sections in the revised guidelines (OECD 2017d), whereas the US government pushes for binding arbitration to ensure that the resolution of disputes between tax administrations is swift and informed by an orthodox interpretation of the new language (Finet 2015; Finley 2015). At the time of writing, twenty-five countries—hosting 70 percent of the US outward foreign direct investment (FDI) stock but excluding emerging economies—had agreed to participate (OECD 2017b; UNCTAD 2014).[19] Because the legal certainty provided by binding arbitration constitutes a locational advantage from the perspective of multinationals, more countries are likely to follow (Arel-Bundock and Lechner 2017).[20] At the same time, a shift in the balance of power may also enable emerging economies to resist US demands for binding arbitration, sustain incoherence in the application of BEPS recommendations, and lead to a multiplication of unresolved tax disputes in the future.

The significance of the new PE definition for the taxation of multinationals depends on the willingness of governments to adopt it in their bilateral tax treaties. Yet the Obama administration stuck with the narrower old definition in its 2016 revision of the US model tax treaty, while the Trump administration refuses to sign the MLI through which tax-treaty-related BEPS changes could be adopted (Schwarz 2016; Herzfeld 2017a). At the same time, Ireland and Luxembourg, the countries hosting the controlled entities to which US multinationals shift profits from the rest of the EU, signed the MLI but opted out of the new PE definition (OECD 2017b). That is, if France or Germany wanted to tax more of a US multinational's activity at source by applying the new wording, they would first need to get the United States, Ireland, and Luxembourg to agree to a corresponding revision of their respective bilateral tax treaties. As a result of the power differential in such bilateral negotiations, a French or German attempt at convincing the United States to deviate from its model treaty is likely to fail. Likewise, the principle of nondiscrimination in EU law should prevent France and Germany from pressuring Ireland or Luxembourg into compliance with the new definition. The EU's Interest and Royalties Directive would, for instance, override a withholding tax on royalty payments to these countries, as legal commentary on the United Kingdom's diverted profits tax has recently made clear (see below) (European Union 2003; MacLennan 2016; Self 2015).[21] Once more, the adoption of new PE rules at OECD level thus depends on the EU's ability to transcend its internal divisions. If a wider PE definition became EU policy, the outcome of bargaining with the United States would be open. If internal divisions persist, however, individual member states will remain unable to wrestle concessions from the Trump or any future administration.

Another contentious issue in post-BEPS relations between the United States and the EU is the publication of country-by-country reports. In contrast to the final BEPS guidance and the MLI for CbCR adoption, which both include strong safeguards against the publication of reports, the European Commission and several member states seek to introduce public CbCR unilaterally. Whereas the French National Assembly even passed a corresponding law—which was, however, scrapped by the Constitutional Court for discouraging free enterprise by divulging company secrets (Assemblée Nationale 2016; Conseil Constitutionnel 2016)—the Commission's proposal is still in abeyance. First proposed as part of its "action plan for a fair and efficient tax system" (European Commission 2015b), the Commission promotes public CbCR to "enable citizens to better assess the contribution of multinational undertakings to welfare in each Member State" (European Commission 2016c, para. 9). From its perspective, "enhanced public scrutiny of corporate income taxes . . . is an essential element to further foster corporate responsibility, to contribute to the welfare through taxes, to promote fairer tax competition . . . and to restore public trust in the fairness of national tax systems" (European Commission 2016c, para. 5). To circumvent the unanimity requirement for Council decisions on taxation, the Commission proposes public CbCR as an amendment to the Accounting Directive, which already provides for public reporting in the banking and extractive industry sectors (European Commission 2016c, 4). On accounting matters, justice instead of finance ministers decide through qualified majority voting. Still, the proposal faces considerable opposition. Although the European Parliament has already adopted the amendments,[22] Germany and twelve other member states continue to oppose public CbCR in the Council (European Parliament 2017; Becker 2016). In parallel, the United States threatens to stop the exchange of country-by-country reports with any country publishing the data and contemplates additional sanctions (Johnston 2016).[23] In contrast to CbCR to tax authorities only, which has been adopted by the United States and the EU (European Union 2016; IRS 2016), the adoption and effectiveness of public CbCR in the EU thus remains highly uncertain.

As these examples illustrate, many governments that are primarily source countries from the US perspective are dissatisfied with the status quo–preserving recommendations of the final BEPS reports and now attempt to defend their interests through divergent implementation. In addition, unilateral measures expanding the taxation of nonresident multinationals at source have recently proliferated (Elliott and Sheppard 2016; Herzfeld 2017b). China has, for instance, tightened exchange controls, thereby keeping local subsidiaries of foreign multinationals from paying dividends to their parent companies (Clover 2016). Most prominently, the UK government introduced a diverted profits tax in response to public outrage over tax minimization by Google and other tech firms (Houlder 2014).[24] The measure enables Her Majesty's Revenue and Customs to withhold 25 percent of profits sent offshore if it suspects a multinational of engaging in a "contrived arrangement" to avoid a taxable presence in the United Kingdom (Houlder 2015a, 2015b). The finance ministers of France, Germany, Italy, and Spain recently proposed the introduction of an EU-wide equalization tax on payments from resident customers to nonresident companies. This measure targets the digital economy in particular, which can sell online services to customers in the entire common market without having a PE in every member state (Le Maire et al. 2017). While this proposal is still at an early stage and faces considerable opposition among member states, it demonstrates that important European governments do not believe that BEPS recommendations will end tax avoidance by US multinationals in the common market. As this goal had been one of the key motivators for EU governments to enter the BEPS project, they obviously failed to defend their agenda against the US government.

Toward More Regulatory Centralization at the EU Level?

The recent political entrepreneurship of the European Commission may, however, turn the preservation of the international tax system's status quo into a Pyrrhic victory for the United States. So far, the internal division between small capital-importing and large capital-exporting member states, paired with the unanimity requirement for Council decisions on taxation, has ensured that the EU would make little progress in fighting tax avoidance in the common market (Dehejia and Genschel 1999; Wasserfallen 2014). Since the BEPS project also failed to provide a solution to this politically increasingly salient problem, the European Commission—led by Pierre Moscovici, the French socialist commissioner for taxation and customs, and Margarete Vestager, the Danish socialliberal commissioner for competition—now seems committed to finally exit the joint decision trap in taxation by other means.[25] To this end, Vestager used the Commission's executive powers in competition policy to launch state aid investigations against Ireland, Luxembourg, and the Netherlands for the provision of selective tax advantages to Amazon, Apple, Fiat, GDF Suez, McDonald's and Starbucks.

As a result of these investigations, the Commission has to date instructed Ireland to claw back €13 billion in corporate tax from Apple, Luxembourg to claw back €270–€280 million from Amazon and Fiat, and the Netherlands to claw back €20–€30 million from Starbucks (European Commission 2017a). By creating uncertainty over the legality of sweetheart deals offered to multinationals, these decisions remove a locational advantage from member states making such offers and may eventually unsettle their opportunity structures in the Council. Therefore, Moscovici flanked the state aid decisions with the action plan on fair and efficient taxation, a relaunch of the common consolidated corporate tax base (CCCTB) proposal, and the proposal for public CbCR discussed earlier (European Commission 2015b, 2015a). Although none of these initiatives has yet been adopted, they perpetuate a public discourse on tax avoidance, create political demand for solutions, and may thereby pressurize member states into action.[26] If this dynamic eventually enabled the EU to overcome its internal divisions and adopt the CCCTB, there would also be consequences for the US tax base.

Currently, US multinationals exploit the mismatch between the free circulation of capital in the common market and twenty-eight national tax policies to shift profits first to a low-tax member state and then to a tax haven outside the EU. This shift usually happens through royalty and dividend payments between group branches (see chapters 1 and 2). From the US perspective, such payments constitute passive income taxable at residence. If the deferral and check-the-box loopholes were closed, profits shifted out of the common market would thus increase tax revenue in the United States. If the EU adopted the CCCTB, however, profits generated in the common market would be consolidated at a multinational's EU headquarters and then divided among member states based on local sales, production, and assets (European Commission 2015a). Accordingly, US multinationals could no longer concentrate their EU profits in a low-tax member state that does not withhold taxes on dividend payments to parent companies outside the EU. As a result, the US multinationals' European tax bill would rise, while the amount of passive income potentially taxable in the United States would shrink.

This perspective, which has in part already become reality through the back taxes US firms have to pay to Ireland, Luxembourg, and the Netherlands, led Jack Lew, the Obama administration's last Treasury secretary, to request an end of the state aid investigations in a letter to Commission President Jean-Claude Juncker. In his letter, Lew accused the Commission of setting "disturbing international tax policy precedents" that were "inconsistent with, and likely contrary to, the BEPS project" (Lew 2016b, 1). He insists that US multinationals' deferral of tax payments on foreign profits in the US "does not give EU Member States the legal right to tax this income," and concludes by urging Juncker "to reconsider pursuing these unilateral actions" (Lew 2016b, 2–3). Although the US Treasury reinforced these requests by threatening to impose retaliatory measures on EU firms (Chee 2016; Lynch 2016), Vestager defended her directorate's approach in her response to Lew, and has since launched further investigations leading to additional decisions against US multinationals (Vestager 2016). By preventing EU governments from effectively addressing their tax avoidance problems through the BEPS project, the United States may thus have given the EU the decisive impetus to finally harness its great power potential in international taxation. The conflict over state aid decisions could thus be the first stage in a protracted EU-US battle over taxing rights.

Theoretical Implications

The BEPS project materialized in 2012 because important G20 members simultaneously had to respond to domestic concerns over corporate tax avoidance. Whereas the conservative finance ministers in the United Kingdom and Germany responded to public outrage over revelations that multinationals like Starbucks paid little to no tax in the common market, the Obama administration was bound by its campaign commitment to restore tax fairness for the middle class, a central theme in Democratic party ideology since World War II. As a result of these constraints, governments on both sides of the Atlantic could not react to tax avoidance merely by lowering taxes on corporate profits. To address the fairness concerns that were either voiced by the electorate or rooted in the decision makers' normative convictions, governments had to credibly commit to countermeasures. Accordingly, the G20 mandated the OECD to find solutions to the observed mismatch between taxation and value creation, to which the organization responded with the creation of the BEPS project.

Although there was agreement that something had to be done, the EU and US governments disagreed over the instruments. Whereas the EU governments in the G20 were open to making limited concessions to source countries—partly to bring US multinationals within the reach of the EU governments' tax administrations, and partly to coopt emerging economies into the OECD process—the US envisaged a solution fully geared toward the interests of residence countries. However, business opposition prevented the Obama administration from adopting strengthened CFC rules and anti-deferral measures domestically. Therefore, the US lacked a regulatory model it could impose on other governments through the OECD process. Since the Obama administration was normatively committed to fighting tax avoidance, it could not convert the resulting lack of purpose into a complete withdrawal from the BEPS project. Hence, the only remaining strategy was to respond to business interests and defend the international tax system's fundamental principles against the more far-reaching reform proposals from European governments.

The Obama administration implemented this strategy through a successful rearguard action against European attempts at expanding tax administrations' leeway in the recharacterization of controlled transactions; broadening the Model Tax Convention's PE definition; and including internal royalty, interest, and service fee payments in country-by-country reports. Yet by preventing the international community from reforming a dysfunctional international tax system, the United States may have undermined its future ability to dominate international tax matters. Whereas FATCA provides other governments with a US-defined solution to tax evasion by individuals, the US administration's inability to provide such a solution to corporate tax avoidance invites other governments to create their own. Therefore, the number of unilateral initiatives against corporate tax avoidance has multiplied in the aftermath of the BEPS project. Most important, it apparently motivated the European Commission to develop strategies to overcome the EU's regulatory dispersion in matters of direct taxation. If these strategies enable the European Union to finally harness its great power potential, international tax policy may be shaped by a power duopoly rather than a single hegemon in the future.

7

FROM HEGEMONY TO TRANSATLANTIC TAX BATTLE?

Over the past decades, the United States has dominated decision making on tax matters in the Organisation for Economic Co-operation and Development (OECD). Democratic and Republican administrations have consistently defended the international tax system's status quo when reform proposals threatened to increase the foreign tax burden of US multinationals. Thereby US administrations have perpetuated a number of legal principles, including separate entity accounting and the arm's-length standard, that enable tax avoidance by multinational corporations both in source and residence countries. The United States has enforced change in global tax policy only when a Democratic administration committed to a progressive domestic tax system could shift associated adjustment costs from powerful domestic interest groups onto foreign firms and governments. For this reason, the Obama administration neither offered reciprocal automatic exchange of information (AEI) in bilateral FATCA agreements, nor joined the multilateral AEI agreement. As a result of the Obama administration's reluctance to introduce new reporting requirements domestically, US financial institutions now benefit from an exclusive competitive advantage in the provision of financial secrecy to foreign investors.

Successive US administrations have been able to defend their redistributive hypocrisy because no other government melds control of comparably sized financial and consumer markets with similar regulatory capacity. Most important, the EU and its member states have so far been unable to overcome regulatory dispersion in tax matters, the crucial prerequisite for harnessing the power of the common market. As long as a check on US hegemony is missing, however, US multinationals can shift profits out of the common market untaxed, whereas wealth managers in secretive US states can offer European investors anonymity from their local tax offices. The result is a persistent drain of taxable income from the EU to the United States that shifts the overall tax burden in the EU away from multinationals and wealthy individuals and toward local businesses, workers, and consumers. Before presenting this book's overall conclusions, I will thus use the first part of this final chapter to discuss the most recent developments in transatlantic bargaining over countermeasures to financial secrecy and corporate profit-shifting, and sketch several future scenarios based on the theory developed in chapter 2.

The Future of International Tax Politics

If further progress in the fight against tax evasion and avoidance depends on the EU's rise to great power status, what are the chances that member states will centralize regulatory authority over direct taxation and sanctions? As the following subsections show, dissatisfaction with nonreciprocal AEI and the BEPS project's failure to limit tax avoidance in the common market has motivated the European Commission and several member states to push for a common reaction. The EU has since produced an integrated blacklist of third countries not complying with its tax good governance standards and ordered several member states to claw back taxes lost to sweetheart deals granting selective advantages to individual firms. Moreover, finance ministers debate the introduction of a digital services tax (DST) and a common consolidated corporate tax base (CCCTB) to curb profit-shifting in the common market. However, regulatory dispersion and internal conflict continue to limit the effectiveness of already adopted measures and prevent consensus on more far-reaching proposals. Interestingly, resistance from small capital-importing member states may no longer be the biggest obstacle to a robust external taxation strategy. Instead, export-dependent member states such as Germany currently shy away from a confrontation with the United States on tax.

Demanding Reciprocal Information Exchange from the United States

From the outset of negotiations on AEI, the US government refused to provide other countries with the same type of account data it requests from them. Accordingly, neither the bilateral FATCA agreements, nor the Multilateral Competent Authority Agreement (MCAA), which it has not signed, oblige the United States to reciprocate the routine reporting of account information. The result of this unbalanced distribution of regulatory obligations is a major competitive advantage for US banks in the attraction of hidden capital. For European governments, persistent financial secrecy in the United States implies that tax evaders among their citizens may shift undeclared financial wealth from Switzerland to Nevada to avoid the submission of corrected returns as well as the associated back taxes and fines (Casi, Spengel, and Stage 2018; Hakelberg and Schaub 2018). Still, large EU member states and the OECD remained silent about the nonreciprocity of bilateral FATCA agreements and the US government's nonparticipation in multilateral AEI during negotiations. Instead, they acknowledged the importance of FATCA for the multilateral process and expressed their understanding for domestic resistance in the United States. In an exemplary statement on the occasion of the MCAA's signature, German minister of finance Wolfgang Schäuble told reporters:

> Without FATCA we would not have seen the same progress on automatic exchange of information in Europe, which underlines the importance of the United States for global economic stability. Congress will have to draw its own conclusions on the progress achieved at the international level, and it will not necessarily appreciate counsel from foreign governments. (Bundesministerium der Finanzen 2014)[1]

In fact, large EU member states and the OECD had several reasons not to stress nonreciprocity from the United States. First, there was little the member states and the OECD could do about it. Whereas European financial institutions faced sanctions without the conclusion of FATCA agreements, disunity in the Council of the European Union prevented EU governments from linking nonreciprocity to the imposition of similar costs on US banks. As a senior German tax official explained, "Even if several European countries negotiate with the United States there is still a difference in power. Because we are more interested in market access for our institutions in the United States than the other way around."[2] Second, it was far more important for large EU members to impose AEI on traditional secrecy jurisdictions such as Switzerland and Luxembourg. At the time, the largest share of European offshore wealth was managed in these countries and tax officials in large EU member states still believed they did not have a tax evasion problem with the United States (Zucman 2014).[3] Accordingly, they refused to delegitimize the political process that was getting them closer than ever to their main goal by criticizing FATCA on fairness grounds. As the head of the OECD's tax department recently confessed in an interview: "[Ignoring nonreciprocity from the US] was extremely embarrassing, but no one wanted to crash the party" (Besson 2016).

After coercive pressure from the United States had forced Austria and Luxembourg to abandon bank secrecy, however, the dynamic changed. In fact, the two countries became just as eager as France and Germany to avoid competitive disadvantages by also imposing the standard on third states. This attitude was evident in their eventual support of a mandate for negotiations on an AEI agreement between the Commission and Switzerland and in the wording of European Council conclusions on the adoption of a revised Savings Directive. In these conclusions, EU heads of state and government called on the Commission to conclude negotiations on AEI with third states and report back by the end of 2014. "If sufficient progress is not made," they requested, "the Commission's report should explore possible options to ensure compliance with the new global standard" (European Council 2014, 3). Although the Commission has managed to strike AEI agreements with Switzerland, Liechtenstein, San Marino, Andorra, and Monaco since then, the Commission still developed an "external strategy for effective taxation" in response to the Council's request. The purpose of this strategy is to project transparency and other tax good governance standards practiced in the EU onto third states (European Commission 2016d, 2). In the area of information exchange, tools include a consolidated EU blacklist of noncooperative tax havens, comprising third countries that do not comply with the OECD's AEI standard, and collective defense measures against jurisdictions that fail to reform despite being listed. As to countermeasures, the Commission proposes "withholding taxes and non-deductibility of costs for transactions done through listed jurisdictions" (European Commission 2016d, 12).

Yet regulatory authority over the blacklist and countermeasures remains dispersed among member states. Whereas the Commission drew up a long list of countries posing a risk to the EU's tax base, member states set the exact screening criteria, assessed third countries, and decided unanimously on additions to the list (Council of the European Union 2016). Hence, many countries matching the EU's criteria were not included in the blacklist when its first edition was eventually published in December 2017 (Council of the European Union 2017; Lips and Cobham 2017). Most important, the United States was missing, although the Trump administration had not taken any steps to mitigate nonreciprocity under FATCA, and still had not signed the multilateral AEI agreement. For these reasons, the United States had initially figured on the Commission's long list of countries failing to respect international transparency standards (European Commission 2016e, 5). Still, EU finance ministers merely included American Samoa and Guam in the final list, albeit with an interesting justification. The ministers concluded that the two US territories in the Pacific "[did]not apply any automatic exchange of financial information, and [had] not signed and ratified, *including through the jurisdiction they are dependent on*, the OECD Multilateral Convention on Mutual Administrative Assistance" (Council of the European Union 2017, 8–9, emphasis added).

As it seems, actors within the EU still struggle to find consensus on how to address the Trump administration in tax matters. Whereas Valère Moutarlier, the Commission's director of direct taxation, told the European Parliament the United States would be placed on the blacklist if it did not agree to fully reciprocal AEI by June 2019 (Kirwin 2018), some member states still shy away from an open confrontation in the tax area. They request to make any blacklisting decision conditional on the outcome of the peer review the OECD's Global Forum on Transparency and Exchange of Information for Tax Purposes is preparing on AEI implementation by the United States. This is likely to let the Trump administration off the hook as the OECD is already tweaking the compliance criteria to prevent a negative rating (Lips and Cobham 2017; Knobel 2018). This time, however, it is not the small capital-importing member states blocking progress. Instead, several export-dependent member states, including Germany, fear a unilateral decision by the EU to blacklist the United States could stoke the existing trade dispute with the Trump administration, potentially resulting in higher tariffs on cars and other manufactures.[4] Despite internal consensus on AEI and the redistributive consequences of US hypocrisy, German preoccupation with its national export surplus thus prevents the EU from challenging US hegemony in international tax politics.

Against this background, we can conceive of two future scenarios. The US government's first option is to stick to a logic of pure dominance, which could however fuel doubts about the benefits of the existing order among powerful European interest groups and eventually increase support for a challenge of American hegemony. The second option is to accommodate European criticism through limited concessions, thereby reestablishing the legitimacy of US hegemony over international tax politics (Anderson 2017; Gilpin 1981). If it were to choose the first option, the US government would defend the current level of nonreciprocity despite the naming and shaming this defense could provoke. In the short term, the United States can afford a confrontational strategy, because even if it was eventually blacklisted by the EU, it would not be subject to direct economic sanctions. In the long term, however, sustained hypocrisy from the United States could foster growing frustration among EU elites over the arbitrary use of US power against key sectors of the European economy.

Since the Trump administration reactivated the US sanctions regime against Iran in 2018, forcing EU financial institutions to end transactions with the country despite their legality under European law, manufacturers across the common market have not been paid for their exports (Brüggmann, Atzler, and Wiebe 2018). Likewise, Austrian, Dutch, French, German, and Italian energy companies currently face a threat of US sanctions because of their participation in North Stream 2, a pipeline project with Russia threatening European demand for liquefied natural gas from the United States (Bidder 2019). Along with depressing the profits of influential business groups, these cases of US coercion also interfere with the strategic interests of EU governments, which want to maintain a deal with Iran, promising investment in exchange for nuclear disarmament, and seek to ease tensions with Russia through economic cooperation. If a future data leak showed— on top of these concerns—that nonreciprocal AEI from the United States abetted tax evasion by named European individuals, demand for countermeasures may eventually be large enough across the political spectrum to overcome the uncertainty linked to a challenge of US hegemony (cf. Lew 2016a).

Instead of adding fuel to the fire, however, a future US government could also pursue the second option through an amendment of its FATCA treaties with EU countries. Currently, the United States commits to report interest and dividends from US sources received by residents of its treaty partners. The main point of criticism is, however, that US financial institutions—unlike foreign banks—are not obliged to look through legal entities when identifying account holders for FATCA purposes (US Treasury 2012a, Art. 2). Therefore, foreign residents can avoid the reporting of their US accounts by transferring formal ownership to a shell company. A future administration could respond to this concern by committing US banks to use beneficial ownership information, which they have to collect since new know-your-customer (KYC) rules entered into force in 2018, in FATCA reporting also. This commitment would send a sign of goodwill to European treaty partners at virtually no cost for the US financial industry, as these rules request the identification of the beneficiaries of a company but not of a trust (FinCEN 2016). As a result, EU governments would leave the negotiating table with a concession from the United States, whereas US wealth managers could preserve their foreign clients' anonymity by advising them to put their financial wealth into the hands of a trustee. While this scenario would merely be an incremental step toward universal financial transparency, it could focus regulatory attention on the Anglo-Saxon trust, which—as well as abetting tax evasion[5]—also perpetuates wealth inequality across generations and shields reckless investors from their creditors (Harrington 2016).

The Prospects for Tackling Tax Avoidance by Multinationals

In the fight against tax evasion, the EU was able to overcome its internal divisions because the US government imposed the AEI on recalcitrant member states through FATCA. Still, regulatory dispersion remains in the implementation of defensive measures against noncompliant third countries, particularly the United States, as a result of a fear of retaliation among export-dependent member states like Germany. In the fight against tax avoidance, the main challenge for the EU is not to wrestle concessions from the US administration. Instead, member states have to prevent multinationals from shifting profits out of the common market untaxed. To this end, finance ministers currently debate the introduction of a DST and have relaunched discussions on a CCCTB. At the same time, the European Commission has used its executive powers in competition policy to push corporate tax havens in the EU toward more cooperation. Still, the DST is bound to fail as Germany fears repercussions for European firms in the United States. Likewise, member states hesitate to pool administrative authority over the definition of the corporate tax base, as they face considerable uncertainty over the redistributive impact of such a decision. Ironically, the Trump administration's tax reform of 2017, which dramatically reduces the tax burden of US multinationals, may provide arguments for adoption of the CCCTB.

As discussed in chapter 6, large EU members had hoped the OECD's base erosion and profit shifting (BEPS) project would limit tax avoidance in the common market, in particular by US multinationals dominating the digital economy. Yet the Obama administration's successful defense of the status quo prevented the desired outcome. Therefore, member states began to discuss two countermeasures to profit-shifting that could be adopted at the EU level without involvement of the United States. The less ambitious measure, originally proposed by France and further elaborated by the European Commission, is a DST of 3 percent on the revenues created from the sale of online services in the common market. The measure's main objective is to make firms that provide services online taxable in all EU member states although the firms do not need a physical presence there to access customers. As such, the measure is a departure from the international tax system's benefits principle, which links a country's right to tax a company to the presence of a permanent establishment on its territory. From the perspective of the Commission, however, this is the only means to prevent distortion of competition between local and digital service providers as long as meaningful reforms cannot be achieved at the OECD level (European Commission 2018).

Because US tech companies dominate the provision of digital services in the common market and could claim credits on their US taxes for additional taxes paid to EU countries, the Trump administration interpreted the measure as an unfair revenue grab (Thomas 2018). Accordingly, US Treasury Secretary Steven Mnuchin (2018) announced firm opposition to "proposals by any country to single out digital companies," insisting in OECD discussions on the matter that income, not sales, was the appropriate base for the taxation of any type of corporation (Rappeport et al. 2018). Whereas the French government was unimpressed by the US response, the scientific advisory council to the German ministry of finance soon fell into line, arguing that a DST would set a dangerous precedent inviting the United States and China to also tax German manufacturers on their local sales. As the revenue loss precipitated by retaliatory measures would by far exceed the gains from a DST, the measure should be abandoned (Wissenschaftlicher Beirat 2018). As a result, Olaf Scholz, Germany's social-democratic minister of finance, withdrew support from the Commission's proposal, forcing France into a compromise on a stripped-down version of the tax that will be introduced only if the OECD does not provide a global solution to the taxation of digital services by 2020 (Mühlauer 2018). Once more, German dependence on exports prevented the EU from introducing countermeasures to tax dodging against the will of the United States.

The second, more ambitious measure, adoption of the CCCTB, is still pending and would introduce unitary taxation and formulary apportionment in the EU. In contrast to the international tax system, which is based on separate entity accounting and the arm's-length standard, the Commission's CCCTB proposal provides for the consolidation of the profits and losses made by the EU branches of a multinational group, a method often applied in federal state systems (European Commission 2016a, Art. 4–7). That is, no matter in which national subsidiary a multinational concentrates revenue from EU sources, it is always included in the group's consolidated income tax statement. Accordingly, the current incentive for profit shifts between EU subsidiaries disappears. Instead, the group's consolidated profit is divided among member states based on a formula that includes sales, workforce, payroll, and tangible assets but explicitly excludes intangible assets (European Commission 2016a, Art. 28 & 34). As a result, member states that host a multinational's research and development and production sites, or that account for a lot of its turnover, also receive the largest share of the group's income, which these member states can then tax at their preferred rate.

To prevent companies from moving headquarters, assets, or activities outside the scope of the CCCTB, the Commission's proposal also includes several safeguards. A provision for exit taxation would enable member states to withhold 100 percent of the market value of any asset a multinational shifts to a subsidiary in a third country (European Commission 2016b, Art. 29). A common set of controlled foreign company (CFC) rules would, moreover, empower (or oblige) national tax authorities to include nondistributed profits of subsidiaries in corporate tax havens in the parent company's tax base (European Commission 2016b, Art. 59). Finally, a harmonized interest barrier would prevent companies from artificially inflating the cost of foreign borrowing to minimize tax payments in the EU (European Commission 2016b, Art. 13). The consistent application of these provisions across the EU would ensure that no member state provides a tax-free channel for profit shifts to third countries, thereby preventing an erosion of the CCCTB. Hence, its introduction would finally realize the BEPS project's initial objective: a realignment of taxation with real economic activity.

The European Commission pitched its proposal to member states in 2016. From its perspective, the introduction of an effective countermeasure to corporate tax avoidance would demonstrate the EU's ability to protect ordinary Europeans from the redistributive consequences of globalization. Hence, the measure could bolster the legitimacy of a union facing Brexit and other right-wing populist backlashes against European integration (Morgan 2017). Moreover, the measure would complete the common market in corporate taxation by removing the need to file income tax statements in every member state. To persuade governments in the Council, Margarete Vestager, the Danish social-liberal commissioner for competition, and Pierre Moscovici, the French socialist commissioner for taxation and customs, try to unsettle the opportunity structures of particularly tax-competitive member states and mobilize business support through targeted incentives.

For the unsettling, Vestager uses the Commission's executive powers in competition policy against selective tax advantages member states granted to individual firms. Her directorate has to date instructed Ireland, Luxembourg, and the Netherlands to claw back a total of €13.3 billion in foregone tax payments from Amazon, Apple, Fiat, and Starbucks, with further decisions impending (European Commission 2017a). By qualifying selective tax advantages as illegal state aid, the Commission creates uncertainty over the validity of these sweetheart deals among multinationals, thereby reducing the attractiveness of corresponding offers made by member states. Accordingly, government officials from the targeted member states have repeatedly criticized the Commission's investigations for reducing business confidence (Lamer 2017a). In contrast, Commissioner Moscovici argues that "legal certainty will come from common rules across the EU to tackle fraud" (Lamer 2017b). Therefore, member states willing to restore business confidence should support the CCCTB.

Along with swinging the stick, however, the Commission also reminds business of the carrots included in the proposal. In particular, the Commission emphasizes the administrative relief achieved through the replacement of twenty-eight income tax statements with a single statement for the entire European group and the omission of transfer pricing analyses for controlled transactions inside the EU (European Commission 2016b, 2). Moreover, the Commission highlights the incentive for innovation provided by the introduction of a super-deduction, allowing corporations to reduce their taxable revenue by 150 percent of their expenses for research and development (R&D) in member states (European Commission 2016b, Art. 9). Finally, the Commission promises to end the bias against equity financing created by a focus on interest deductions in national tax codes. To this end, the Commission proposes the introduction of an allowance for growth and investment, enabling corporations to also deduct increases in their equity from their taxable base (European Commission 2016b, Art. 11). Together, these measures are supposed to mobilize national business associations in favor of the CCCTB proposal.

When considering responses to a public consultation on the CCCTB, this strategy seems to have had some success. The umbrella organizations of French and German business generally support the proposal because of the reduction in compliance costs and double taxation achieved through a European consolidation of the tax base. Unsurprisingly, these organizations are also in favor of a super-deduction for R&D expenses and the proposed allowance for growth and investment (BDI 2016; MEDEF 2016). Accordingly, the French and German governments also agreed to support the adoption of the CCCTB, coordinating a common position on the Commission's proposal (Bundesministerium der Finanzen and Ministère de l'Economie et des Finances 2018). From the perspective of Emmanuel Macron (2017), the French president, "fiscal divergence feeds discord among member states, disaggregates national economic models and fragilizes all of Europe." Therefore, member states should harmonize the corporate tax base and define a binding range for corporate tax rates. Despite general support from the EU's pivotal member states (cf. Moravcsik 2013; Krotz and Schild 2013), however, the adoption of the CCCTB remains uncertain.

In fact, even France and Germany still hesitate to pool administrative authority over a core state power like corporate taxation at the European level. In their coordinated position on the Commission's proposal, for instance, they argue against the harmonization of R&D incentives. Instead, member states should retain the right to reward corresponding activities through the provision of tax credits, which should fall outside the scope of the CCCTB (Bundesministerium der Finanzen and Ministère de l'Economie et des Finances 2018). Likewise, the scientific advisory council to the German ministry of finance warns that the proposed allowance for growth and investment would have important spillover effects on national income tax systems, thereby infringing upon member states' exclusive competence in this area (Wissenschaftlicher Beirat 2017). If tax incentives were not harmonized, however, member states could still use expenditures to lure well-paid jobs in R&D away from one another. Divergence between national rules would continue, undermining the CCCTB's original intent and perpetuating targeted tax competition among member states.

Beyond the loss of formal regulatory authority, the redistributive consequences of a switch to formulary apportionment also remain a source of concern. Available estimates vary widely, depending on the data used and the assumptions made. The most recent study, for instance, expects an increase in corporate tax revenue by 8 percent in Germany and a reduction of 86 percent in Ireland (Hentze 2019). In contrast, an earlier study, testing different apportionment factors, predicts declines of 2 to 15 percent for both countries (Devereux and Loretz 2008). Moreover, both studies assume that firms do not adjust their behavior to the CCCTB. This is a simplifying assumption that masks intense debate over the impact of a switch to formulary apportionment on the location of production. Whereas some argue that such a switch provides firms with incentives to shift jobs rather than profits to corporate tax havens (Wissenschaftlicher Beirat 2007, 2017), others maintain that the geographic distribution of facilities, production, and sales—the apportionment factors proposed by the Commission—is not primarily determined by tax concerns (Clausing 2018; Eichner and Runkel 2008). As a result, member states have to overcome fundamental uncertainty when seeking consensus on the formula underpinning the CCCTB.

Finally, US tax reform, which often affects the tax policy choices of other developed countries (Swank 2006), may also impact the likelihood of CCCTB adoption by the EU. Some argue that the reduction of the US corporate tax rate from 35 to 21 percent in 2017 increases competitive pressure on EU member states. Against this background, they should become more reluctant to cede authority over tax incentives and carve-outs to the EU, particularly since the unanimity requirement makes the decision-making process slow and uncertain (Fuest 2018). The misinterpretation of sovereignty as the right to cut, but never raise, taxes when competition commands may thus prevent member states from pursuing the CCCTB. Yet the Trump administration's tax reform could also have an unintended effect in the opposite direction. So far, US tech companies attribute the rights to the foreign use of their intellectual property (IP) to subsidiaries in Ireland, Luxembourg, and the Netherlands. These lowly taxed branches collect license fee payments from the rest of the EU and accumulate the resulting profits. Since 2018, however, the Trump reform's global intangible low-taxed income provision enables US firms to repatriate profits from the lease of IP at a reduced rate of 10.5 percent. Moreover, the reform's provision on foreign-derived intangible income reduces taxes on future income from the export of IP-related services to 3 percent (Pfatteicher et al. 2018). As US tech companies no longer need to shift their IP out of the United States to benefit from tax haven conditions, tax incentives for locating R&D and financing activities in Ireland, Luxembourg, or the Netherlands disappear. By outcompeting EU corporate tax havens, the Trump administration could thus end up raising their interest in common policies that keep the taxable income of US companies in the EU.

Conclusion

US hegemony has marked the politics of international taxation over the past three decades. Whenever the US administration was in favor of change and did not face opposition from powerful domestic interest groups, the administration managed to shape international standards and the domestic tax policies of other governments accordingly, no matter how fundamental the requested changes were for foreign countries. Likewise, the US administration successfully defended the status quo whenever foreign initiatives threatened to increase the tax burden on US business or to erode the virtual tax base of the United States. The preferences and normative claims of other countries mattered only insofar as they determined the strategy used by the US government to enforce its goals or provided additional justification for an already defined policy agenda. When secrecy jurisdictions refused to lift financial secrecy, the Clinton and Obama administrations used economic coercion to break their opposition. When EU governments sought to limit tax avoidance by multinationals from the US and elsewhere, the Bush and Obama administrations withdrew from multilateral initiatives or threatened to reserve against proposals they considered harmful. As such, the politics of international taxation bear great resemblance to bargaining over global financial regulation, which usually leads to the multilateral adoption of the US regulatory model (cf. Helleiner 2014; Simmons 2001).

The source of US power over international tax politics is a unique combination of market size and regulatory capacity. The dominant share of the United States in global demand for capital, goods, and services makes foreign business more dependent on access to the US market than US business is dependent on access to any foreign market. A private bank located in a secrecy jurisdiction, for instance, could not offer its wealth management clients competitive rates of return if the bank had to divest from US assets. If there is no yield, however, the tax advantages linked to the anonymity the jurisdiction provides become pointless from the perspective of the investor. Likewise, a holding company loses its purpose if the US multinational to which it belongs can no longer shift assets and revenues between the United States and the corporate tax haven in which it is located. Therefore, continued access to the US market is a crucial precondition for the business models of both secrecy jurisdictions and corporate tax havens. The US administration can exploit their dependence because it has the regulatory capacity to dictate the terms under which foreign firms transact with US firms and consumers. Under FATCA, the US Treasury may impose a 30 percent withholding tax on payments to foreign banks refusing to report US account holders to the IRS. Even divestment from US assets does not protect a recalcitrant bank from the tax, because the bank still needs access to US dollars and the corresponding clearing infrastructure to process international transactions. At the same time, the Treasury Department has statutory authority over CFC, transfer pricing, and thin capitalization rules, which have an important impact on the assessment of intragroup transactions for tax purposes.

In contrast, regulatory dispersion prevents the EU from harnessing the power of the common market in bargaining over global tax policy. Under the Lisbon treaty, member states have to make decisions on direct taxation and economic sanctions by unanimity. Hence, individual member states can veto additional reporting requirements for European banks as well as defensive measures against foreign banks or governments that refuse to comply with reporting standards applicable within the union. Because direct taxation is an exclusive competence of member states, individual member states can moreover grant foreign companies access to the common market while applying national tax law. This ability has prevented individual governments from credible threats of market closure, intensified tax competition within the EU, and divided small capital-importing and large capital-exporting member states in bargaining over international taxation at the OECD. In contrast to the situation in policy fields in which the EU has managed to centralize regulatory authority at the supranational level—such as data protection, trade, and product safety—the EU thus remains a taker of global tax norms essentially developed by the United States (cf. Bach and Newman 2007, 2010; Meunier and Nicolaïdis 2006).

Since the EU is unable to check US power, the Obama and Trump administrations have gotten away with a considerable degree of hypocrisy in the implementation of standards they have projected on other countries. After the Obama administration had used bilateral FATCA agreements to spread the principle of AEI across the world, the administration eventually refused to fully reciprocate the automatic reporting of accounts. Moreover, the Obama administration did not join a multilateral agreement on the implementation of the OECD's AEI standard, which uses FATCA as a model. The unilateral opt-out provides US banks with an exclusive competitive advantage in the provision of financial secrecy to foreign investors, and led to a substantial shift of bank deposits from traditional secrecy jurisdictions into the United States (Casi, Spengel, and Stage 2018; Hakelberg and Schaub 2018). Because the associated export of financial services bolsters the US current account, the hypocritical implementation of AEI can be interpreted as an element in a hegemonic strategy that pushes the burden of deficit reduction onto foreign countries (cf. Gilpin 1981; Oatley 2015). Moreover, sustained US hypocrisy, which can also be observed in the implementation of anti-money-laundering regulation, casts doubt on the significance of international norms for state behavior (Sharman 2011). After all, if compliance is driven by a logic of appropriateness, the creator of a norm should be obligated to consistency.

Yet the powerful can apparently make the powerless follow rules that the powerful themselves do not respect, and get away with doing so over long periods of time.

The need for hypocrisy results from the interaction of party ideology and business power in US domestic politics. For Republican administrations, international tax competition is a welcome justification for regressive tax reform. Accordingly, they have no interest in initiatives that harmonize national tax rules, unless concerns over law enforcement are at stake. As Republican tax policy priorities usually match the preferences of powerful business groups seeking to minimize their tax burden, there is no need to bring about inconsistencies between domestic and international standards. In contrast, Democratic administrations are ideologically committed to a progressive tax system that puts the largest burden onto the strongest shoulders. Hence, they need to ensure that the most potent taxpayers—wealthy individuals and corporations—do not circumvent their fiscal obligations. To this end, Democrats foster international initiatives against tax evasion and avoidance. If such proposals impose costs on powerful business groups, however, the proposals do not survive the domestic policymaking process. Therefore, Democratic administrations need to forge initiatives that shift adjustment costs onto foreign business and powerless domestic actors.

When we look at US international tax policy from this perspective, we understand why FATCA creates new reporting requirements for foreign banks but none for US financial institutions. The Obama administration's main regulatory goal was to curb tax evasion by US individuals with offshore accounts. This group wields limited structural and discursive power over the political process because of its negligible impact on job creation and the illegality of its tax minimization strategy. In contrast, raising domestic transparency standards to keep US banks from abetting tax evasion by foreign individuals would have provoked resistance from the financial sector. Because of US banks' large contribution to job creation and international mobility, they can make credible threats of divestment. Moreover, managing the wealth of foreigners is perfectly legal under US law. The financial sector could thus have employed considerable structural and discursive power to kill the entire legislative project. Hence, the Obama administration forced all foreign banks to report data on US account holders to reach its main regulatory goal but spared domestic banks from a meaningful increase in reporting requirements. In the end, nonreciprocity guaranteed the FATCA initiative's political survival.

Likewise, the interaction between party ideology and business power explains why the Obama administration ended up defending the international tax system's status quo in bargaining over the BEPS project's recommendations. Initially, President Obama and Treasury Secretary Geithner were just as committed to fighting profit-shifting as they were to an increase in financial transparency. But their repeated proposals for a reform of CFC regulation failed as a result of opposition from US multinationals. These firms make credible divestment threats because of their substantial share in US employment and stress the legality of their tax avoidance schemes, thereby shifting the blame to legislators writing incoherent tax codes. Hence, these firms exert significant structural and discursive power over the political process. Without a domestic regulatory template, however, the Obama administration lacked a purpose in negotiations on BEPS. At the beginning, this lack opened agenda space for reform proposals by European governments, which hoped to attribute some of the untaxed income of US multinationals to their coffers. As a result, the Obama administration decided that minimizing the foreign tax burden of US multinationals was still better than having EU countries increase their tax take at the expense of the United States. Accordingly, the administration entered into a successful rearguard battle, paring back unorthodox proposals from European governments.

In many cases, the interaction between party ideology and business power can also explain the global tax policy preferences of other developed countries. Yet citizen support for redistribution is dramatically higher in Europe than in the United States (Koos and Sachweh 2017; Svallfors 2006). Moreover, the possibility of long-term corporatist bargains allows center-left governments in Europe to trade regressive tax reform for business support of redistributive spending (Beramendi and Rueda 2007). Therefore, the fairness concerns of voters may provide a greater barrier to regressive tax reform in EU countries than in the United States, where party preferences over taxation are defined by the most affluent constituents only (Plümper, Troeger, and Winner 2009; Bartels 2009). For this reason, the conservative finance ministers of Germany and the United Kingdom put BEPS on the agenda of the G20 after a series of investigative reports had increased the political salience of corporate tax avoidance in the common market. Depending on the degree of public attention, initiatives for countermeasures to tax evasion and avoidance in EU countries may thus come from center-left governments or conservative governments facing a majority of voters with egalitarian convictions.

Irrespective of the origin of demand for international tax initiatives, however, European governments also adapt their positions to the preferences of powerful domestic interest groups. All governments of small capital-importing EU member states—no matter their ideological leaning—have opposed the introduction of tax standards that went beyond the regulatory status quo at the global level because of expected repercussions for these member states' financial and legal services sectors. Likewise, Germany has repeatedly blocked EU tax initiatives mainly targeting the US government or US firms to prevent retaliation against

Germany's export industry. Combined with the veto power conferred upon EU member states by the unanimity requirement in tax matters, narrow sectoral interests have thus prevented meaningful steps toward the European integration of international tax policy. Against this background, the adoption of a CCCTB remains highly uncertain, whereas a switch to qualified majority voting (QMV) in tax matters, which requires an amendment of the Lisbon treaty, can be excluded in the short to medium term (Wasserfallen 2014).

If member states still decided to share their competence over direct taxation, for instance within the context of a grand political bargain for political integration, the principle of "no taxation without representation" would command a thorough overhaul of the current decision-making process. The president of the Commission, which holds the right to initiative and would therefore elaborate the EU's common tax policy, would have to be elected either directly by European voters or by the European Parliament (EP). As a result, the Commission's tax policy agenda would be further politicized, responding to party ideology and the fairness concerns of voters. To ensure budgetary authority rests with parliament, as is usually the case in democratic systems, the EP would also have to enter the legislative process on an equal footing with the Council of the European Union. Accordingly, the Council would have to switch to QMV on tax matters to prevent individual member states, and their dominant industry sectors, from vetoing reforms supported by the Commission and an EP majority. The locus of lobbying would shift from national capitals to Brussels, where business power would be greatest for groups that can access deputies from across the EU and threaten them with divestment. Hence, influence will depend on Europeanization.

Explanations of government preferences on global tax policy other than the interaction of business power with barriers to regressive tax reform have important shortcomings. The salience of normative claims by ideological groups greatly depends on the ethical predisposition of government parties. Chapters 3 and 4 demonstrate that the arguments of libertarian lobbyists against the OECD's harmful tax competition project had no impact on the position of the Clinton administration and resonated only partially with the Bush administration. Republican officials adopted libertarian arguments when they addressed the officials' normative attachment to competition. Yet they ignored arguments that clashed with their law-and-order instincts. Accordingly, the Bush administration stuck to the OECD's limited information exchange agenda despite concerns over privacy voiced by libertarian lobby groups. This effect is likely to be similar at the other end of the political spectrum. Normative claims by the Tax Justice Network, a left-leaning nongovernmental organization, for instance, should resonate more with center-left than with conservative governments. Accordingly, ideological groups would have to change voter preferences to a considerable degree to impact the tax policy choices of governments from the opposite political camp (cf. Emmenegger and Marx 2019).

Likewise, a recent financial crisis is not a good predictor for government preferences on global tax policy, irrespective of the potential causal mechanism one considers. Chapter 3 shows that the Clinton administration adopted new reporting requirements for foreign banks at a time when the federal budget was balanced. Like FATCA a decade later, the Clinton administration's qualified intermediary program faced little opposition from US finance not because the sector was on the defensive but because the requirements mainly affected foreign banks, thereby creating competitive advantages for US institutions. Moreover, chapter 5 makes clear that President Obama had already defined his tax policy priorities in 2007, before the failure of Bear Stearns and the adoption of the first bailout and stimulus packages. In general, budget constraints are a bad predictor of a government's global tax policy choices because of the many ways in which these constraints can be addressed. A spending cut or a hike in indirect taxes could be just as effective as an increase in tax compliance. Hence, it is more important to know how the government party generally wants to distribute the burden of financing the state among different social groups. Finally, a recent financial crisis may increase the political salience of revelations showing that wealthy individuals and multinational corporations do not pay their fair share of tax. So far, however, popular demand for change has not enabled the implementation of reforms opposed by powerful interest groups in the United States, the international tax system's hegemonic power. Proponents of tax justice will thus have to find ways to change the calculus of US multinationals to further advance their agenda.

Notes

1. CHANGE AND STABILITY IN GLOBAL TAX POLICY

1. Investors may use secrecy jurisdictions for purposes other than tax evasion. Instead of hiding assets from the tax office, investors may hide assets from spouses to frustrate requests for alimony in case of divorce, or from creditors to avoid the repayment of debt. Whatever the main motive, however, it is likely to concur with tax evasion, since declaring assets to the tax office is most likely to also bring them within the reach of spouses and creditors.

2. Interview with former Austrian minister of finance, July 10, 2014.

3. Interviews with member of the Austrian Parliament, July 8, 2014; tax policy adviser to the Austrian Greens, July 9, 2014; tax policy adviser to the Austrian chancellor, July 16, 2014; Austrian OECD diplomat, March 7, 2014.

4. Bank secrecy had existed in Switzerland long before Adolf Hitler was elected Reich chancellor in 1933. The Swiss Bankers Association spun this narrative only once the Allies began to investigate its financing activities for the Axis powers toward the end of World War II (Guex 2000).

5. Interviews with European Commission official on June 13, 2018 and with two academic experts on EU tax policy on August 23, 2018.

6. Interview with partner and manager in Austrian tax law firm on July 7, 2014.

7. Interview with partner in US tax law firm on April 17, 2015.

8. Interviews with former US Treasury officials on April 13 and 15, 2015.

9. According to Clausing (2016) the US fisc lost $77–$111 billion to corporate tax avoidance in 2012. Tørsløv, Wier, and Zucman (2017) estimate that US multinationals diverted 63 percent of their foreign profits to tax havens in 2016, causing a tax revenue loss for the United States of $70 billion. At the same time, Zucman (2014) estimates that the revenue cost of tax evasion by US households with offshore accounts amounts to $36 billion annually.

10. Interview on April 13, 2015.

11. A Nexis search for "Qualified Intermediary Program" in all English-language news retrieved six articles between August 2006, when the first PSI report was released, and December 2007. A Nexis search for "Qualified Intermediary Program" in all English-language news retrieved forty-one articles between July 2008, when the second PSI report was released, and December 2008, but only three articles between January and June of the same year.

12. Alex Cobham is the current director of the Tax Justice Network, a nongovernmental organization (NGO) advocating for tougher international rules against tax evasion and avoidance.

13. According to the benefits principle, a source country is entitled to tax the active business income of a permanent establishment under its jurisdiction. The royalties, dividends, and interest this permanent establishment pays to its parent company, however, are in principle taxable in the latter's country of residence. According to the OECD's model tax treaty, source countries retain the right to levy limited withholding taxes on dividend and interest payments but not on royalty payments (OECD 2014d, Art. 10, 11, & 12). Moreover, the United States strikes bilateral tax treaties with foreign countries that reduce withholding taxes on interest paid to US firms to zero (US Treasury 2016, Art. 11).

2. POWER IN INTERNATIONAL TAX POLITICS

1. Tax evaders invest offshore to strip their capital income of its tax burden. As a result, offshore wealth grows faster than onshore wealth (Alstadsæter, Johannesen, and Zucman 2017a; Harrington 2016). Yet this possibility exists only as long as an individual who is in principle liable to tax on her worldwide income manages to hide her offshore account from her local tax office. Therefore, the level of financial secrecy has a direct effect on the after-tax return to offshore portfolio investment.

2. Since the 1920s, when member states of the League of Nations created the current international tax system, the prevention of double taxation, which requires reconciliation of the source and residence principles, has been the main purpose of international tax law. The OECD's Model Tax Convention provides governments with two reconciliation methods: residence countries can exempt their residents' foreign income from taxation altogether or credit foreign taxes against the domestic tax. The credit method is most widespread but applies only once companies repatriate their foreign profits in the form of dividends, interest, or royalties. Therefore, companies can defer tax payments by hoarding profits offshore for an indefinite amount of time or until the government grants them a repatriation tax holiday (Rixen 2008, 57–60; Pinkernell 2012).

3. The EU has been identified as a single actor with great power status in the regulation of finance, trade, and many other areas of economic governance (Bach and Newman 2007; Drezner 2008; Meunier and Nicolaïdis 2006; Posner 2009).

4. The OECD Model Agreement links source country status to the presence of a PE. A PE is a place of effective management or production. This may also include an Internet server wholly owned or controlled by a foreign company that is used to process product sales and payments. Yet tax authorities have to determine in every case whether the automatic processing of sales and payments is a core element of corporate activity. Source-country status in e-commerce therefore remains a contested issue (Pinkernell 2014, 28–30).

5. FATCA also obliges participating institutions to levy a withholding tax on pass-through payments from the United States to nonparticipating institutions. This requirement is meant to reduce the attractiveness of business with nonparticipating institutions and to extend the reach of FATCA beyond financial institutions with business in the United States (Grinberg 2012).

6. Decisions on administrative assistance in tax matters are decided by unanimity in the Council of Ministers. The directive introducing the AEI in the EU does not provide for sanctions against third states not applying this standard in their relations with member states. Moreover, any mandate for negotiations with third states on an AEI agreement also has to be granted by unanimity (cf. European Union 2014b).

7. According to data from the US Bureau of Labor Statistics (2017), all private households and service providers catering directly to households create about as much employment in the United States as half of the manufacturing sector.

8. The steps are as follows: (1) formation of government preferences at the domestic level, (2) interaction of government preferences in determining great power strategy, (3) great power strategy producing the outcome.

3. COUNTERING HARMFUL TAX PRACTICES

1. Searches of LexisNexis and HeinOnline using various combinatons of the keywords "OECD," "harmful tax," "bankers," "finance," "American," "Florida," and "Texas" do not retrieve any documents suggesting that banking associations from Florida or Texas openly opposed the HTC project. In this context, criticism is always directed against new domestic reporting requirements.

2. In any event, the CFA had first decided to postpone sanctions against uncooperative tax havens to 2001, and later even extended the deadline for full cooperation by tax havens to 2005.

3. Interviews with lobbyist for US multinationals on April 23, 2015, and with partner in tax law firm on June 22, 2015.

4. For further tax planning strategies using hybrids to circumvent subpart F see Office of Tax Policy (2000); IRS (1998b); West (2005).

5. IRS Notice 98–35 revokes Notice 98–11 and corresponding temporary regulations. Notice 98–35 also presents a new set of regulations. However, these were placed under a moratorium until 2000, when Congress expected to have finished its analysis of subpart F (Cooper and Torgersen 1998).

6. Interviews with former US Treasury officials on April 15 and 17, 2015.

4. THE SWIFT RETURN OF TAX COMPETITION

1. The Bush team's calculations apparently relied on an overly optimistic projection of GDP growth at an average 2.7 percent over the following ten years.

2. The group included Nobel Prize winners Milton Friedman, Robert Lucas, James Buchanan, Gary Becker, and Robert Mundell. For the crucial role these economists have played in the "neoliberal thought collective" see Mirowski (2013).

3. Hacker and Pierson argue that Republican representatives in the House are more vulnerable to campaigns by anti-tax lobby groups such as the Club for Growth or Americans for Tax Reform than incumbent senators, which is the reason Republican representatives almost unanimously accede to requests from these groups.

4. The split Senate extended the cuts by two years in 2010, so the cuts eventually expired on January 1, 2013.

5. Interviews with former US Treasury officials on April 15 and 17, 2015.

6. Testifying at a Senate hearing on tax haven abuse, O'Neill was eager to dispel allegations that he was turning a blind eye on breaches of US tax law (cf. O'Neill 2001b).

7. According to Mirowski (2013), the Mont Pelérin Society and George Mason University are key players in what he describes as the "neoliberal thought collective."

8. Interview with former US Treasury official on April 15, 2015.

5. THE EMERGENCE OF MULTILATERAL AEI

1. A Nexis search for "Qualified Intermediary Program" in all English-language news retrieved six articles between August 2006, when the PSI report was released, and December 2007.

2. A Nexis search for "Qualified Intermediary Program" in all English-language news retrieved forty-one articles between July and December 2008, but only three articles between January and June 2008.

3. Interview on March 6, 2014.

4. Interviews with OECD diplomat for large member state on March 6, 2014; member of German parliament on November 14, 2014; and former undersecretary of state in German ministry of finance on January 28, 2015.

5. Interviews with former US Treasury officials on April 13 and 15, 2015.

6. Interview on April 13, 2015.

7. Interviews with senior French tax official on March 14, 2014; former undersecretary of state in German ministry of finance on January 28, 2015; and senior German tax official on March 3, 2015.

8. Interview with former US Treasury official on April 15, 2015.

9. Interviews with members of German parliament on October 8 and 16, 2014, and on November 14, 2014.

10. Interviews with former undersecretary of state in German ministry of finance on January 28, 2015, and senior German tax official on March 3, 2015.

11. Interviews with former US Treasury officials on April 13 and 15, 2015.

12. Interviews with former US Treasury officials on April 13 and 15, 2015.

13. Interviews with former undersecretary of state in German ministry of finance on January 28, 2015, and senior German tax official on March 3, 2015.

14. Interview with senior French tax official on March 14, 2014.

15. Interview on April 15, 2015.

16. According to an OECD tax official interviewed on March 6, 2014, this wording was understood as obliging signatories to cooperate with the OECD in establishing multilateral AEI.

17. Interviews with member of the German parliament on October 15, 2014; with former undersecretary in German ministry of finance on January 28, 2014; and with senior German tax official on March 3, 2015.

18. Interviews with members of the German parliament on October 8 and 16, 2014, and on November 14, 2014.

19. Interview with member of the German parliament on October 16, 2014.

20. Research by academics and journalists later revealed that Swiss and Luxembourgian wealth managers had created or purchased a massive number of mostly Panamanian corporations on behalf of their clients just after the Savings Directive and Agreement entered into force in 2005 (cf. Johannesen 2014; Obermayer et al. 2015).

21. These attempts were made in January 2009, January 2010, May and July 2011, and May and November 2012 (cf. Council of the European Union 2009, 2010, 2011a, 2011b, 2012a, 2012b).

22. For coverage of the negotiations during each of the Council meetings listed in note 21 see Schweizerische Depeschenagentur (2009, 2010, 2011a, 2011b, 2012) and Council of the European Union (2012b).

23. Translation from Luxembourgish by the author.

24. Interview on May 24, 2013.

25. Interviews with OECD diplomat for small member state on March 5, 2014; with OECD diplomat for small member state on March 7, 2014; with senior French tax official on March 14, 2014; with European Commission tax official on March 28, 2014; and with senior German tax official on March 3, 2015.

26. Interview with senior Austrian tax official on July 14, 2014.

27. Interview on March 3, 2015. Translation from German by the author.

28. Translation from German by the author

29. Interview on March 6, 2014.

30. Interviews with OECD ambassador for small member state on March 4, 2014, and with OECD diplomat for large member state on March 6, 2014.

31. Interview on April 15, 2015.

32. Interview on April 13, 2015.

33. Interviews with former Treasury officials on April 13 and 15, 2015.

34. Interview with partner and manager of Austrian tax law firm on July 7, 2014.

35. Interview on April 15, 2015.

36. Interview on January 28, 2015. Translation from German by the author.

37. Interview on March 3, 2015. Translation from German by the author.

38. Interview on April 17, 2015.

6. THE BEPS PROJECT

1. Interview with tax adviser to the German finance ministry on June 22, 2015.

2. Interview with senior German tax official on March 3, 2015.

3. Interviews with tax adviser to the German finance ministry on June 22, 2015, and partner in US tax law firm on April 17, 2015.

4. Interview with senior German tax official on March 3, 2015. Translation from German by the author.

5. Interview on April 21, 2015.

6. Translation from German by the author.

7. Interviews with senior tax lobbyist for US multinationals on April 23, 2015, and partner in US tax law firm on April 17, 2015.

8. Interview on March 3, 2015. Translation from German by the author.

9. The author served as senior adviser to the OECD in the elaboration of the BEPS project.

10. Out of a total of 9,316 pages received by the OECD during public consultations on the BEPS project, 3,014 are devoted to transfer pricing; 1,177 to CbCR; and merely 577 to CFC rules.

11. Submissions from the Silicon Valley Tax Directors Group (SVTDG 2015) and the United States Council on International Business (USCIB 2015) also included in the compendium of public comments convey the same points of criticism.

12. This statement matches the key points of criticism expressed by PwC (2015), another big four accounting firm, in its submission to the OECD.

13. Interview with senior lobbyist for US multinationals on April 23, 2015.

14. Interview on April 23, 2015.

15. Special measures were sometimes interpreted as CFC rules, but they do not appear in the corresponding final BEPS report (cf. OECD 2015b).

16. Interview with tax adviser to the German government on June 22, 2015.

17. The author also shows that Amazon has begun to change its tax structure in Europe so as to unambiguously subject itself to taxation at source.

18. That is, a source country wishing to apply the new definition to corporations residing in the US, Luxembourg, or Ireland faces the difficult task of renegotiating the corresponding bilateral tax treaties and convincing its treaty partners to abandon their general reservation in the process. At present, this result seems highly unlikely, especially when the US government is the treaty partner.

19. The twenty-five countries include Andorra, Australia, Austria, Belgium, Canada, Fiji, Finland, France, Germany, Greece, Ireland, Italy, Japan, Liechtenstein, Luxembourg, Malta, the Netherlands, New Zealand, Portugal, Singapore, Slovenia, Spain, Sweden, Switzerland, and the United Kingdom.

20. The authors show that the diffusion of bilateral tax treaties is in part driven by the competitive advantages such agreements afford corporations interested in investing abroad.

21. With the adoption of the Interest and Royalties Directive in 2003, withholding taxes on interest and royalty payments between related firms of different member states were abolished.

22. Yet the Alliance of Liberals and Democrats for Europe (ALDE) managed to introduce a safeguard clause protecting multinationals against the release of sensitive information (Amendment 82). Deputies on the left fear this will allow many companies to circumvent public reporting (cf. De Masi 2017).

23. According to the draft directive, public CbCR would apply to all firms with a PE in the common market that earn more than €750 million in annual revenue. In contrast to the BEPS recommendations, this provision implies that firms that are not headquartered in the EU would also be obliged to publish information. Therefore, were the United States to withhold information received from parent companies, this would not make much of a difference. Accordingly, alternative sanction mechanisms, including the application of

section 891 of the US tax code through which taxes on companies from a country that is considered to impose discriminatory taxes on US multinationals could be doubled, are currently being debated (cf. Grinberg 2016b).

24. Although the measure was clearly conceived to respond to public concern over tax avoidance, the measure fit in neatly with the conservative government's tax-cut-cum-base-broadening strategy. While the diverted profits tax limits profit shifting out of the United Kingdom, the parallel introduction of a tax break for multinationals' overseas financing activities provides an additional incentive for shifting profits toward the United Kingdom. In addition, the Tories also reduced the statutory corporate tax rate from 26 to 19 percent and introduced another tax break for research and development activity. Overall, the United Kingdom intensified international tax competition instead of limiting it (cf. Hakelberg and Rixen 2017).

25. The term "joint decision trap" was coined by Fritz W. Scharpf (1988) to describe deadlock in decision-making processes that are marked by a unanimity requirement and divergent interests among involved actors.

26. According to Gerda Falkner (2011, 12) "unsettling" and "pressurizing" are two strategies through which the Commission can change member states' opportunity structures and thereby find an exit from the EU's joint decision trap.

7. FROM HEGEMONY TO TRANSATLANTIC TAX BATTLE?

1. Translated from German by the author.

2. Interview on March 3, 2015. Translated from German by the author.

3. Interviews with senior French tax official on March 14, 2014, and senior German tax official on March 3, 2015.

4. Interviews with European Commission official on June 13, 2018, and two academic experts on EU tax policy on August 23, 2018.

5. In common law countries, the beneficiary of a trust is taxed only once she receives distributions. Civil law countries do not recognize trusts. Therefore, a resident beneficiary of an Anglo-Saxon trust would be taxed currently on the trust's earnings. For this reason, residents of continental Europe must keep their trust arrangements secret from the tax office to reap the fiscal benefits of these arrangements.

References

Adam, Ferdy. 2014. "Impact de l'échange automatique d'informations en matière de produits financiers: Une tentative d'évaluation macro-économique appliquée au Luxembourg." *Economie et statistiques: Working papers du STATEC*, no. 73. http://www.statistiques.public.lu/catalogue-publications/economie-statistiques/2014/73-2014.pdf.

Adams, Christopher, Edward Alden, and Michael Peel. 2001. "International Economy & Africa: OECD Fears Tax Haven Reforms May Founder." *Financial Times*, April 28, 2001, International Economy & Africa.

Adams, Christopher, Victor Mallet, and Michael Peel. 2001. "International Economy: Tax Havens to Improve Transparency." *Financial Times*, May 1, 2001, International Economy.

Adams, Christopher, and Michael Peel. 2001. "US Move Jeopardises Tax Haven Reform." *Financial Times*, May 11, 2001, International Economy.

Alden, Edward, and Michael Peel. 2001. "US May Ease Stance over Money Laundering." *Financial Times*, June 1, 2001, International Economy.

Alstadsæter, Annette, Niels Johannesen, and Gabriel Zucman. 2017a. "Tax Evasion and Inequality." Working paper. http://www.nielsjohannesen.net/wp-content/uploads/AJZ2017.pdf.

———. 2017b. "Who Owns the Wealth in Tax Havens? Macro Evidence and Implications for Global Inequality." Working paper 23805, National Bureau of Economic Research. https://doi.org/10.3386/w23805.

Anderson, Perry. 2017. *The H-Word: The Peripeteia of Hegemony*. New York: Verso.

Andersson, Per. 2015. "Electoral Systems and Taxation During the 20th Century." Paper presented at 2015 ECPR Joint Sessions, University of Warsaw.

Arel-Bundock, Vincent. 2017. "The Unintended Consequences of Bilateralism: Treaty Shopping and International Tax Policy." *International Organization* 71 (2): 349–71.

Arel-Bundock, Vincent, and Lisa Lechner. 2017. "The Power of Boilerplate: Decentralized Multilateralism and the International Tax Regime." Paper presented at 2017 APSA Annual Meeting, San Francisco.

Assemblée Nationale. 2016. "Loi no. 2016–1691 du 9 décembre 2016 relatif à la transparence, à la lutte contre la corruption et à la modernisation de la vie économique (1)." Paris: Assemblée Nationale. http://www.assemblee-nationale.fr/14/ta/ta0830.asp.

Associated Press. 2000a. "Clinton Wants Curbs on Tax Shelters." *Associated Press*, February 19, 2000, Washington—General News.

———. 2000b. "OECD Publishes List of Tax Havens, Threatening Sanctions for Those Who Fail to Reform." *Associated Press International*, June 26, 2000, International News.

———. 2000c. "OECD Publishes Tax Havens List." *Associated Press*, June 26, 2000, Financial Pages.

Ault, Hugh J. 2013. "Some Reflections on the OECD and the Sources of International Tax Principles." SSRN Scholarly Paper ID 2287834. Rochester, NY: Social Science Research Network. https://papers.ssrn.com/abstract=2287834.

Avi-Yonah, Reuven S. 2000. "Globalization, Tax Competition, and the Fiscal Crisis of the Welfare State." *Harvard Law Review* 113 (7): 1573–1676.

———. 2005. "All of a Piece Throughout: The Four Ages of U.S. International Taxation." *Virginia Tax Review* 25 (2): 313–38.

———. 2007. *International Tax as International Law: An Analysis of the International Tax Regime.* Cambridge: Cambridge University Press.

Avi-Yonah, Reuven S., and Haiyan Xu. 2016. "Evaluating BEPS." SSRN Scholarly Paper ID 2716125. Rochester, NY: Social Science Research Network. http://papers.ssrn.com/abstract=2716125.

Bach, David, and Abraham L. Newman. 2007. "The European Regulatory State and Global Public Policy: Micro-Institutions, Macro-Influence." *Journal of European Public Policy* 14 (6): 827–46.

———. 2010. "Governing Lipitor and Lipstick: Capacity, Sequencing, and Power in International Pharmaceutical and Cosmetics Regulation." *Review of International Political Economy* 17 (4): 665–95.

Barandun, Angela, Walter Niederberger, and Andreas Valda. 2012. "Die Baustellen Des Schweizer Finanzplatzes." *Tages-Anzeiger*, November 23, 2012, Wirtschaft.

Bartels, Larry M. 2009. *Unequal Democracy: The Political Economy of the New Gilded Age.* Princeton, NJ: Princeton University Press.

Basinger, Scott J., and Mark Hallerberg. 2004. "Remodeling the Competition for Capital: How Domestic Politics Erases the Race to the Bottom." *The American Political Science Review* 98 (2): 261–76.

Baucus, Max. 2009. "S.1934—111th Congress (2009–2010): Foreign Account Tax Compliance Act of 2009." Introduced October 27, 2009. https://www.congress.gov/bill/111th-congress/senate-bill/1934?q=%7B%22search%22%3A%5B%22foreign+account+tax+compliance+act%22%5D%7D&resultIndex=6.

BDI (Federation of German Industries). 2014. "Comments of BDI on the OECD Discussion Draft on Transfer Pricing Documentation and CbC Reporting from January 30, 2014." In *Discussion Draft on Transfer Pricing Documentation and CbC Reporting—Public Comments Received,* edited by Organisation for Economic Cooperation and Development (OECD), 1: 83–86. Paris: OECD Publishing.

———. 2016. *CCCTB Public Consultation Results—2b Published—Organisations Registered.* Brussels: European Commission. https://circabc.europa.eu/sd/a/fcfcc0b7-c26f-4908-9467-3c56e64e02c4/CCCTB%20Public%20Consultation%20Results%20-%202b%20published%20-%20Organisations%20registered.xlsx.

Beattie, Alan. 2001. "US Assailed at OECD Meeting on Tax Havens, Climate." *Financial Times,* May 18, 2001, International Economy.

Becker, Markus. 2016. "Streit mit EU-Kommission: Schäuble will Steuerdaten von Konzernen geheim halten." *Spiegel Online,* December 19, 2016, Wirtschaft. http://www.spiegel.de/wirtschaft/soziales/eu-kommission-schaeuble-will-konzern-steuern-geheim-halten-a-1126544.html.

Bennett, Andrew, and Alexander George. 1997. "Process Tracing in Case Study Research." Paper presented at MacArthur Foundation Workshop on Case Study Methods, October 17-19, Harvard University. https://www.uzh.ch/cmsssl/suz/dam/jcr:00000000-5103-bee3-0000-000059b16b9d/05.19.bennett_george.pdf.

Beramendi, Pablo, and David Rueda. 2007. "Social Democracy Constrained: Indirect Taxation in Industrialized Democracies." *British Journal of Political Science* 37 (4): 619–41.

Bergin, Tom. 2012. "Special Report: How Starbucks Avoids UK Taxes." *Reuters,* October 15, 2012. https://uk.reuters.com/article/us-britain-starbucks-tax-idUKBRE89E0EX20121015.

Besson, Sylvain. 2016. "Sous pression, le paradis fiscal américain promet de s'amender." *Le Temps*, March 31, 2016. https://www.letemps.ch/economie/2016/03/31/pression -paradis-fiscal-americain-promet-s-amender.

Bidder, Benjamin. 2019. "US-Attacken auf Nord Stream 2: Die Sabotage." *Spiegel Online*, January 14, 2019, Wirtschaft. http://www.spiegel.de/wirtschaft/unternehmen/richard -grenell-und-nord-stream-2-darum-bekaempft-us-botschafter-die-pipeline-a -1247942.html.

BIS (Bank for International Settlements). 2016a. "Glossary from 'Guidelines for Report-ing the BIS International Banking Statistics.'" Basel: Bank for International Settle-ments. http://www.bis.org/statistics/bankstatsguide_glossary.pdf.

———. 2016b. "Reporting Countries." Accessed January 21, 2016. http://www.bis.org/statistics /rep_countries.htm.

———. 2018. "Locational Banking Statistics." 2018. Accessed March 19, 2018. http://www .bis.org/statistics/bankstats.htm?m=6%7C31%7C69.

Blocher, Christoph. 2006. "'Der Unternehmer, die Schweiz und Europa' Ein dreifacher Sonderfall." Speech given at Schweizerisch-Deutscher Wirtschaftsclub, Frankfurt am Main. https://www.ejpd.admin.ch/ejpd/de/home/aktuell/reden---interviews /reden/archiv/reden_christoph_blocher/2006/2006-05-22.html.

Blyth, Mark. 2013. "Paradigms and Paradox: The Politics of Economic Ideas in Two Mo-ments of Crisis." *Governance* 26 (2): 197–215.

Bramerdorfer, Norbert. 2015. "FATCA und seine Umsetzung in Österreich." WU Wien, September 28, 2015. https://www.wu.ac.at/fileadmin/wu/d/i/taxlaw/events.main /int.events/CDG-symposium09-2015/01_FATCA_Pr%C3%A4sentation _20150928_-_Kurzfassung.pdf.

Brüggmann, Mathias, Elisabeth Atzler, and Frank Wiebe. 2018. "Sanktionen: Banken le-gen Iran-Geschäft lahm—Mittelständler kommen nicht an ihr Geld." *Handelsblatt*, January 10, 2018. https://www.handelsblatt.com/finanzen/banken-versicherungen /sanktionen-banken-legen-iran-geschaeft-lahm-mittelstaendler-kommen-nicht -an-ihr-geld/23136410.html.

Brunetti, Aymo. 2013. "Regulatorische Herausforderungen für die grenzüberschreitende Schweizer Vermögensverwaltung und strategische Optionen." Bern: Eidgenös-sisches Finanzdepartement. http://www.news.admin.ch/NSBSubscriber/message /attachments/31569.pdf.

Bundesministerium der Finanzen. 2008. *Monatsbericht des BMF—März 2008*. Berlin: Bundesministerium der Finanzen.

———. 2014. *Pressekonferenz anlässlich der Berlin Tax Conference 2014*. Berlin: Bundes-ministerium der Finanzen. http://www.bundesfinanzministerium.de/Content /DE/Video/2014/2014-10-29-global-forum-pk/2014-10-29-global-forum-pk .html.

Bundesministerium der Finanzen and Ministère de l'Economie et des Finances. 2018. "Ge-meinsames Positionspapier Deutschlands und Frankreichs zum GKB-Vorschlag." Bundesministerium der Finanzen. https://www.bundesfinanzministerium.de /Content/DE/Standardartikel/Themen/Europa/2018-06-20-Meseberg-Anl2.pdf?_ _blob=publicationFile&v=1.

Bundesministerium für Finanzen. 1988. "Bundesgesetz, mit dem das Kreditwesengesetz geändert wird." Ministerialentwurf 130/ME XVII. GP. Vienna: Bundesministerium für Finanzen. https://www.parlament.gv.at/PAKT/VHG/XVII/ME/ME_00130/imf name_542008.pdf.

Bundesrat. 2012. "Stenographischer Bericht, 903. Sitzung." Berlin: Bundesrat. http:// www.bundesrat.de/SharedDocs/downloads/DE/plenarprotokolle/2012 /Plenarprotokoll-903.pdf?__blob=publicationFile&v=3.

Bundestag. 2010. "Stenographischer Bericht 77. Sitzung." Plenarprotokoll 17/77. Berlin: Deutscher Bundestag. http://dipbt.bundestag.de/dip21/btp/17/17077.pdf.

——. 2012a. "Stenographischer Bericht 175. Sitzung." Plenarprotokoll 17/175. Berlin: Deutscher Bundestag. http://dip21.bundestag.de/dip21/btp/17/17175.pdf.

——. 2012b. "Finanzausschuss Wortprotokoll 98. Sitzung." Protokoll Nr. 17/98. Berlin: Deutscher Bundestag. http://webarchiv.bundestag.de/cgi/show.php?fileToLoad=5097&id=1223.

Burgess, John. 2000. "35 Countries Named as Unfair Tax Havens." *Washington Post*, June 27, 2000, Financial.

Bush Campaign. 2000. 4President.org. "George W. Bush for President 2000 Campaign Brochure: 'Opportunity, Security and Responsibility—A Fresh Start for America.'" http://www.4president.org/brochures/georgewbush2000brochure.htm.

Büthe, Tim. 2002. "Taking Temporality Seriously: Modeling History and the Use of Narratives as Evidence." *American Political Science Review* 96 (3): 481–93.

Büttner, Tim, and Matthias Thiemann. 2017. "Breaking Regime Stability? The Politicization of Expertise in the OECD/G20 Process on BEPS and the Potential Transformation of International Taxation." *Accounting, Economics, and Law: A Convivium* 7 (1).

Calmes, Jackie, and Edmund Andrews. 2009. "Obama Asks Curb on Use of Havens to Reduce Taxes." *New York Times*, May 5, 2009, Business/Financial Desk.

Camp, David. 2015. "The OECD BEPS Action Plan and the Need for US Tax Reform." Speech to the 2015 OECD International Tax Conference, Washington, DC. http://www.uscib.org/docs/OECD_SPEECH_JUNE_10_2015.pdf.

Camp, David, and Orrin Hatch. 2014. "Hatch, Camp Statement on 2014 OECD Tax Conference." U.S. Senate, Committee on Finance. June 2, 2014. https://www.finance.senate.gov/ranking-members-news/hatch-camp-statement-on-2014-oecd-tax-conference.

Canute, James. 2001a. "Grenada Shuts Down 17 Banks in Clean-up of Financial Sector." *Financial Times*, March 13, 2001, International Economy.

——. 2001b. "Offshore Centres Head for Firmer Ground." *Financial Times*, January 5, 2001, International Economy.

Carroll, Joseph. 2007. "Americans Say Federal Income Taxes Too High, But Not Unfair." Gallup News Service, April 13, 2007. http://www.gallup.com/poll/27199/Americans-Say-Federal-Income-Taxes-Too-High-Unfair.aspx.

Carson, Shawn, Alan Cinnamon, and Zigurds Kronbergs. 1998. "US Hybrids: The Changing Landscape." *International Tax Review* 9 (10): 25–29.

Casi, Elisa, Christoph Spengel, and Barbara Stage. 2018. "Cross-Border Tax Evasion After the Common Reporting Standard: Game Over?" ZEW Discussion Paper No. 18–036. Mannheim: Leibnitz Centre for European Economic Research. http://ftp.zew.de/pub/zew-docs/dp/dp18036.pdf.

Cassard, Marcel. 1994. "The Role of Offshore Centers in International Financial Intermediation." Working Paper No. 94/107. Washington, DC: International Monetary Fund. https://www.imf.org/external/pubs/cat/longres.cfm?sk=1200.0.

Center for Responsive Politics. 2015. "OpenSecrets.Org: Money in Politics—See Who's Giving & Who's Getting." Accessed June 30, 2015. https://www.opensecrets.org/.

Chee, Foo Yun. 2016. "U.S. Demands EU Reconsiders Tax Probes of Its Companies." *Reuters*, February 11, 2016. http://www.reuters.com/article/us-eu-usa-taxavoidance-idUSKCN0VK1N0.

Chisik, Richard, and Ronald B Davies. 2004. "Asymmetric FDI and Tax-Treaty Bargaining: Theory and Evidence." *Journal of Public Economics, OTPR*, 88 (6): 1119–48.

Christensen, John, Nick Shaxson, and Duncan Wigan. 2016. "The Finance Curse: Britain and the World Economy." *The British Journal of Politics and International Relations* 18 (1): 255–69.

Christians, Allison. 2013. "What You Give and What You Get: Reciprocity Under a Model 1 Intergovernmental Agreement on FATCA." SSRN Scholarly Paper ID 2292645. Rochester, NY: Social Science Research Network. http://papers.ssrn.com/abstract =2292645.

———. 2014. "Tax, Society & Culture: IRS Claims Statutory Authority for FATCA Agreements Where No Such Authority Exists." *Tax, Society & Culture* (blog). July 4, 2014. http://taxpol.blogspot.com.au/2014/07/irs-claims-statutory-authority-for.html.

Chung, Joanna. 2008. "UBS 'Regrets' Bank Failings, Executive Tells Tax Inquiry." *Financial Times*, July 18, 2008.

Citizens for Tax Justice. 2000. "Summary and Analysis of George W. Bush's Tax Plan— Updated August 2000." Campaign 2000 information page. https://www.ctj.org /html/revised-analysis-of-bush-plan/.

Clausing, Kimberly A. 2016. "The Effect of Profit Shifting on the Corporate Tax Base in the United States and Beyond." SSRN Scholarly Paper ID 2685442. Rochester, NY: Social Science Research Network. https://papers.ssrn.com/abstract=2685442.

———. 2018. "Does Tax Drive the Headquarters Locations of the World's Biggest Companies?" SSRN Scholarly Paper ID 3232887. Rochester, NY: Social Science Research Network. https://papers.ssrn.com/abstract=3232887.

Clinton, Hillary. 2007a. "Hillary Clinton: Remarks on Economic Blueprint for the 21st Century." August 10, 2007. http://www.presidency.ucsb.edu/ws/index.php?pid =77059.

———. 2007b. "Hillary Clinton: Policy Address in Knoxville, Iowa on America's Economic Challenges." November 19, 2007. http://www.presidency.ucsb.edu/ws/index.php ?pid=77078.

Clover, Charles. 2016. "Foreign Companies in China Hit by New Exchange Controls." *Financial Times*. December 6, 2016.

Cobham, Alex. 2015a. "The Politics of Country-by-Country Reporting." *Uncounted* (blog), June 15, 2015. http://uncounted.org/2015/06/15/the-politics-of-country-by-country -reporting/.

———. 2015b. "OECD Country-by-Country Reporting: Strangled at Birth." *Uncounted* (blog), June 8, 2015. http://uncounted.org/2015/06/08/oecd-country-by-country -reporting-strangled-at-birth/.

Cobham, Alex, and Petr Janský. 2017. "Global Distribution of Revenue Loss from Tax Avoidance." United Nations University, WIDER Working Paper 55/2017.

Cohn, Peter. 2009. "Industry Cheers Summers' Comments on Code Changes." *National Journal's Congress Daily*, June 18, 2009.

Committee on Payment and Settlement Systems. 2011. "Statistics on Payment and Settlement Systems in the CPSS Countries—Figures for 2009." CPMI Paper 95. Basel: Bank for International Settlements. https://www.bis.org/cpmi/publ/d95.pdf.

Committee on Payments and Market Infrastructures. 2017. "Statistics on Payment, Clearing and Settlement Systems in the CPMI Countries—Figures for 2016." CPMI Paper 172. Basel: Bank for International Settlements. https://www.bis.org/cpmi/publ/d172.pdf.

Conseil Constitutionnel. 2016. "Décision No. 2016–741 DC du 8 décembre 2016." December 8, 2016. http://www.conseil-constitutionnel.fr/conseil-constitutionnel /francais/les-decisions/acces-par-date/decisions-depuis-1959/2016/2016-741-dc /decision-n-2016-741-dc-du-8-decembre-2016.148310.html.

Cooper, Michael J., and Stan Torgersen. 1998. "US Pauses for Breath on Subpart F." *International Tax Review* 9 (8): 67–70.

Council of the European Union. 2004. "Agreement in the Form of an Exchange of Letters between the European Community and the Swiss Confederation." *Official Journal of the European Union* L385 (December): 51–54.

——. 2009. "Report on proceedings in the Council's other configurations." https://data .consilium.europa.eu/doc/document/ST-5440-2009-INIT/en/pdf

——. 2010. "Provisional Agenda 2990th Meeting of the Council of the European Union." http://data.consilium.europa.eu/doc/document/ST-5311-2010-INIT/en/pdf.

——. 2011a. "Provisional Agenda 3088th Meeting of the Council of the European Union." http://data.consilium.europa.eu/doc/document/ST-10035-2011-INIT/en/pdf.

——. 2011b. "Provisional Agenda 3105th Meeting of the Council of the European Union." http://data.consilium.europa.eu/doc/document/ST-12505-2011-INIT/en/pdf.

——. 2012a. "Provisional Agenda 3167th Meeting of the Council of the European Union." http://data.consilium.europa.eu/doc/document/ST-9817-2012-REV-1/en/pdf.

——. 2012b. "ECOFIN Report to the European Council on Tax Issues." http://data .consilium.europa.eu/doc/document/ST-16327-2012-INIT/en/pdf.

——. 2013. "Council conclusions on tax evasion and tax fraud." Brussels: Council of the European Union. https://www.consilium.europa.eu/uedocs/cms_data/docs/pressdata /en/ecofin/137120.pdf.

——. 2016. "Council Conclusions on an External Taxation Strategy and Measures against Tax Treaty Abuse." Press Release 281/16. Brussels: Council of the European Union.

——. 2017. "Council Conclusions on the EU List of Non-Cooperative Jurisdictions for Tax Purposes." *Official Journal of the European Union* C 438 (December): 5–24.

Couzin, Robert. 2000. "Fighting for Harmony, Not Balance." *International Tax Review* 11: 17.

Coy, Peter. 2000. "Commentary: How Compassionate Is Bush's Tax Plan?" *Businessweek*, September 18, 2000. http://www.businessweek.com/2000/00_38/b3699246.htm.

Danziger, Sheldon, and Peter Gottschalk. 1997. *America Unequal*. Cambridge, MA: Harvard University Press.

Day, Matt. 2015. "How Microsoft Moves Profits Offshore to Cut Its Tax Bill." *Seattle Times*, December 12, 2015. https://www.seattletimes.com/business/microsoft/how -microsoft-parks-profits-offshore-to-pare-its-tax-bill/.

De Masi, Fabio. 2017. "Country-by-Country Reporting: European Parliament Gives in to Tax Tricks of Multinationals." *Fabio De Masi* (blog), June 13, 2017. http://www .fabio-de-masi.de/en/article/1580.country-by-country-reporting-european -parliament-gives-in-to-tax-tricks-of-multinationals.html.

Dean, Steven. 2006. "Attractive Complexity: Tax Deregulation, the Check-the-Box Election and the Future of Tax Simplification." *Hofstra Law Review* 34 (2): Article 5.

DeCarlo, Joseph, Alan Granwell, and Dirk Suringa. 1998. "Hybrid Branches Face Stern Test." *International Tax Review* 9 (3): 19–21.

Dehejia, Vivek, and Philipp Genschel. 1999. "Tax Competition in the European Union." *Politics & Society* 27: 403–30.

DeLay, Tom. 2001. "Letter to Secretary of the Treasury Paul O'Neill." In Carl Levin and Joseph Lieberman (chairs). 2001. *What Is the U.S. Position on Offshore Tax Havens? Hearing before the Permanent Subcommittee on Investigations of the Committee on Governmental Affairs, United States Senate*, 107th Cong., 101.

DeLong, J. Bradford, and Barry Eichengreen. 2001. "Between Meltdown and Moral Hazard: The International Monetary and Financial Policies of the Clinton Administration." National Bureau of Economic Research, Working Paper No. 8443.

Der Standard. 2013. "Bankgeheimnis wackelt; US-Steuergesetz setzt Österreich und Schweiz zu." *Der Standard*, January 10, 2013.

Desai, Mihir A, and Dhammika Dharmapala. 2010. "Dividend Taxes and International Portfolio Choice." *Review of Economics and Statistics* 93 (1): 266–84.

Devereux, Michael P., and Simon Loretz. 2008. "The Effects of EU Formula Apportionment on Corporate Tax Revenues." *Fiscal Studies* 29 (1): 1–33.

Dharmapala, Dhammika. 2014. "Base Erosion and Profit Shifting: A Simple Conceptual Framework." SSRN Scholarly Paper ID 2497770. Rochester, NY: Social Science Research Network. http://papers.ssrn.com/abstract=2497770.

Dionne, J. 1999. "Bush's Tax Taming." *Washington Post*, July 12, 1999, Opinions.

——. 2000. "Republican Tax Twists." *Washington Post*, November 1, 2000, Opinions.

DoJ (US Department of Justice). 2008. "Swiss Bank Executive Charged with Aiding U.S. Taxpayers Evade Income Tax." Press release, December 11, 2008. http://www.justice.gov/archive/opa/pr/2008/November/08-tax-1001.html.

Drawbaugh, Kevin, and Andy Sullivan. 2013. "Insight: How Treasury's Tax Loophole Mistake Saves Companies Billions Each Year." *Reuters*, May 31, 2013. http://www.reuters.com/article/2013/05/31/us-usa-tax-checkthebox-insight-idUSBRE94T17K20130531.

Drezner, Daniel W. 2008. *All Politics Is Global: Explaining International Regulatory Regimes*. Princeton, NJ: Princeton University Press.

Drucker, Jesse. 2016. "The World's Favorite New Tax Haven Is the United States." *Bloomberg Businessweek*, January 27, 2016. http://www.bloomberg.com/news/articles/2016-01-27/the-world-s-favorite-new-tax-haven-is-the-united-states.

——. 2018. "Companies Warn of Hits From Tax Cuts. Don't Be Fooled." *New York Times*, January 20, 2018, Business Day.

Easson, Alex. 2004. "Harmful Tax Competition: An Evaluation of the OECD Initiative." *Tax Notes International* 34: 1037–77.

ECB (European Central Bank). 2015. "National Tables: Euro Area—National Tables—MFI Balance Sheets—Monetary Statistics—ECB Statistical Data Warehouse." Accessed March 5, 2015. http://sdw.ecb.europa.eu/reports.do?node=1000003158.

Eccleston, Richard. 2012. *The Dynamics of Global Economic Governance: The Financial Crisis, the OECD and the Politics of International Tax Cooperation*. Northampton, MA: Edward Elgar.

Eccleston, Richard, and Felicity Gray. 2014. "Foreign Accounts Tax Compliance Act and American Leadership in the Campaign against International Tax Evasion: Revolution or False Dawn?" *Global Policy* 5 (3): 321–33.

Eccleston, Richard, and Richard Woodward. 2014. "Pathologies in International Policy Transfer: The Case of the OECD Tax Transparency Initiative." *Journal of Comparative Policy Analysis: Research and Practice* 16 (3): 216–29.

ECJ (European Court of Justice). 2006. "Judgment of the Court in Case C-196/04," September 12, 2006. http://curia.europa.eu/juris/document/document.jsf;jsessionid=9ea7d2dc30ddedf4993cb93c47888caa98edb18421d8.e34KaxiLc3qMb40Rch0SaxuQahj0?text=&docid=63874&pageIndex=0&doclang=EN&mode=lst&dir=&occ=first&part=1&cid=315389.

Eden, Lorraine, and Robert T. Kudrle. 2005. "Tax Havens: Renegade States in the International Tax Regime?" *Law & Policy* 27 (1): 100–127.

Edwards, John. 2007. "John Edwards: Remarks at Cooper Union in New York City: 'Building One America.'" June 21, 2007. http://www.presidency.ucsb.edu/ws/index.php?pid=77256.

Eggenberger, Katrin, and Patrick Emmenegger. 2015. "Economic Vulnerability and Political Responses to International Pressure: Liechtenstein, Switzerland and the Struggle for Banking Secrecy." *Swiss Political Science Review* 21 (4): 491–507.

Eichner, Thomas, and Marco Runkel. 2008. "Why the European Union Should Adopt Formula Apportionment with a Sales Factor." *The Scandinavian Journal of Economics* 110 (3): 567–89.

Eidgenössisches Finanzdepartement. 2013. "Weiterentwicklung der Finanzmarktstrate-gie." Bern: Eidgenössisches Finanzdepartement. https://www.efd.admin.ch/dam /efd/de/dokumente/alt/wirtschaft_waehrungfinanzplatz/faktenblaetter/faktenblatt_ weiterentwicklungderfinanzmarktstrategie.pdf.download.pdf/faktenblatt_weiterent wicklungderfinanzmarktstrategie.pdf.

Elliott, Amy S., and Lee Sheppard. 2016. "News Analysis: BEPS Failure and Multilateral Ini-tiatives." *Tax Notes*, September 15, 2016. http://www.taxnotes.com/worldwide-tax -daily/multijurisdictional-taxation/news-analysis-beps-failure-and-multilateral -initiatives/2016/09/15/hd6z?highlight=BEPS&United%20States&Robert%20Stack.

Elsayyad, May, and Kai A. Konrad. 2012. "Fighting Multiple Tax Havens." *Journal of In-ternational Economics* 86 (2): 295–305.

Emmenegger, Patrick. 2015. "The Long Arm of Justice: U.S. Structural Power and Inter-national Banking." *Business & Politics* 17 (3): 473–93.

——. 2017. "Swiss Banking Secrecy and the Problem of International Cooperation in Tax Matters: A Nut Too Hard to Crack?" *Regulation & Governance* 11 (1): 24–40.

Emmenegger, Patrick, and Paul Marx. 2019. "The Politics of Inequality as Organised Spectacle: Why the Swiss Do Not Want to Tax the Rich." *New Political Economy* 24 (1): 103–24.

EU G5 Finance Ministers. 2013. "Pierre Moscovici et ses homologues demandent à la Com-mission européenne la mise en oeuvre dans les meilleurs délais d'un FATCA euro-péen." Ministère de l'Economie et des Finances. Communiqué de presse no. 533, April 10, 2013. http://proxy-pubminefi.diffusion.finances.gouv.fr/pub/document /18/14730.pdf.

European Commission. 2001. "Towards an Internal Market without Tax Obstacles, a Strat-egy for Providing Companies with a Consolidated Corporate Tax Base for Their EU-Wide Activities." Communication from the Commission to the Council, the Euro-pean Parliament, and the Economic and Social Committee: COM(2001) 582 final, October 23, 2001. Brussels: European Commission. http://eur-lex.europa.eu/legal -content/EN/TXT/PDF/?uri=CELEX:52001DC0582&from=EN.

——. 2008a. "Proposal for a Council Directive Amending Directive 2003/48/EC on Taxa-tion of Savings Income in the Form of Interest Payments." COM(2008) 727 final, November 13, 2008. Brussels: European Commission. https://eur-lex.europa .eu/legal-content/EN/TXT/PDF/?uri=CELEX:52008PC0727&qid=1558105 348687&from=EN.

——. 2008b. "Report from the Commission to the Council in Accordance with Article 18 of Council Directive 2003/48/EC on Taxation of Savings Income in the Form of Interest Payments." COM(2008) 552 final, September 15, 2008. Brussels: Euro-pean Commission. https://eur-lex.europa.eu/legal-content/EN/TXT/PDF/?uri=CEL EX:52008DC0552&qid=1558105526143&from=EN.

——. 2009. "Proposal for a Council Directive on Administrative Cooperation in the Field of Taxation." COM(2009)029, February 2, 2009. http://eur-lex.europa.eu /LexUriServ/LexUriServ.do?uri=COM:2009:0029:FIN:EN:PDF.

——. 2015a. "Proposal for a Council Directive on a Common Consolidated Corporate Tax Base (CCCTB)—State of Play." 14509/15, December 1, 2015. Brussels: European Commission. http://data.consilium.europa.eu/doc/document/ST-14509-2015-INIT /en/pdf.

——. 2015b. "Communication from the Commission to the European Parliament and the Council: A Fair and Efficient Tax System in the European Union: 5 Key Areas for Action." COM(2015)302 final, June 17, 2015. Brussels: European Commission. https://eur-lex.europa.eu/resource.html?uri=cellar:5e1fd1b0-15b7-11e5-a342 -01aa75ed71a1.0003.01/DOC_1&format=PDF.

——. 2016a. "Proposal for a Council Directive on a Common Consolidated Corporate Tax Base (CCCTB)." COM/2016/0683 final-2016/0336 (CNS), October 25, 2016. Brussels: European Commission. http://eur-lex.europa.eu/legal-content/EN/TXT /?qid=1508228750541&uri=CELEX:52016PC0683.

——. 2016b. "Proposal for a Council Directive on a Common Corporate Tax Base." COM(2016) 685 final-2016/0337 (CNS), October 25, 2016. Brussels: European Commission. https://ec.europa.eu/taxation_customs/sites/taxation/files/com_2016 _685_en.pdf.

——. 2016c. "Proposal for a Directive of the European Parliament and of the Council Amending Directive 2013/34/EU as Regards Disclosure of Income Tax Information by Certain Undertakings and Branches." COM/2016/0198 final-2016/0107 (COD), April 12, 2016. Brussels: European Commission. http://eur-lex.europa.eu /legal-content/EN/TXT/?uri=CELEX%3A52016PC0198.

——. 2016d. "Communication from the Commission to the European Parliament and the Council on an External Strategy for Effective Taxation." COM(2016)24, January 28, 2016. Brussels: European Commission. https://ec.europa.eu/transparency /regdoc/rep/1/2016/EN/1-2016-24-EN-F1-1.PDF.

——. 2016e. "First Step towards a New EU List of Third Country Jurisdictions: Scoreboard." Brussels: European Commission—DG Taxation and Customs Union, September 2016. https://ec.europa.eu/taxation_customs/sites/taxation/files/2016-09 -15_scoreboard-indicators.pdf.

——. 2017a. "State Aid—Tax Rulings." Tax Planning Practices—European Commission. Accessed October 12, 2017. http://ec.europa.eu/competition/state_aid/tax_rulings /index_en.html.

——. 2017b. "Commission Decision (EU) 2017/502 of 21 October 2015 on State Aid SA.38374 (2014/C Ex 2014/NN) Implemented by the Netherlands to Starbucks (Notified under Document C(2015) 7143)." *Official Journal of the European Union* L (83): 38–115.

——. 2017c. "Commission Decision of 4.10.2017 on State Aid SA.38944 (2014/C) (Ex 2014/NN) Implemented by Luxembourg to Amazon." C(2017) 6740 final, October 4, 2017. Brussels: European Commission. http://ec.europa.eu/competition /state_aid/cases/254685/254685_1966181_892_4.pdf.

——. 2017d. "Commission Decision (EU) 2017/1283 of 30 August 2016 on State Aid SA.38373 (2014/C) (Ex 2014/NN) (Ex 2014/CP) Implemented by Ireland to Apple (Notified under Document C(2017) 5605)." *Official Journal of the European Union* L (187): 1–110.

——. 2018. "Proposal for a Council Directive on the Common System of a Digital Services Tax on Revenues Resulting from the Provision of Certain Digital Services." COM(2018) 148 final, March 21, 2018. Brussels: European Commission. https://ec .europa.eu/taxation_customs/sites/taxation/files/proposal_common_system _digital_services_tax_21032018_en.pdf.

European Community. 2003. "Council Directive 2003/48/EC of 3 June 2003 on Taxation of Savings Income in the Form of Interest Payments." *Official Journal of the European Union* L 157: 38.

European Council. 2014. "European Council 20/21 March 2014 Conclusions." March 21, 2014. https://www.consilium.europa.eu/uedocs/cms_data/docs/pressdata/en/ec /141749.pdf.

European Parliament. 2017. "Amendments Adopted by the European Parliament on 4 July 2017 on the Proposal for a Directive of the European Parliament and of the Council Amending Directive 2013/34/EU as Regards Disclosure of Income Tax Information by Certain Undertakings and Branches." COM(2016)0198-C8-0146/2016

-2016/0107 (COD). Brussels: European Parliament. http://www.europarl.europa.eu /sides/getDoc.do?pubRef=-//EP//NONSGML+TA+P8-TA-2017-0284+ 0+DOC+PDF+V0//EN.

European Union. 2003. "Council Directive 2003/49/EC of 3 June 2003 on a Common System of Taxation Applicable to Interest and Royalty Payments Made between Associated Companies of Different Member States." *Official Journal of the European Union* L 157 (49). http://eur-lex.europa.eu/LexUriServ/LexUriServ.do?uri =CELEX:32003L0049:en:HTML.

——. 2011. "Council Directive 2011/16/EU of 15 February 2011 on Administrative Co-operation in the Field of Taxation and Repealing Directive 77/799/EEC." *Official Journal of the European Union* L 54 (64): 1–12.

——. 2014a. "Council Directive 2014/48/EU of 24 March 2014 Amending Directive 2003/48/EC on Taxation of Savings Income in the Form of Interest Payments." *Official Journal of the European Union* L 111 (50).

——. 2014b. "Council Directive 2014/107/EU of 9 December 2014 Amending Directive 2011/16/EU as Regards Mandatory Automatic Exchange of Information in the Field of Taxation." September 12, 2014. http://eur-lex.europa.eu/legal-content/EN /TXT/PDF/?uri=CELEX:32014L0107&from=EN.

——. 2016. "Council Directive (EU) 2016/881 of 25 May 2016 Amending Directive 2011/16/EU as Regards Mandatory Automatic Exchange of Information in the Field of Taxation." *Official Journal of the European Union* L 146 (8): 8–21.

Eurostat. 2018. "National Accounts Aggregates by Industry (up to NACE A*64)." Luxembourg: Eurostat. http://ec.europa.eu/eurostat/data/database#.

Fairfield, Tasha. 2010. "Business Power and Tax Reform: Taxing Income and Profits in Chile and Argentina." *Latin American Politics and Society* 52 (2): 37–71.

Falkner, Gerda. 2011. "Introduction: The EU's Decision Traps and Their Exits." In *The EU's Decision Traps: Comparing Policies*, edited by Gerda Falkner, 1–18. Oxford: Oxford University Press.

Farquet, Christophe, and Matthieu Leimgruber. 2014. "Catch Me If You Can! Tax Havens, the Market for Tax Evasion and Fiscal Diplomacy from the League of Nations to the OECD, 1920–1990." Paper Presented at the Workshop on International Tax Competition and Financial Secrecy, University of St. Gallen.

FATF (Financial Action Task Force). 2006. "Summary of the Third Mutual Evaluation Report on Anti-Money Laundering and Combating the Financing of Terrorism— United States of America." Paris: Financial Action Task Force. http://www.fatf-gafi .org/media/fatf/documents/reports/mer/MER%20US%20ES.pdf.

Fehling, Daniel. 2015. "Das BEPS-Projekt auf der Zielgeraden—Was Bedeutet dies für Deutschland?" *FR Finanz-Rundschau Ertragssteuerrecht*, 97 (18): 817–823.

Feldstein, Martin. 1999. "Bush's Tax Plan Makes Sense." *Wall Street Journal*, June 12, 1999, sec. A.

——. 2000. "Bush's Tax Plan Is Even Better Than the Campaign Says." *Wall Street Journal*, March 28, 2000, sec. A.

Finanzverwaltung des Landes Nordrhein-Westfalen. 2018. "Zahlen, Daten, Fakten: Zusammenfassende Informationen rund um das Thema Selbstanzeige." December 31, 2018. https://www.finanzverwaltung.nrw.de/de/steuerhinterziehung/zahlen -daten-fakten.

FinCEN (Financial Crimes Enforcement Network). 2012. "Customer Due Diligence Requirements for Financial Institutions." *Federal Register* 77 (53): 13046–56.

——. 2016. "Customer Due Diligence Requirements for Financial Institutions; Final Rule." *Federal Register* 81 (91): 29398–460.

Finet, J. P. 2015. "U.S. Will Participate in Drafting Multilateral Instrument, Stack Says." *Tax Notes*, October 19, 2015. http://www.taxnotes.com/news-documents/base-ero sion-and-profit-shifting-beps/us-will-participate-drafting-multilateral-instru ment-stack-says/2015/10/19/16848076?highlight=BEPS&United%20States &Robert%20Stack.

Finley, Ryan. 2015. "Stack Gives U.S. Perspective on BEPS Recommendations." *Tax Notes*, October 13, 2015. http://www.taxnotes.com/worldwide-tax-daily/base-erosion-and -profit-shifting-beps/stack-gives-us-perspective-beps-recommendations/2015/10 /13/h4vx?highlight=BEPS&United%20States&Robert%20Stack.

———. 2016. "BEPS Report on Transfer Pricing 'Could Have Been Worse,' Hickman Says." *Tax Notes*, August 6, 2016. http://www.taxnotes.com/worldwide-tax-daily/transfer -pricing/beps-report-transfer-pricing-could-have-been-worse-hickman-says /2016/06/08/hb7c.

———. 2017a. "Stack Reflects on Turbulent Days at Treasury, Future of the OECD." *Tax Notes*, March 15, 2017. http://www.taxnotes.com/news-documents/base-erosion- and-profit-shifting-beps/stack-reflects-turbulent-days-treasury-future-oecd /2017/03/15/18870411?highlight=BEPS&United%20States&Robert%20Stack.

———. 2017b. "The Year in Review: The Year of the Many Arm's-Length Standards." *Tax Notes*, May 1, 2017. http://www.taxnotes.com/worldwide-tax-daily/base-erosion -and-profit-shifting-beps/year-review-year-many-arms-length-standards/2017/01 /05/hgl9?highlight=BEPS&United%20States&Robert%20Stack.

Flubacher, Rita. 2012. "Jetzt ist Plan B zu Prüfen." *Tages-Anzeiger*, December 22, 2012, Analyse.

Fournier, Ron. 1999. "Bush Tax Plan Would Aid Very Rich and Working Poor." *Associated Press*, January 12, 1999, Political News.

Fram, Alan. 1993. "Clinton Plan Reverses Reaganomics But Leaves Deficits Untamed." *Associated Press*, June 8, 1993, Washington Dateline.

Freedberg, Sydney. 2002. "Enron Allies Helped Stave off Tax Haven Crackdown." *St. Petersburg Times* (Florida), January 19, 2002.

Frenkel, Jacob A., Assaf Razin, and Efraim Sadka. 1991. *International Taxation in an Integrated World*. Cambridge, MA: MIT Press.

Frieden, Jeffry A. 1991. "Invested Interests: The Politics of National Economic Policies in a World of Global Finance." *International Organization* 45 (04): 425–51.

Fuchs, Doris, and Markus Lederer. 2008. "The Power of Business." *Business and Politics* 9 (3): 1–17.

Fuest, Clemens. 2018. "Why Germany Must React to Trump's Tax Reform." *Handelsblatt Global Edition*, May 15, 2018. https://global.handelsblatt.com/opinion/germany -must-react-trumps-tax-reform-921824.

G7 Leaders. 1996. "1996 Lyon Economic Communiqué." University of Toronto, Trinity College, Munk School of Global Affairs and Public Policy, G7 Information Centre: G7/8 Summits. http://www.g8.utoronto.ca/summit/1996lyon/communique .html.

G7 Ministers of Finance. 2001. "Statement of G-7 Finance Ministers and Central Bank Governors, April 28, 2001." University of Toronto, Trinity College, Munk School of Global Affairs and Public Policy, G7 Information Centre: G8 Finance Ministers' Meetings. http://www.g8.utoronto.ca/finance/fm010428.htm.

G20 Leaders. 2008. "Declaration of the Summit on Financial Markets and the World Economy, Washington, DC, November 15, 2008." University of Toronto, Trinity College, Munk School of Global Affairs and Public Policy, G20 Information Centre: G20 Summits. http://www.g20.utoronto.ca/2008/2008declaration1115.html.

——. 2012. "G20 Los Cabos Summit 2012—Leaders Declaration." University of Toronto, Trinity College, Munk School of Global Affairs and Public Policy, G20 Information Centre: G20 Summits. http://www.g20.utoronto.ca/2012/2012-0619-loscabos.html.

——. 2013. "Tax Annex to the St. Petersburg G20 Leaders' Declaration." St. Petersburg: G20. https://www.oecd.org/g20/summits/saint-petersburg/Tax-Annex-St-Petersburg-G20 -Leaders-Declaration.pdf.

G20 Ministers. 2012. "Communiqué, Meeting of Finance Ministers and Central Bank Governors," February 26, 2012. University of Toronto, Trinity College, Munk School of Global Affairs and Public Policy, G7 Information Centre: G8 Finance Ministers' Meetings. http://www.g20.utoronto.ca/2012/2012-120226-finance-en.html.

Gamperl, Elisabeth, Frederik Obermaier, and Bastian Obermayer. 2017. "Just Do It." *Paradise Papers—The Shadowy World of Big Money* (blog), June 11, 2017. https:// projekte.sueddeutsche.de/paradisepapers/politik/nike-and-its-system-of-tax -avoidance-e727797/.

Ganghof, Steffen. 2000. "Adjusting National Tax Policy to Economic Internationalization Strategies and Outcomes." In *Welfare and Work in the Open Economy Volume II: Diverse Responses to Common Challenges in Twelve Countries*, edited by Fritz W. Scharpf and Vivien A. Schmidt, 597–646. Oxford: Oxford University Press.

——. 2006. *The Politics of Income Taxation: A Comparative Analysis*. Colchester, UK: ECPR Press.

Garrett, Geoffrey. 1995. "Capital Mobility, Trade, and the Domestic Politics of Economic Policy." *International Organization* 49 (04): 657–87.

Garst, Brian. 2014. "Don't Expect U.S. FATCA Reciprocation Any Time Soon." *Center for Freedom and Prosperity*, October 13, 2014. http://freedomandprosperity.org/2014 /featured/dont-expect-u-s-fatca-reciprocation-any-time-soon/.

Genschel, Philipp. 2002. *Steuerharmonisierung und Steuerwettbewerb in der Europäischen Union*. Frankfurt am Main: Campus Verlag.

Genschel, Philipp, Achim Kemmerling, and Eric Seils. 2011. "Accelerating Downhill: How the EU Shapes Corporate Tax Competition in the Single Market." *JCMS: Journal of Common Market Studies* 49 (3): 585–606.

Genschel, Philipp, and Thomas Rixen. 2015. "The International Tax Regime: Historical Evolution and Political Change." In *Transnational Legal Orders*, edited by G. Shaffer and T. Halliday, 154–83. Cambridge: Cambridge University Press.

Genschel, Philipp, and Peter Schwarz. 2011. "Tax Competition: A Literature Review." *Socio-Economic Review* 9 (2): 339–70.

——. 2013. "Tax Competition and Fiscal Democracy." In *Politics in the Age of Austerity*, edited by Wolfgang Streeck and Armin Schäfer, 59–83. Cambridge: Polity.

Genschel, Philipp, and Laura Seelkopf. 2015. "The Competition State." In *The Oxford Handbook of Transformations of the State*, edited by Stephan Leibfried, Evelyn Huber, Matthew Lange, Jonah D. Levy, Frank Nullmeier, and John D. Stephens, 237–52. Oxford: Oxford University Press.

Gerring, John. 2007. *Case Study Research: Principles and Practices*. Cambridge: Cambridge University Press.

Gilpin, Robert. 1981. *War and Change in World Politics*. Cambridge: Cambridge University Press.

Giridharadas, Anand. 2001. "Saved Havens; The Treasury Coddles Tax Cheats." *The New Republic* 225 (9/10): 23.

Global Forum. 2014. "Agreements." *Exchange of Tax Information Portal*. Accessed April 14, 2014. http://www.eoi-tax.org/jurisdictions/US#agreements.

Gordon, Roger H. 1992. "Can Capital Income Taxes Survive in Open Economies?" *The Journal of Finance* 47 (3): 1159–80.

Government Accountability Office. 2007. "Tax Compliance: Qualified Intermediary Program Provides Some Assurance That Taxes on Foreign Investors Are Withheld and Reported, but Can Be Improved." December 19, 2007. http://www.gao.gov/products /GAO-08-99.

Government of Bermuda. 2000. "Bermuda Advance Commitment Letter." Letter to Mr. Donald J. Johnston, OECD Secretary General, May 15, 2000. https://www .oecd.org/ctp/harmful/1903535.pdf.

Governor of the Cayman Islands. 2000. "Cayman Islands Advance Commitment Letter." Letter to Mr. Donald J. Johnston, OECD Secretary General, May 15, 2000. https:// www.oecd.org/ctp/harmful/1903543.pdf.

GovTrack.us. 2015. "President Barack Obama: Former President of the United States." Accessed May 20, 2019. https://www.govtrack.us/congress/members/barack_obama /400629.

Graetz, Michael J. 1993. "Tax Policy at the Beginning of the Clinton Administration." *Yale Journal on Regulation* 10: 561.

———. 2000. "The David R. Tillinghast Lecture—Taxing International Income: Inadequate Principles, Outdated Concepts, and Unsatisfactory Policies." *Tax Law Review* 54: 261.

Griffiths, Ian. 2012. "Amazon: £7bn Sales, No UK Corporation Tax." *The Guardian*, April 4, 2012, Technology. https://www.theguardian.com/technology/2012/apr/04 /amazon-british-operation-corporation-tax.

Grinberg, Itai. 2012. "Beyond FATCA: An Evolutionary Moment for the International Tax System." *Georgetown Law Faculty Working Papers*, Paper 160. http://scholarship .law.georgetown.edu/fwps_papers/160.

———. 2015. "The New International Tax Diplomacy." *Georgetown Law Journal* 104: 1137.

———. 2016a. "Does FATCA Teach Broader Lessons about International Tax Multilateralism?" In *Global Tax Governance*, edited by Peter Dietsch and Thomas Rixen, 158–74. Colchester: ECPR Press.

———. 2016b. "A Constructive U.S. Counter to EU State Aid Cases." *Tax Notes*, November 1, 2016. http://www.taxnotes.com/worldwide-tax-daily/international-taxation /constructive-us-counter-eu-state-aid-cases/2016/01/11/h6wh?highlight =BEPS&United%20States&Robert%20Stack.

Guex, Sébastien. 2000. "The Origins of the Swiss Banking Secrecy Law and Its Repercussions for Swiss Federal Policy." *Business History Review* 74 (02): 237–66.

Guttentag, Joseph H. 1995. "An Overview of International Tax Issues." *University of Miami Law Review* 50: 445.

Hacker, Jacob S., and Paul Pierson. 2002. "Business Power and Social Policy: Employers and the Formation of the American Welfare State." *Politics & Society* 30 (2): 277–325.

———. 2005. "Abandoning the Middle: The Bush Tax Cuts and the Limits of Democratic Control." *Perspectives on Politics* 3 (01): 33–53.

Hakelberg, Lukas. 2015a. "Redistributive Tax Cooperation: Automatic Exchange of Information, US Power, and the Absence of Joint Gains." In *Global Tax Governance*, edited by Peter Dietsch and Thomas Rixen, 123–56. Colchester: ECPR Press.

———. 2015b. "The Power Politics of International Tax Co-Operation: Luxembourg, Austria and the Automatic Exchange of Information." *Journal of European Public Policy* 22 (3): 409–28.

Hakelberg, Lukas, and Thomas Rixen. 2017. "Is Neoliberalism Still Spreading? The Impact of International Cooperation on Capital Taxation." Paper presented as part of "Fighting Tax Avoidance and Tax Crimes in the European Union" panel, European Consortium for Political Research General Conference, University of Oslo.

Hakelberg, Lukas, and Max Schaub. 2018. "The Redistributive Impact of Hypocrisy in International Taxation." *Regulation & Governance* 12 (3): 353–70.

Hall, Peter A. 1993. "Policy Paradigms, Social Learning, and the State: The Case of Economic Policymaking in Britain." *Comparative Politics* 25 (3): 275–96.

Hammer, Richard. 2001. "Statement of the United States Council for International Business." In Carl Levin and Joseph Lieberman (chairs). 2001. *What Is the U.S. Position on Offshore Tax Havens? Hearing before the Permanent Subcommittee on Investigations of the Committee on Governmental Affairs, United States Senate,* 107th Cong., 163–65.

Hammer, Richard M., and Jeffrey Owens. 2001. "Promoting Tax Competition." *Tax Notes International* 22 (11): 1302–5.

Harrington, Brooke. 2016. *Capital without Borders: Wealth Managers and the One Percent.* Cambridge, MA: Harvard University Press.

Hässig, Lukas. 2010. *Paradies perdu: Vom Ende des Schweizer Bankgeheimnisses.* Hamburg: Hoffmann und Campe.

Helleiner, Eric. 1995. "Explaining the Globalization of Financial Markets: Bringing States Back In." *Review of International Political Economy* 2 (2): 315–41.

——. 1996. *States and the Reemergence of Global Finance: From Bretton Woods to the 1990s.* Ithaca, NY: Cornell University Press.

——. 2002. "The Politics of Global Financial Regulation: Lessons from the Fight Against Money Laundering." In *International Capital Markets: Systems in Transition,* edited by John Eatwell and Lance Taylor, 177–206. Oxford: Oxford University Press.

——. 2014. *The Status Quo Crisis: Global Financial Governance After the 2008 Financial Meltdown.* Oxford: Oxford University Press.

Hentze, Tobias. 2019. "The Challenge of Moving to a Common Consolidated Corporate Tax Base in the EU." IW-Report 2/19. Cologne: Institut der deutschen Wirtschaft. https://www.iwkoeln.de/fileadmin/user_upload/Studien/Report/PDF/2019/IW -Report_2019_Common_Corporate_Tax_Base.pdf.

Herzfeld, Mindy. 2015a. "News Analysis: The U.S. Treasury and the BEPS Mess." *Tax Notes,* June 22, 2015. http://www.taxnotes.com/worldwide-tax-daily/base-erosion -and-profit-shifting-beps/news-analysis-us-treasury-and-beps-mess/2015/06/22 /h2k6?highlight=BEPS&United%20States&Robert%20Stack.

——. 2015b. "News Analysis: Will the United States Take Action on the BEPS Action Plan?" *Tax Notes,* August 9, 2015. http://www.taxnotes.com/beps-expert/base -erosion-and-profit-shifting-beps/news-analysis-will-united-states-take-action -beps-action-plan/2015/09/08/16722736?highlight=BEPS&United%20States.

——. 2017a. "News Analysis: What's Next for the OECD Under Trump?" *Tax Notes,* January 23, 2017. http://www.taxnotes.com/worldwide-tax-daily/tax-policy/news-analy sis-whats-next-oecd-under-trump/2017/01/23/hgw6?highlight=BEPS&Uni ted%20States&Robert%20Stack.

——. 2017b. "The Year in Review: Whither the International Tax System?" *Tax Notes,* March 1, 2017. http://www.taxnotes.com/worldwide-tax-daily/base-erosion-and -profit-shifting-beps/year-review-whither-international-tax-system/2017/01/03 /hgk7?highlight=BEPS&United%20States&Robert%20Stack.

Hong, Qing, and Michael Smart. 2010. "In Praise of Tax Havens: International Tax Planning and Foreign Direct Investment." *European Economic Review* 54 (1): 82–95.

Hotz, V. Joseph. 2003. "The Earned Income Tax Credit." In *Means-Tested Transfer Programs in the United States,* 141–98. Chicago: University of Chicago Press.

Houlder, Vanessa. 2014. "Crackdown on Tax Abuses by Technology Companies." *Financial Times,* December 1, 2014.

——. 2015a. "US Multinationals Fight UK Chancellor George Osborne's Google Tax." *Financial Times,* February 9, 2015.

——. 2015b. "CBI Urges Restraint in Crackdown on Tax Dodging by Multinationals." *Financial Times*, September 24, 2015.

Huizinga, Harry, and Gaëtan Nicodème. 2004. "Are International Deposits Tax-Driven." *Journal of Public Economics* 88 (6): 1093–1118.

Inland Revenue Department. 2011. "Departmental Interpretation and Practice Notes—No.49." Hong Kong: Inland Revenue Department. https://www.ird.gov.hk/eng/pdf/e_dipn49.pdf.

International Monetary Fund. 2018. "Coordinated Portfolio Investment Survey (CPIS)." Accessed February 21, 2018. http://data.imf.org/?sk=B981B4E3-4E58-467E-9B90-9DE0C3367363.

IPB Tax. 2013. "Robert B. Stack Appointed U.S. Deputy Assistant Treasury Secretary for International Tax Policy: Ivins, Phillips & Barker." http://www.ipbtax.com/firm-news-123.html.

IRS (Internal Revenue Service). 1995. "Notice 95–14 Simplification of Entity Classification Rules." *Internal Revenue Service Cumulative Bulletin* 1995 (1): 297–99.

——. 1997. "T.D. 8697 Simplification of Entity Classification Rules." *Internal Revenue Service Cumulative Bulletin* 1997 (1): 215–25.

——. 1998a. "Notice 98–11 Treatment If Hybrid Arrangements under Subpart F." *Internal Revenue Bulletin* 1998 (6): 18–19.

——. 1998b. "Notice 98–35 Treatment of Hybrid Arrangements Under Subpart F." *Internal Revenue Bulletin* 1998 (27): 35–38.

——. 1999. "Notice 99–8 Proposed Changes to Final Withholding Regulations Under Section 1441; Proposed Model Qualified Intermediary Withholding Agreement." *Internal Revenue Bulletin* 1999 (5): 26–51.

——. 2000. "Rev. Proc. 2000–12 Application Procedures for Qualified Intermediary Status Under Section 1441; Final Qualified Intermediary Withholding Agreement." *Internal Revenue Service Cumulative Bulletin* 2000 (1): 387–413.

——. 2015. "History of the Whistleblower/Informant Program." https://www.irs.gov/uac/History-of-the-Whilstleblower-Informant-Program.

——. 2016. "Country-by-Country Reporting—Final Regulations [TD 9773]." *Federal Register* 81 (126): 42482–91.

——. 2018. "REG-132197-17 Eliminating Unnecessary Tax Regulations." *Federal Register* 83 (32): 6808–14.

IRS (Internal Revenue Service) and Treasury. 1996. "Simplification of Entity Classification Rules." *Federal Register* 61 (93): 21989–94.

Irvine, Martha. 2000. "Working Poor to Get 5 Percent Worth of State Income Tax Relief." *Associated Press State & Local Wire*, May 12, 2000.

Israel, Stephan, Andreas Flütsch, and David Nauer. 2010. "Die Schweiz will für Deutschland den Steuereintreiber spielen." *Tages-Anzeiger*, October 19, 2010, Wirtschaft.

Javers, Eamon. 2009. "Obama Targets Offshore Havens." *Politico.com*, May 5, 2009. https://www.politico.com/story/2009/05/obama-targets-offshore-havens-022094.

Johannesen, Niels. 2014. "Tax Evasion and Swiss Bank Deposits." *Journal of Public Economics* 111: 46–62.

Johannesen, Niels, and Gabriel Zucman. 2014. "The End of Bank Secrecy? An Evaluation of the G20 Tax Haven Crackdown." *American Economic Journal: Economic Policy* 6 (1): 65–91.

Johnston, Stephanie Soong. 2016. "U.S. May Stop Information Exchange With Partners Who Publish CbC Reports." *Tax Notes*, March 11, 2016. http://www.taxnotes.com/news-documents/base-erosion-and-profit-shifting-beps/us-may-stop-information-exchange-partners-who-publish-cbc-reports/2016/03/11/18281921?highlight=BEPS&United%20States&Robert%20Stack.

Juncker, Jean-Claude. 2013. *Déclaration de politique générale sur l'état de la nation de M. Jean-Claude Juncker, Premier Ministre, Ministre d'Etat.* Luxembourg: Grand Duché. https://www.chd.lu/wps/PA_ArchiveSolR/FTSShowAttachment?mime=application%2fpdf&id=CDFF383419BD08B455811B80E5B46802$DA8553DECA23014CA584B79B9E54EFAD&fn=CDFF383419BD08B455811B80E5B46802$DA8553DECA23014CA584B79B9E54EFAD.pdf.

Karier, Thomas. 1997. *Great Experiments in American Economic Policy: From Kennedy to Reagan.* Westport, CT: Praeger Publishers.

Katsushima, Toshiaki. 1999. "Harmful Tax Competition." *Intertax* 27 (11): 396–97.

Keen, Michael, and Kai A. Konrad. 2014. "The Theory of International Tax Competition and Coordination." SSRN Scholarly Paper ID 2111895. Rochester, NY: Social Science Research Network. http://papers.ssrn.com/abstract=2111895.

Kentouris, Chris. 1997. "Foreign-Investor Tax Change Complicates Life for Banks." *American Banker*, November 17, 1997.

Kirchler, Erich, Boris Maciejovsky, and Friedrich Schneider. 2003. "Everyday Representations of Tax Avoidance, Tax Evasion, and Tax Flight: Do Legal Differences Matter?" *Journal of Economic Psychology* 24 (4): 535–53.

Kirwin, Joe. 2018. "U.S. on Course to Land on European Tax Blacklist: EU Official." *Bloomberg Tax*, May 15, 2018. https://www.bna.com/us-course-land-n73014475976/.

Knobel, Andres. 2018. "The US Can Be Blacklisted under the OECD's New Rules Due to a Forgotten Commitment." *Tax Justice Network* (blog), December 12, 2018. https://www.taxjustice.net/2018/12/12/the-us-can-be-blacklisted-under-the-oecds-new-rules-due-to-a-forgotten-commitment/.

Koos, Sebastian, and Patrick Sachweh. 2017. "The Moral Economies of Market Societies: Popular Attitudes towards Market Competition, Redistribution and Reciprocity in Comparative Perspective." *Socio-Economic Review*, December 15, 2017. https://doi.org/10.1093/ser/mwx045.

KPMG. 2014. "Manal S. Corwin Speaker Bio." Accessed June 30, 2014. https://www.kpmginstitutes.com/events/speakers/manal-corwin.aspx.

———. 2015. "Comments on the Discussion Draft on Revisions to Chapter I of the Transfer Pricing Guidelines (Including Risk, Recharacterization and Special Measures)." In *Comments Received on Public Discussion Draft—BEPS Actions 8, 9 and 10: Revisions to Chapter I of the Transfer Pricing Guidelines (Including Risk, Recharacterisation, and Special Measures)*, edited by Organisation for Economic Co-operation and Development (OECD), 2:527–47. Paris: OECD Publishing.

Krasner, Stephen D. 1976. "State Power and the Structure of International Trade." *World Politics* 28 (03): 317–47.

Kreienbaum, Martin. 2014. "Kreienbaum: Base Erosion and Profit Shifting (BEPS): Erste Ergebnisse werden G20-Finanzministern vorgelegt." *Internationales Steuerrecht* 18: 637–38.

Krippner, Greta R. 2005. "The Financialization of the American Economy." *Socio-Economic Review* 3 (2): 173–208.

Krotz, Ulrich, and Joachim Schild. 2013. *Shaping Europe: France, Germany, and Embedded Bilateralism from the Elysée Treaty to Twenty-First Century Politics.* Oxford: Oxford University Press.

Kudrle, Robert T. 2003. "Hegemony Strikes Out: The U.S. Global Role in Antitrust, Tax Evasion, and Illegal Immigration." *International Studies Perspectives* 4 (1): 52–71.

———. 2008. "The OECD's Harmful Tax Competition Initiative and the Tax Havens: From Bombshell to Damp Squib." *Global Economy Journal* 8 (1): 1–23.

Lamer, Elodie. 2017a. "EU Presidency Addresses Tax Certainty Ahead of Finance Ministers' Meeting." *Tax Notes*, May 4, 2017. http://www.taxnotes.com/worldwide-tax

-daily/harmonization/eu-presidency-addresses-tax-certainty-ahead-finance
-ministers-meeting/2017/04/05/lslt.

———. 2017b. "CCCTB Best Tool Against Tax Uncertainty, EU Commission Says." *Tax Notes*, November 4, 2017. http://www.taxnotes.com/worldwide-tax-daily/tax-reform /ccctb-best-tool-against-tax-uncertainty-eu-commission-says/2017/04/11/mbdf.

Le Maire, Bruno, Wolfgang Schäuble, Pier-Carlo Padoan, and Luis De Guindos. 2017. "Political Statement—Joint Initiative on the Taxation of Companies Operating in the Digital Economy." http://g8fip1kplyr33r3krz5b97d1.wpengine.netdna-cdn.com/wp -content/uploads/2017/09/170907-joint-initiative-digital-taxation252c-signed -letter-by-4-ministers.pdf.

Legro, Jeffrey W., and Andrew Moravcsik. 1999. "Is Anybody Still a Realist?" *International Security* 24 (2): 5–55.

Leone, Marie. 2009. "Watch Out for the Expense-Deferral Rule." *CFO.com* | Accounting & Tax, May 5, 2009. https://www.cfo.com/accounting-tax/2009/05/watch-out-for -the-expense-deferral-rule/

Levin, Carl. 2005. "S.1565—109th Congress (2005–2006): Tax Shelter and Tax Haven Reform Act of 2005." Introduced July 29, 2005. https://www.congress.gov/bill/109th -congress/senate-bill/1565?q=%7B%22search%22%3A%5B%22stop+tax+haven+ abuse+act%22%5D%7D&resultIndex=19.

———. 2007. "S.681—110th Congress (2007–2008): Stop Tax Haven Abuse Act." Introduced February 17, 2007. https://www.congress.gov/bill/110th-congress/senate-bill /681?q=%7B%22search%22%3A%5B%22stop+tax+haven+abuse+act%22%5D% 7D&resultIndex=11.

———. 2008. Interview by Larry Kudlow. *Kudlow & Company*, July 17, 2008. CNBC.

Levin, Carl, and Norm Coleman. 2006. "Tax Haven Abuses: The Enablers, the Tools, and Secrecy." Washington, DC: US Senate. http://www.hsgac.senate.gov/download /report-tax-haven-abuses-the-enablers-the-tools-and-secrecy.

———. 2008. "Tax Haven Banks and U.S. Tax Compliance." Washington, DC: US Senate. http://www.gpo.gov/fdsys/pkg/CHRG-110shrg44127/html/CHRG-110shrg44127 .htm.

Levin, Carl, and Joseph Lieberman (chairs). 2001. *What Is the U.S. Position on Offshore Tax Havens? Hearing before the Permanent Subcommittee on Investigations of the Committee on Governmental Affairs, United States Senate*, 107th Cong.

Levin, Carl, and John McCain. 2013. "Offshore Profit Shifting and the U.S. Tax Code— Part 2 (Apple Inc.)." Memorandum to members of the Permanent Subcommittee on Investigations, US Senate, May 21, 2013. https://www.hsgac.senate.gov/imo /media/doc/EXHIBIT%201a%20-%20Subcommittee%20Memo%20on%20Off- shore%20Profit%20Shifting%20&%20Apple%20(May%2021%202013).pdf.

———. 2014. *Offshore Tax Evasion: The Effort to Collect Unpaid Taxes on Billions in Hidden Offshore Accounts*. Majority and minority staff report released in conjunction with 26 February 2014 hearing of the Permanent Subcommittee on Investigations, US Senate. https://www.hsgac.senate.gov/imo/media/doc/REPORT%20 %20OFFSHORE%20TAX%20EVASION%20(Feb%2026%202014,%208-20 -14%20FINAL).pdf.

Lew, Jacob J. 2016a. "U.S. Treasury Secretary Jacob J. Lew on the Evolution of Sanctions and Lessons for the Future." Carnegie Endowment for International Peace, March 30, 2016. https://carnegieendowment.org/2016/03/30/u.s.-treasury-secretary-jacob-j. -lew-on-evolution-of-sanctions-and-lessons-for-future-event-5191.

———. 2016b. Letter to Mr. Jean-Claude Juncker, president of the European Commission, November 2, 2016. https://www.treasury.gov/resource-center/tax-policy/treaties /Documents/Letter-State-Aid-Investigations.pdf.

Lincoln, Blanche. 2005. "S.Amdt.2652 to S.2020—109th Congress (2005–2006)." Introduced November 17, 2005. https://www.congress.gov/amendment/109th-congress/senate-amendment/2652?q=%7B%22search%22%3A%5B%22%5C%22child+ta x+credit%5C%22%22%5D%7D&resultIndex=4.

Lindblom, Charles Edward. 1977. *Politics and Markets: The World's Political Economic Systems.* New York: Basic Books.

Lips, Wouter. 2019. "Great Powers in Global Tax Governance: A Comparison of the US Role in the CRS and BEPS." *Globalizations* 16 (1): 104–19.

Lips, Wouter, and Alex Cobham. 2017. "Paradise Lost: Who Will Feature on the Common EU Blacklist of Non-Cooperative Tax Jurisdictions?" Open Data for Tax Justice, November 27, 2017. https://datafortaxjustice.net/paradiselost/.

Lynch, Suzanne. 2016. "US and EU Clash over Tax Practice Clampdown." *Irish Times,* September 3, 2016. http://www.irishtimes.com/business/economy/us-and-eu-clash -over-tax-practice-clampdown-1.2565150.

MacLennan, Stuart. 2016. "The Questionable Legality of the Diverted Profits Tax Under Double Taxation Conventions and European Union Law." *Intertax* 44 (12): 903–12.

Macron, Emmanuel. 2017. "Initiative pour l'Europe—Discours d'Emmanuel Macron pour une Europe souveraine, unie, démocratique." *L'Élysée,* September 28, 2017. https://www.elysee.fr/emmanuel-macron/2018/01/09/initiative-pour-l-europe -discours-d-emmanuel-macron-pour-une-europe-souveraine-unie-democratique.

Maloney, Carolyn. 2017. "H.R. 3089—115th Congress (2017–2018): Corporate Transparency Act of 2017." Introduced June 28, 2017. https://www.congress.gov/bill /115th-congress/house-bill/3089.

Martin, Julie. 2015. "US Disappointed with BEPS Plan Guidance, Treasury Officials Say." *MNE Tax* (blog). December 6, 2015. http://mnetax.com/us-officials-detail -position-on-beps-output-9269.

Mastromarco, Dan. 2001. "Memorandum/ Request for Meeting." In Carl Levin and Joseph Lieberman (chairs). 2001. *What Is the U.S. Position on Offshore Tax Havens? Hearing before the Permanent Subcommittee on Investigations of the Committee on Governmental Affairs, United States Senate,* 107th Cong., 103–4.

Mazzoni, Gianluca, and Reuven S. Avi-Yonah. 2016. "The Apple State Aid Decision: A Wrong Way to Enforce the Benefits Principle?" *Tax Notes,* December 14, 2016. http://www.taxnotes.com/worldwide-tax-daily/base-erosion-and-profit-shifting -beps/apple-state-aid-decision-wrong-way-enforce-benefits-principle/2016/12/14 /hg54?highlight=BEPS&United%20States&Robert%20Stack.

MEDEF (Mouvement des entreprises de France). 2014. "MEDEF's Comments on Transfer Pricing Documentation and CbC Reporting Draft (30.01.14)." In *Discussion Draft on Transfer Pricing Documentation and CbC Reporting—Public Comments Received,* edited by Organisation for Economic Co-operation and Development (OECD), 3:62–75. Paris: OECD Publishing.

——. 2016. *CCCTB Public Consultation Results -2b Published—Organisations Registered.* Brussels: European Commission. https://circabc.europa.eu/sd/a/fcfcc0b7-c26f -4908-9467-3c56e64e02c4/CCCTB%20Public%20Consultation%20Results%20 -%202b%20published%20-%20Organisations%20registered.xlsx.

Meunier, Sophie, and Kalypso Nicolaïdis. 2006. "The European Union as a Conflicted Trade Power." *Journal of European Public Policy* 13 (6): 906–25.

Ministerium für Finanzen und Wirtschaft Baden-Württemberg. 2014. "Über 25.000 Selbstanzeigen von Steuersündern im Südwesten." November 16, 2014. https://fm.baden -wuerttemberg.de/de/service/presse-und-oeffentlichkeitsarbeit/pressemitteilung /pid/ueber-25000-selbstanzeigen-von-steuersuendern-im-suedwesten-2/.

Mirowski, Philip. 2013. *Never Let a Serious Crisis Go to Waste: How Neoliberalism Survived the Financial Meltdown*. New York: Verso.

Mitchell, Daniel J. 2001a. "CFP Press Statement, 28 June 2001." In Carl Levin and Joseph Lieberman (chairs). 2001. *What Is the U.S. Position on Offshore Tax Havens? Hearing before the Permanent Subcommittee on Investigations of the Committee on Governmental Affairs, United States Senate*, 107th Cong., 108.

——. 2001b. "CFP Strategic Memo, June 16, 2001." In Carl Levin and Joseph Lieberman (chairs). 2001. *What Is the U.S. Position on Offshore Tax Havens? Hearing before the Permanent Subcommittee on Investigations of the Committee on Governmental Affairs, United States Senate*, 107th Cong., 105–6.

——. 2001c. "The Taxing OECD: A Congressman's Salient Questions Receive No Answer." *Investor's Business Daily*, March 27, 2001.

Mnuchin, Steven. 2018. "Statement On OECD's Digital Economy Taxation Report." US Department of the Treasury. March 16, 2018. https://home.treasury.gov/news/press-releases/sm0316.

Mollohan, Alan. 2010. "H.R.2847—111th Congress (2009–2010): Hiring Incentives to Restore Employment Act." Introduced March 18, 2010. https://www.congress.gov/bill/111th-congress/house-bill/2847?q=%7B%22search%22%3A%5B%22hiring+incentives+restore+employment%22%5D%7D&resultIndex=4.

Montgomery, Lori, and Scott Wilson. 2009. "Obama Targets Overseas Tax Dodge; Plan Would Crack Down On Individuals, Firms With Money Abroad." *Washington Post*, May 5, 2009, sec. A.

Moravcsik, Andrew. 2013. *The Choice for Europe: Social Purpose and State Power from Messina to Maastricht*. Abingdon-on-Thames, UK: Routledge.

Mordi, Francisca. 2011. "IRS Proposed Regulations on Reporting Interest Paid to Nonresident Alien Individuals." American Bankers Association. April 7, 2011. https://www.dropbox.com/s/zz79zanz0s9e16d/NRaliens4811.pdf?dl=0.

Morgan, Jamie. 2017. "Taxing the Powerful, the Rise of Populism and the Crisis in Europe: The Case for the EU Common Consolidated Corporate Tax Base." *International Politics* 54 (5): 533–51.

Moschella, Manuela, and Eleni Tsingou. 2014. *Great Expectations, Slow Transformation: Incremental Change in Financial Governance*. London: ECPR Press.

Mühlauer, Alexander. 2018. "Frankreichs Digitalsteuer-Pläne drohen zu platzen." *sueddeutsche.de*, November 29, 2018, Politik. https://www.sueddeutsche.de/politik/europaeische-union-frankreichs-digitalsteuer-plaene-drohen-zu-platzen-1.4232109.

Mullis, Kenan. 2011. "Check-the-Box and Hybrids: A Second Look at Elective U.S. Tax Classification for Foreign Entities." *Tax Analysts Featured News*, November 4, 2011. http://www.taxanalysts.com/www/features.nsf/Articles/58D8A3375C8ECCD18525793E0055EB9B?OpenDocument.

Murphy, Richard. 2009. "Google's Tax." *Tax Research UK* (blog). April 19, 2009. https://www.taxresearch.org.uk/Blog/2009/04/19/googles-tax/.

Mussler, Werner. 2008. "EU-Steuerpolitik Steinbrücks Feldzug." *Frankfurter Allgemeine Zeitung*, March 9, 2008. http://www.faz.net/aktuell/wirtschaft/eu-steuerpolitik-steinbruecks-feldzug-1510780.html.

Naegeli, Kathrin. 2010. "Merz bekräftigt Nein zu automatischem Informationsaustausch." *SDA—Basisdienst Deutsch*, February 14, 2010.

——. 2011. "EU sucht Lösung im Streit um automatischen Informationsaustausch: Schweiz und weitere Drittstaaten dienen als Manövriermasse." *SDA—Basisdienst Deutsch*, January 28, 2010.

National Foreign Trade Council. 2015. "Statement of Catherine Schultz Vice President for Tax Policy, National Foreign Trade Council Before the House Ways and Means Tax Policy Subcommittee." National Foreign Trade Council. December 1, 2015. http://www.nftc.org/default/Tax%20Policy/2015WM%20Testimony%20 NFTC%20BEPS%20123015.pdf.

Naumann, Manfred, and Bernhard Groß. 2014. "Die Dokumentation von Verrechnungspreisen: Der OECD Bericht zu Maßnahme 13 des BEPS Action Plan." *Internationales Steuerrecht*, no. 21: 792–97.

NFTC (National Foreign Trade Council). 2014. "Comments on OECD Discussion Draft on Transfer Pricing Documentation and Country by Country Reporting." In *Discussion Draft on Transfer Pricing Documentation and CbC Reporting—Public Comments Received*, edited by Organisation for Economic Co-operation and Development (OECD), 3:84–91. Paris: OECD Publishing.

———. 2015. "Comments on Discussion Draft on BEPS Actions 8, 9, and 10: Risk, Recharacterisation, and Special Measures." In *Comments Received on Public Discussion Draft - BEPS Actions 8, 9 and 10: Revisions to Chapter I of the Transfer Pricing Guidelines (Including Risk, Recharacterisation, and Special Measures)*, edited by Organisation for Economic Co-operation and Development (OECD), 2:601–16. Paris: OECD Publishing.

Niederberger, Walter. 2012. "USA spielen Stärke des Finanzplatzes voll aus." *Tages-Anzeiger*, November 30, 2012, Wirtschaft.

Novak, Robert. 2001. "Global Tax Police." *Washington Post*, April 19, 2001.

NYSBA (New York State Bar Association). 1995. "Report on the 'Check the Box' Entity Classification System Proposed in Notice 95–14." Albany: New York State Bar Association. http://www.nysba.org/workarea/DownloadAsset.aspx?id=49928.

Oatley, Thomas. 2015. *A Political Economy of American Hegemony: Buildups, Booms, and Busts*. 1st edition. Cambridge: Cambridge University Press.

Oatley, Thomas, and Robert Nabors. 1998. "Redistributive Cooperation: Market Failure, Wealth Transfers, and the Basle Accord." *International Organization* 52 (1): 35–54.

Obama, Barack. 2006. "S.2257—109th Congress (2005–2006): Hurricane Katrina Working Family Tax Relief Act of 2006." Introduced February 8, 2006. https://www .congress.gov/bill/109th-congress/senate-bill/2257?q=%7B%22search%22%3A% 5B%22%5C%22child+tax+credit%5C%22%22%5D%7D&resultIndex=3.

———. 2007. "Remarks in Washington, DC: 'Tax Fairness for the Middle Class.'" September 18, 2007. http://www.presidency.ucsb.edu/ws/index.php?pid=77013.

———. 2009. "Remarks by the President on International Tax Policy Reform." May 4, 2009. https://obamawhitehouse.archives.gov/the-press-office/remarks-president -international-tax-policy-reform.

Obermayer, Bastian Brinkmann, Hans Leyendecker, Bastian, and Klaus Ott. 2015. "Ermittlungen wegen Steuerhinterziehung: Wie Fahnder gegen das System Luxemburg losschlagen." *sueddeutsche.de*, February 25, 2015, Wirtschaft. http://www .sueddeutsche.de/wirtschaft/ermittlungen-wegen-steuerhinterziehung-wie -fahnder-gegen-das-system-luxemburg-losschlagen-1.2366065.

O'Donnell, T., Philip Marcovici, and M. Michaels. 2000. "The New US Withholding Tax Regime: To Be or Not To Be, a Qualified Intermediary." *Tax Planning International Rev.* 27: 3, 4.

OECD. 1998. *Harmful Tax Competition*. Paris: Organisation for Economic Co-operation and Development. http://www.oecd-ilibrary.org/content/book/9789264162945-en.

———. 2000. "Towards Global Tax Co-operation: Report to the 2000 Ministerial Council Meeting and Recommendations by the Committee on Fiscal Affairs." Paris: OECD Publishing. http://www.oecd.org/ctp/harmful/2090192.pdf.

——. 2001. "The 2001 Progress Report." Paris: OECD Publishing. http://www.oecd.org
/ctp/harmful/2664450.pdf.

——. 2009. "A Progress Report on the Jurisdictions Surveyed by the OECD Global Forum in Implementing the Internationally Agreed Tax Standard." Paris: OECD
Publishing. http://www.oecd.org/ctp/42497950.pdf.

——. 2013a. "Action Plan on Base Erosion and Profit Shifting." Paris: OECD Publishing.
https://www.oecd.org/ctp/BEPSActionPlan.pdf.

——. 2013b. "Addressing Base Erosion and Profit Shifting." Paris: OECD Publishing.
http://www.keepeek.com/Digital-Asset-Management/oecd/taxation/addressing
-base-erosion-and-profit-shifting_9789264192744-en.

——. 2014a. "AEOI: Status of Commitments." Paris: OECD Publishing. http://www
.oecd.org/tax/transparency/AEOI-commitments.pdf.

——. 2014b. "BEPS Actions 8, 9 and 10: Discussion Draft on Revisions to Chapter I of
the Transfer Pricing Guidelines (Including Risk, Recharacterisation, and Special
Measures)." Paris: OECD Publishing.

——. 2014c. "Discussion Draft on Transfer Pricing Documentation and CbC Reporting."
Paris: OECD Publishing.

——. 2014d. "Model Tax Convention on Income and on Capital 2014 (Full Version)."
Paris: OECD Publishing. http://www.keepeek.com/Digital-Asset-Management
/oecd/taxation/model-tax-convention-on-income-and-on-capital-2015-full
-version_9789264239081-en.

——. 2014e. "Multilateral Competent Authority Agreement." Exchange of Tax Information. 2014. http://www.oecd.org/ctp/exchange-of-tax-information/multilateral-com
petent-authority-agreement.pdf.

——. 2014f. "Public Discussion Draft—BEPS Action 7: Preventing the Artificial Avoidance of PE Status." Paris: OECD Publishing.

——. 2014g. *Standard for Automatic Exchange of Financial Account Information in Tax Matters.*
Paris: OECD Publishing. http://www.keepeek.com/Digital-Asset-Management/oecd
/taxation/standard-for-automatic-exchange-of-financial-account-information
-for-tax-matters_9789264216525-en#page1.

——. 2015a. "Aligning Transfer Pricing Outcomes with Value Creation—Actions 8–10:
BEPS Final Reports." Paris: OECD Publishing.

——. 2015b. "Designing Effective Controlled Foreign Company Rules—Action 3: 2015
Final Report." Paris: OECD Publishing.

——. 2015c. "Preventing the Artificial Avoidance of Permanent Establishment Status—
Action 7: 2015 Final Report." Paris: OECD Publishing. http://www.oecd-ilibrary
.org/docserver/download/2315341e.pdf?expires=1506699134&id=id&accname
=guest&checksum=8A5583674260CEA7E37FB1BCF1C6C9D9.

——. 2015d. "Transfer Pricing Documentation and Country-by-Country Reporting—
Action 13: 2015 Final Report." Paris: OECD Publishing.

——. 2015e. "Preventing the Artificial Avoidance of Permanent Establishment Status,
Action 7—2015 Final Report." OECD/G20 Base Erosion and Profit Shifting Project. Paris: OECD Publishing. http://www.oecd-ilibrary.org/taxation/preventing
-the-artificial-avoidance-of-permanent-establishment-status-action-7-2015-final
-report_9789264241220-en.

——. 2017a. "CRS by Jurisdiction." Accessed June 30, 2017. https://www.oecd.org/tax
/automatic-exchange/crs-implementation-and-assistance/crs-by-jurisdiction/crs
-by-jurisdiction-2018.htm.

——. 2017b. "Matrix of Options and Reservations." MLI Database. Accessed April 10, 2017.
http://www.oecd.org/tax/treaties/mli-database-matrix-options-and-reservations
.htm.

———. 2017c. "Multilateral Convention to Implement Tax Treaty Related Measures to Prevent Base Erosion and Profit Shifting." Paris: OECD Publishing. http://www .oecd.org/tax/treaties/multilateral-convention-to-implement-tax-treaty-related -measures-to-prevent-BEPS.pdf.

———. 2017d. "Previous Requests for Input." Accessed September 19, 2017. https://www .oecd.org/fr/ctp/previous-requests-for-input.htm.

———. 2018a. "Gross Domestic Expenditure on R&D by Sector of Performance and Source of Funds." OECD.Stat. Accessed October 13, 2018. http://stats.oecd.org/Index .aspx?DataSetCode=GERD_SOF#.

———. 2018b. "Signatories of the Multilateral Competent Authority Agreement and Intended First Information Exchange Date." Paris: OECD Publishing. https://www .oecd.org/tax/automatic-exchange/international-framework-for-the-crs/MCAA -Signatories.pdf.

Office of Management and Budget. 2009. "A New Era of Responsibility: Renewing America's Promise." Washington, DC: Office of Management and Budget. http://www.gpo .gov/fdsys/pkg/BUDGET-2010-BUD/pdf/BUDGET-2010-BUD.pdf.

———. 2013. "Fiscal Year 2014: Analytical Perspectives Budget of the U.S. Government." 2013. http://www.whitehouse.gov/sites/default/files/omb/budget/fy2014/assets/spec .pdf.

Office of Tax Policy. 2000. "The Deferral of Income Earned Through U.S. Controlled Foreign Corporations." Washington, DC: Department of the Treasury. https:// www.treasury.gov/resource-center/tax-policy/Documents/subpartf.pdf.

Office of the Press Secretary, the White House. 2009. "Leveling the Playing Field: Curbing Tax Havens and Removing Tax Incentives for Shifting Jobs Overseas." Press release, May 4, 2009. https://obamawhitehouse.archives.gov/the-press-office/leveling-playing -field-curbing-tax-havens-and-removing-tax-incentives-shifting-jobs.

O'Neill, Paul. 2001a. "Letter to Ministers Brown, Eichel, Fabius, Martin, Shiokawa, and Visco." In Carl Levin and Joseph Lieberman (chairs). 2001. *What Is the U.S. Position on Offshore Tax Havens? Hearing before the Permanent Subcommittee on Investigations of the Committee on Governmental Affairs, United States Senate*, 107th Cong., 81–82.

———. 2001b. "Statement of Paul H. O'Neill Before the Senate Committee on Governmental Affairs Permanent Subcommittee on Investigations." In Carl Levin and Joseph Lieberman (chairs). 2001. *What Is the U.S. Position on Offshore Tax Havens? Hearing before the Permanent Subcommittee on Investigations of the Committee on Governmental Affairs, United States Senate*, 107th Cong., 45–55.

———. 2001c. "Treasury Secretary O'Neill Statement on OECD Tax Havens." In Carl Levin and Joseph Lieberman (chairs). 2001. *What Is the U.S. Position on Offshore Tax Havens? Hearing before the Permanent Subcommittee on Investigations of the Committee on Governmental Affairs, United States Senate*, 107th Cong., 83–84.

Ota, Alan K. 2003. "Tax Cut Package Clears Amid Bicameral Rancor." *CQ Weekly*, May 24, 2003.

Owens, Jeffrey. 1993. "Globalisation: The Implications for Tax Policies." *Fiscal Studies* 14 (3): 21–44.

Palan, Ronen, Richard Murphy, and Christian Chavagneux. 2010. *Tax Havens: How Globalization Really Works*. Cornell Studies in Money. Ithaca, NY: Cornell University Press.

Palan, Ronen, and Duncan Wigan. 2014. "Herding Cats and Taming Tax Havens: The US Strategy of 'Not in My Backyard.'" *Global Policy* 5 (3): 334–43.

Parillo, Kristen A. 2014. "Robert Stack—BEPS and the United States." *Tax Notes*, December 22, 2014. http://www.taxnotes.com/worldwide-tax-daily/base-erosion-and

-profit-shifting-beps/robert-stack-beps-and-united-states/2014/12/22/gymb
?highlight=BEPS&United%20States&Robert%20Stack.

Parker, Andrew, and John Burton. 2003. "Is the Global Crackdown on Tax Evasion 'Slow-ing to the Speed of the Last Ship in the Convoy'?" *Financial Times*, December 1, 2003, Comment & Analysis.

Peel, Michael. 2001a. "OECD and US near Deal on Tax Havens Crackdown." *Financial Times*, June 14, 2001, International Economy.

———. 2001b. "OECD May Have Deal to Fight Tax Evasion." *Financial Times*, June 28, 2001, International Economy.

Pfatteicher, Linda, Jeremy Cape, Mitch Thompson, and Matthew Cutts. 2018. "GILTI and FDII: Encouraging U.S. Ownership of Intangibles and Protecting the U.S. Tax Base." Bloomberg Tax. February 27, 2018. https://www.bna.com/gilti-fdii -encouraging-n57982089387/.

Picciotto, Sol. 1992. *International Business Taxation: A Study in the Internationalisation of Business Regulation*. London: Weidenfield & Nicolson.

———. 2015. "Indeterminacy, Complexity, Technocracy and the Reform of International Corporate Taxation." *Social & Legal Studies* 24 (2): 165–84.

Piltz, Detlev J. 2015. "BEPS und das staatliche Interesse." *Internationales Steuerrecht*, no. 15: 529–33.

Pinkernell, Reimar. 2012. "Ein Musterfall zur internationalen Steuerminimierung durch US-Konzerne." *StuW*, no. 4: 369–74.

———. 2014. "Internationale Steuergestaltung im Electronic Commerce." 494. Ifst-Schrift. Berlin: Institut Finanzen und Steuern e.V. http://www.ifst.de/images/schriften /2014/494/494.pdf.

Plümper, Thomas, Vera E. Troeger, and Hannes Winner. 2009. "Why Is There No Race to the Bottom in Capital Taxation?" *International Studies Quarterly* 53 (3): 761–86.

Posner, Elliot. 2009. "Making Rules for Global Finance: Transatlantic Regulatory Coopera-tion at the Turn of the Millennium." *International Organization* 63 (04): 665–699.

PwC. 2015. "PwC's Comments on BEPS Actions 8, 9, and 10: Discussion Draft on Revi-sions to Chapter I of the Transfer Pricing Guidelines (Including Risk, Recharacteri-sation, and Special Measures)." In *Comments Received on Public Discussion Draft— BEPS Actions 8, 9 and 10: Revisions to Chapter I of the Transfer Pricing Guidelines (Including Risk, Recharacterisation, and Special Measures)*, edited by Organisation for Economic Co-operation and Development (OECD), 2:669–75. Paris: OECD Publishing.

Quinlan, Andrew, and Daniel J. Mitchell. 2001. "CFP Special Alert, 06-15-01." Carl Levin and Joseph Lieberman (chairs). 2001. *What Is the U.S. Position on Offshore Tax Havens? Hearing before the Permanent Subcommittee on Investigations of the Com-mittee on Governmental Affairs, United States Senate*, 107th Cong., 105.

Radaelli, Claudio M. 1999. "Harmful Tax Competition in the EU: Policy Narratives and Advocacy Coalitions." *JCMS: Journal of Common Market Studies* 37 (4): 661–82.

Ralph, Oliver. 1999. "Corporates Revolt at CFC Expansion." *International Tax Review*, Jan-uary 6, 1999. http://www.internationaltaxreview.com/Article/2611541/Corporates -revolt-at-CFC-expansion.html.

———. 2000. "How Business Stands up to the OECD." *Int'l Tax Rev.* 11: 47.

Rangel, Charles. 2009. "H.R.3933—111th Congress (2009–2010): Foreign Account Tax Compliance Act of 2009." Introduced October 27, 2009. https://www.congress.gov /bill/111th-congress/house-bill/3933?q=%7B%22search%22%3A%5B%22foreign +account+tax+compliance+act%22%5D%7D&resultIndex=5.

Rappeport, Alan, Milan Schreuer, Jim Tankersley, and Natasha Singer. 2018. "Europe's Planned Digital Tax Heightens Tensions With U.S." *New York Times*, October 19,

2018, Business. https://www.nytimes.com/2018/03/19/us/politics/europe-digital-tax
-trade.html.

Rixen, Thomas. 2008. *The Political Economy of International Tax Governance*. Transformations of the State. New York: Palgrave Macmillan.

———. 2010. "Bilateralism or Multilateralism? The Political Economy of Avoiding International Double Taxation." *European Journal of International Relations* 16 (4): 589–614.

———. 2013. "Why Reregulation after the Crisis Is Feeble: Shadow Banking, Offshore Financial Centers, and Jurisdictional Competition." *Regulation & Governance* 7 (4): 435–59.

Rixen, Thomas, and Peter Schwarz. 2012. "How Effective Is the European Union's Savings Tax Directive? Evidence from Four EU Member States." *JCMS: Journal of Common Market Studies* 50 (1): 151–68.

Rosenbaum, David E. 1993. "The Budget Struggle: Clinton Wins Approval of His Budget Plan as Gore Votes to Break Senate Deadlock." *New York Times*, July 8, 1993.

Rubenfeld, Samuel. 2017. "U.S. Congress Tries, Again, on Corporate Transparency." *WSJ* (blog). June 28, 2017. https://blogs.wsj.com/riskandcompliance/2017/06/28/u-s
-congress-tries-again-on-corporate-transparency/.

Rubin, Richard, and Jesse Drucker. 2014. "Obama Tax Rhetoric on Offshore Profit Falls Shy of Action." Bloomberg. February 5, 2014. http://www.bloomberg.com/news
/2014-02-05/obama-tax-rhetoric-on-offshore-profit-falls-shy-of-action.html.

Rubin, Robert, and Jacob Weisberg. 2003. *In an Uncertain World: Tough Choices from Wall Street to Washington*. New York: Random House.

Ruding, Onno. 1992. *Report of the Committee of Independent Experts on Company Taxation*. Luxembourg: Office for Official Publications of the European Communities.

Ruf, Martin, and Alfons J. Weichenrieder. 2013. "CFC Legislation, Passive Assets and the Impact of the ECJ's Cadbury-Schweppes Decision." SSRN Scholarly Paper ID 2353336. Rochester, NY: Social Science Research Network. http://papers.ssrn.com
/abstract=2353336.

Rutishauser, Arthur. 2012a. "Es darf beim Bankgeheimnis kein Denkverbot geben." *Tages-Anzeiger*, February 28, 2012, Wirtschaft.

———. 2012b. "Die Vorteile der Abgeltungssteuer halten nur zwei Jahre." *Tages-Anzeiger*, September 28, 2012, Wirtschaft.

Sabo, Martin Olav. 1993. "H.R.2264—103rd Congress (1993–1994): Omnibus Budget Reconciliation Act of 1993." Introduced May 25, 1993. https://www.congress.gov
/bill/103rd-congress/house-bill/2264.

Scannell, Kara, and Vanessa Houlder. 2016. "US Tax Havens—the New Switzerland." *Financial Times*, May 8, 2016. http://www.ft.com/intl/cms/s/0/cc46c644-12dd-11e6
-839f-2922947098f0.html#axzz48719fIAD.

Scharpf, Fritz W. 1988. "The Joint-Decision Trap: Lessons from German Federalism and European Integration." *Public Administration* 66 (3): 239–78.

Schaub, Martin. 2011. "Zur völkerrechtlichen Zulässigkeit des amerikanischen Editionsbefehls an die UBS im Streit um die Kundendaten." *Zeitschrift Für Ausländisches Öffentliches Recht und Völkerrecht, ZAORV= Heidelberg Journal of International Law, HJIL* 71 (4): 807–24.

Schwarz, Jonathan. 2016. "US Model Treaty 2016: What Does It Say about the US and BEPS?" Kluwer International Tax Blog. http://kluwertaxblog.com/2016/02/21/us
-model-treaty-2016-what-does-it-say-about-the-us-and-beps/.

Schweizerische Depeschenagentur. 2009. "EU-Finanzminister: Kein Entscheid im Steuerpaket: Auf Schweiz wartet am Ende automatischer Informationsaustausch." *SDA—Basisdienst Deutsch*, December 2, 2009.

———. 2010. "Informationsaustausch: EU-Finanzminister einig bei Amtshilfe: EU-Steuerkommissar sieht Bankgeheimnis zurückgebunden." *SDA—Basisdienst Deutsch,* December 7, 2010.

———. 2011a. "Italien blockiert Einigung im EU-Steuerstreit - Fordert Sanktionen: Tremonti: 'Die EU ist der Schweiz beigetreten.'" *SDA—Basisdienst Deutsch,* May 17, 2011.

———. 2011b. "Schwierige Lösungssuche im EU-Steuerstreit—Vorerst keine Verhandlungen zwischen EU-Kommission und Schweiz." *SDA—Basisdienst Deutsch,* July 12, 2011.

———. 2012. "Weiterhin keine Verhandlungen EU-Schweiz zu Zinsbesteuerung." *SDA—Basisdienst Deutsch,* May 15, 2012.

———. 2013a. "Patrick Odier will rasche Lösung im Steuerstreit mit den USA." *SDA—Basisdienst Deutsch,* May 6, 2013.

———. 2013b. "Privatbankiers Für internationale Standards in Steuerfragen." *SDA—Basisdienst Deutsch,* June 7, 2013.

Schweizerischer Bundesrat. 2012. "Bericht des Bundesrates 'Die Behörden unter dem Druck der Finanzkrise und der Herausgabe von UBS-Kundendaten an die USA' in Erfüllung des Postulates 10.3390 GPK NR/ 10.3629 GPK SR vom 30. Mai 2010." Bern: Schweizerische Eidgenossenschaft. https://www.newsd.admin.ch/newsd/message/attachments/35770.pdf.

———. 2015. "Erläuternder Bericht zur multilateralen Vereinbarung der zuständigen Behörden über den automatischen Informationsaustausch über Finanzkonten und zu einem Bundesgesetz über den internationalen automatischen Informationsaustausch in Steuersachen." Bern: Schweizerischer Bundesrat. https://www.admin.ch/ch/d/gg/pc/documents/2620/Automatischer-Informationsaustausch_Erl.-Bericht_de.pdf.

Scott, Jeremy. 2014. "Check The Box For Tax Avoidance." *Forbes,* February 19, 2014. http://www.forbes.com/sites/taxanalysts/2014/02/19/check-the-box-for-tax-avoidance/.

Seabrooke, Leonard, and Duncan Wigan. 2016. "Powering Ideas through Expertise: Professionals in Global Tax Battles." *Journal of European Public Policy* 23 (3): 357–74.

Self, Heather. 2015. "The UK's New Diverted Profits Tax: Compliance with EU Law." *Intertax* 43 (4): 333–36.

Semeta, Algirdas. 2014. "Letter to Mr Yannis Stournaras, Minister of Finance of the Hellenic Republic." Ares(2014)574281. Commission of the European Union. http://ec.europa.eu/archives/commission_2010-2014/semeta/headlines/news/2014/03/ares(2014)574281.pdf.

Sharman, Jason Campbell. 2006a. *Havens in a Storm: The Struggle for Global Tax Regulation.* Ithaca, NY: Cornell University Press.

———. 2006b. "Norms, Coercion and Contracting in the Struggle against 'Harmful' Tax Competition." *Australian Journal of International Affairs* 60 (1): 143–69.

———. 2011. "Testing the Global Financial Transparency Regime." *International Studies Quarterly* 55 (4): 981–1001.

Shaxson, Nicholas. 2012. *Treasure Islands: Tax Havens and the Men Who Stole the World.* New York: Vintage.

Shay, Stephen E., J. Clifton Fleming, and Robert J. Peroni. 2002. "The David R. Tillinghast Lecture—What's Source Got to Do with It—Source Rules and US International Taxation." *Tax Law Review* 56: 81.

Sheppard, Lee. 2015. "News Analysis: Stack's BEPS Update." *Tax Notes,* April 20, 2015. http://www.taxnotes.com/beps-expert/base-erosion-and-profit-shifting-beps/news-analysis-stacks-beps-update/2015/04/20/16718201?highlight=BEPS&United%20States&Robert%20Stack.

——. 2016. "News Analysis: BEPS and EU Progress Report." *Tax Notes*, June 27, 2016. http://www.taxnotes.com/worldwide-tax-daily/base-erosion-and-profit-shifting -beps/news-analysis-beps-and-eu-progress-report/2016/06/27/hbm8.

Silicon Valley Tax Directors Group. 2015. Letter to Senators Portman, Schumer, Thune, and Cardin from Jeffrey K. Bergmann, co-chair, Silicon Valley Tax Directors Group, April 15, 2015. http://www.svtdg.org/docs/svtdg_sfc_wg_comments_4-15-15.pdf.

Simmons, Beth A. 2001. "The International Politics of Harmonization: The Case of Capital Market Regulation." *International Organization* 55 (03): 589–620.

Simonian, Haig. 2008. "Top UBS Banker Detained by US." *Financial Times*, May 7, 2008. http://www.ft.com/intl/cms/s/0/c4db77f0-1b98-11dd-9e58-0000779fd2ac.html.

Singer, David Andrew. 2007. *Regulating Capital: Setting Standards for the International Financial System*. Ithaca, NY: Cornell University Press.

Sinn, Stefan. 1992. "The Taming of Leviathan: Competition among Governments." *Constitutional Political Economy* 3 (2): 177–96.

Slemrod, Joel, and Jon Bakija. 2008. *Taxing Ourselves: A Citizen's Guide to the Debate over Taxes*, 4th ed. Cambridge, MA: MIT Press.

Stack, Robert B. 2015. "Stack Discusses the Progress and Future of BEPS." *Tax Notes*, June 29, 2015. http://www.taxnotes.com/beps-expert/base-erosion-and-profit -shifting-beps/stack-discusses-progress-and-future-beps/2015/06/29/16717656 ?highlight=BEPS&United%20States&Robert%20Stack.

States News Service. 2008. "Obama Applauds Subcommittee's Report Supporting Stop Tax Haven Abuse Act." *States News Service*, July 17, 2008.

Steinmo, Sven. 1994. "The End of Redistribution? International Pressures and Domestic Tax Policy Choices." *Challenge* 37 (6): 9–17.

Steuerle, C. Eugene. 2008. *Contemporary U.S. Tax Policy*. Washington, DC: Urban Institute Press.

Stevenson, Richard W. 1999. "At Bush's Ear, A Supply-Sider With a Heart." *New York Times*, December 12, 1999, sec. 3.

——. 2000. "Bush Tax Plan: The Debate Takes Shape." *New York Times*, August 24, 2000, sec. A.

Stewart, David D. 2014. "Stack Describes U.S. Goals and Concerns on BEPS Drafts." *Tax Notes*, March 26, 2014. http://www.taxnotes.com/beps-expert/information -reporting/stack-describes-us-goals-and-concerns-beps-drafts/2014/03/26 /16717256?highlight=BEPS&United%20States&Robert%20Stack.

Strache, Heinz-Christian. 2013. *204. Sitzung des Nationalrates der Republik Österreich— XXIV. Gesetzgebungsperiode*. Vienna: Parlamentsdirektion. https://www.parlament .gv.at/PAKT/VHG/XXIV/NRSITZ/NRSITZ_00204/fname_324912.pdf.

Streeck, Wolfgang, and Kathleen Ann Thelen. 2005. *Beyond Continuity: Institutional Change in Advanced Political Economies*. Oxford: Oxford University Press.

Stuntz, William J. 2001. "The Pathological Politics of Criminal Law." *Michigan Law Review* 100 (3): 505–600.

Sullivan, Ronald. 1993. "The Budget Struggle: The Region; Backlash to Tax Rise Splits New Jersey Democrats." *New York Times*, July 8, 1993.

Sultzer, Scott. 1995. "Money Laundering: The Scope of the Problem and Attempts to Combat It." *Tennessee Law Review* 63: 143.

Svallfors, Stefan. 2006. *The Moral Economy of Class: Class and Attitudes in Comparative Perspective*. Stanford, CA: Stanford University Press.

SVTDG (Silicon Valley Tax Directors Group). 2015. "Comment Letter on the OECD Public Discussion Draft BEPS Actions 8, 9 and 10." In *Comments Received on Public Discussion Draft—BEPS Actions 8, 9 and 10: Revisions to Chapter 1 of the Transfer Pricing Guidelines (Including Risk, Recharacterisation, and Special Measures)*, edited by Organisation for Economic Co-operation and Development (OECD), 2:723–73. Paris: OECD Publishing.

Swank, Duane. 2006. "Tax Policy in an Era of Internationalization: Explaining the Spread of Neoliberalism." *International Organization* 60 (4): 847–82.

Switzerland Global Enterprise. 2014. "Überblick über das schweizer Steuersystem." Bern: Switzerland Global Enterprise. https://www.s-ge.com/sites/default/files/cserver /publication/free/ihb-10-ueberblick-ueber-das-schweizer-steuersystem-s-ge.pdf.

Szigetvari, András. 2014. "Österreich lüftet Bankgeheimnis für USA." *Der Standard*, April 30, 2014. http://derstandard.at/1397522015449/Oesterreich-lueftet-sein -Bankgeheimnis-fuer-USA.

Tanenbaum, Edward. 2012. "Here They Come: FATCA Intergovernmental Agreements." *Tax Management International Journal* 41 (11): 623–25.

Tanzi, Vito. 1995. *Taxation in an Integrating World*. Washington, DC: Brookings Institution Press.

Task Force on Information Exchange and Financial Privacy. 2002. "Report on Financial Privacy, Law Enforcement and Terrorism." Washington, DC: Institute for Research on the Economics of Taxation. http://iret.org/pub/Final_ReportR15small _forIRET1.doc.

Taylor, Andrew. 2000. "Law Designed for Curbing Deficits Becomes GOP Tool for Cutting Taxes." *CQ Weekly*, July 4, 2000.

Thatcher, Mark, and Vivien A. Schmidt. 2013. *Resilient Liberalism in Europe's Political Economy*. Cambridge: Cambridge University Press.

The Economist. 2014. "Putting the Squeeze on Miami Vice." *The Economist*'s Schumpeter blog, January 17, 2014. http://www.economist.com/blogs/schumpeter/2014/01 /banks-and-tax-evasion.

The President. 2017. "Executive Order 13789 of April 21, 2017—Identifying and Reducing Tax Regulatory Burdens." *Federal Register* 82 (79): 19317–19.

Thomas, Leigh. 2018. "EU Ministers Fail to Break Digital Tax Deadlock." *Reuters*, December 4, 2018. https://www.reuters.com/article/us-eu-tax-digital-idUSKBN1O22MR.

Tørsløv, Thomas, Ludvig Wier, and Gabriel Zucman. 2018. "The Missing Profits of Nations." Working Paper 24701, National Bureau of Economic Research. https://doi .org/10.3386/w24701.

UNCTAD (United Nations Conference on Trade and Development). 2014. "Bilateral FDI Statistics 2014." http://unctad.org/en/Pages/DIAE/FDI%20Statistics/FDI-Statistics -Bilateral.aspx.

US Bureau of Economic Analysis. 2018a. "Direct Investment & Multinational Enterprises (MNEs)." International Data. Accessed June 17, 2018. https://www.bea.gov/iTable /index_MNC.cfm.

———. 2018b. "International Transactions, International Services, and International Investment (IIP) Tables." International Data. Accessed June 17, 2018. https://www .bea.gov/iTable/index_ita.cfm.

US Bureau of Labor Statistics. 2017. "Employment, Hours, and Earnings from the Current Employment Statistics Survey (National)." US Department of Labor. Accessed October 19, 2017. https://data.bls.gov/cgi-bin/dsrv?ce.

US House of Representatives. 2009. *Foreign Bank Account Reporting and Tax Compliance: Hearing before the Subcommittee on Select Revenue Measures of the Committee on Ways and Means, U.S. House of Representatives*, 111th Cong. November 5, 2009. http://www .gpo.gov/fdsys/pkg/CHRG-111hhrg63014/pdf/CHRG-111hhrg63014.pdf.

US Senate. 2008a. *Nomination of Douglas H. Shulman: Hearing before the Committee on Finance, United States Senate*, 110th Cong., January 29, 2008. https://www.finance .senate.gov/imo/media/doc/42222.pdf.

——. 2008b. *Tax Haven Banks and U.S. Tax Compliance: Hearings before the Permanent Subcommittee on Investigations of the Committee on Homeland Security and Governmental Affairs, United States Senate,* 110th Cong., July 17 and 25, 2008. https://www.hsgac.senate.gov/subcommittees/investigations/hearings/tax-haven-banks-and-u-s-tax-compliance.

US Treasury. 2000. "General Explanations of the Administration's Fiscal Year 2001 Revenue Proposals." Washington, DC: Department of the Treasury. https://www.treasury.gov/resource-center/tax-policy/Documents/General-Explanations-FY2001.pdf.

——. 2001. "The President's Agenda for Tax Relief." Washington, DC: Department of the Treasury. https://www.treasury.gov/press-center/press-releases/Documents/report30652.pdf.

——. 2009. "General Explanations of the Administration's Fiscal Year 2010 Revenue Proposals." Washington, DC: Department of the Treasury. http://www.treasury.gov/resource-center/tax-policy/Documents/General-Explanations-FY2010.pdf.

——. 2010. "General Explanations of the Administration's Fiscal Year 2011 Revenue Proposals." Washington, DC: Department of the Treasury. http://www.treasury.gov/resource-center/tax-policy/Documents/General-Explanations-FY2011.pdf.

——. 2012a. "Model Intergovernmental Agreement to Improve Tax Compliance and to Implement FATCA." https://www.treasury.gov/press-center/press-releases/Documents/reciprocal.pdf.

——. 2012b. "Joint Statement from the US and Switzerland Regarding a Framework for Cooperation to Facilitate the Implementation of FATCA." http://www.treasury.gov/resource-center/tax-policy/treaties/Documents/FATCA-Joint-Statement-US-Switzerland-06-21-2012.pdf.

——. 2012c. "Joint Statement From the United States, France, Germany, Italy, Spain and the United Kingdom Regarding an Intergovernmental Approach to Improving International Tax Compliance and Implementing FATCA." http://www.treasury.gov/press-center/press-releases/Documents/020712%20Treasury%20IRS%20FATCA%20Joint%20Statement.pdf.

——. 2013. "General Explanations of the Administration's Fiscal Year 2014 Revenue Proposals." Washington, DC: Department of the Treasury. http://www.treasury.gov/resource-center/tax-policy/Documents/General-Explanations-FY2014.pdf.

——. 2014a. "General Explanations of the Administration's Fiscal Year 2015 Revenue Proposals." http://www.treasury.gov/resource-center/tax-policy/Documents/General-Explanations-FY2015.pdf.

——. 2014b. "Model 2 IGA, Preexisting TIEA or DTC." https://www.treasury.gov/resource-center/tax-policy/treaties/Documents/FATCA-Model-2-Agreement-Preexisting-TIEA-or-DTC-6-6-14.pdf.

——. 2016. "United States Model Income Tax Convention." Washington, DC: Department of the Treasury. https://www.treasury.gov/resource-center/tax-policy/treaties/Documents/Treaty-US%20Model-2016.pdf.

——. 2017a. "Treasury International Capital System." Washington, DC: Department of the Treasury. http://www.treasury.gov/resource-center/data-chart-center/tic/Pages/index.aspx.

——. 2017b. "Second Report to the President on Identifying and Reducing Tax Regulatory Burdens (Executive Order 13789)." Washington, DC: Department of the Treasury. https://www.treasury.gov/press-center/press-releases/Documents/2018-03004_Tax_EO_report.pdf.

——. 2018a. "Foreign Account Tax Compliance Act (FATCA)." http://www.treasury.gov/resource-center/tax-policy/treaties/Pages/FATCA.aspx.

———. 2018b. "Regulatory Reform Accomplishments Under President Trump's Executive Orders." Washington, DC: Department of the Treasury. https://home.treasury.gov /sites/default/files/2018-04/20180423%20Regulatory%20Reform%20Report_0 .pdf.

USCIB (United States Council on International Business). 2014. "USCIB Comments on the OECD Discussion Draft on Transfer Pricing Documentation and Country by Country Reporting." In *Discussion Draft on Transfer Pricing Documentation and CbC Reporting—Public Comments Received*, edited by Organisation for Economic Co-operation and Development (OECD), 4:156–62. Paris: OECD Publishing.

———. 2015. "USCIB Comment Letter on OECD Discussion Draft on BEPS Actions 8, 9, and 10." In *Comments Received on Public Discussion Draft—BEPS Actions 8, 9 and 10: Revisions to Chapter I of the Transfer Pricing Guidelines (Including Risk, Recharacterisation, and Special Measures)*, edited by Organisation for Economic Co-operation and Development (OECD), 2:842–53. Paris: OECD Publishing.

Valda, Andreas. 2012a. "Bekenntnis zum Datenaustausch." *Tages-Anzeiger*, December 21, 2012, Schweiz.

———. 2012b. "Regeln zur Bekämpfung von Schwarzgeld delegiert." *Tages-Anzeiger*, December 15, 2012, Wirtschaft.

———. 2013. "Unser Land will keine Namen ausliefern." *Tages-Anzeiger*, May 11, 2013, Wirtschaft.

Vasagar, Jeevan, and Vanessa Houlder. 2014. "Governments Sign Deal against Tax Evasion." *Financial Times*, October 29, 2014. http://www.ft.com/intl/cms/s/0 /5ec1d4e0-5f99-11e4-8c27-00144feabdc0.html#axzz3LU6ZM7Tq.

Vestager, Margarete. 2016. "Letter to Mr. Jacob J. Lew, Secretary of the Treasury," February 29, 2016. http://static.politico.com/cf/ba/b7725d194d84a1df018c28160048 /margrethe-vestager-letter-to-secty-lew-on-eu-tax-investigations.pdf.

Vogel, David. 1997. "Trading Up and Governing Across: Transnational Governance and Environmental Protection." *Journal of European Public Policy* 4 (4): 556–71.

Wasserfallen, Fabio. 2014. "Political and Economic Integration in the EU: The Case of Failed Tax Harmonization." *JCMS: Journal of Common Market Studies* 52 (2): 420–35.

Webb, Michael. 2004. "Defining the Boundaries of Legitimate State Practice: Norms, Transnational Actors and the OECD's Project on Harmful Tax Competition." *Review of International Political Economy* 11 (4): 787–827.

Wechsler, William. 2001. "Follow the Money." *Foreign Affairs*, July/August 2001. https:// www.foreignaffairs.com/articles/2001-07-01/follow-money.

West, Philip R. 1996. "Foreign Law in US International Taxation: The Search for Standards." *Florida Tax Review* 3: 147.

———. 2005. "Re-thinking Check-the-Box: Subpart F." *Taxes* 2005 (March): 33–38.

Williams, Phil. 1997. "Money Laundering." *South African Journal of International Affairs* 5 (1): 71–96.

Wilson, John Douglas. 1999. "Theories of Tax Competition." *National Tax Journal* 52: 269–304.

Wissenschaftlicher Beirat. 2007. "Gutachten: Einheitliche Bemessungsgrundlage der Körperschaftsteuer in der Europäischen Union." Berlin: Bundesministerium der Finanzen. https://www.bundesfinanzministerium.de/Content/DE/Standardartikel/Ministerium /Geschaeftsbereich/Wissenschaftlicher_Beirat/Gutachten_und_Stellungnahmen /Ausgewaehlte_Texte/0703231a3003.pdf?__blob=publicationFile&v=3.

———. 2017. "Finanzierungsneutrale Unternehmensbesteuerung in der Europäischen Union? Stellungnahme zum Richtlinienvorschlag der EU-Kommission vom Oktober 2016." Berlin: Bundesministerium der Finanzen. https://www.bundesfinanzministerium.de

/Content/DE/Standardartikel/Ministerium/Geschaeftsbereich/Wissenschaftlicher
_Beirat/Gutachten_und_Stellungnahmen/Ausgewaehlte_Texte/2017-11-16
-Finanzierungsneutrale-Unternehmensbesteuerung-in-der-EU-anlage.pdf?__blob
=publicationFile&v=4.

———. 2018. "Stellungnahme zu den EU-Vorschlägen für eine Besteuerung der digitalen Wirtschaft." Berlin: Bundesministerium der Finanzen. https://www.bundesfinanzministerium.de/Content/DE/Standardartikel/Ministerium/Geschaeftsbereich/Wissenschaftlicher_Beirat/Gutachten_und_Stellungnahmen/Ausgewaehlte_Texte/2018-09-27-digitale-Wirtschaft-anl.pdf?__blob=publicationFile&v=3.

World Bank. 2018. "Market Capitalization of Listed Domestic Companies (Current US$)." Accessed June 5, 2018. http://data.worldbank.org/indicator/CM.MKT.LCAP.CD.

World Inequality Database. 2018. "Data—WID—World Inequality Database." Accessed June 10, 2018. http://wid.world/data/.

WTO (World Trade Organization). 2019a. "WTO Data—International trade statistics—Merchandise trade values." Accessed May 20, 2019. https://data.wto.org/.

———. 2019b. "WTO Data—International trade statistics—Trade in commercial services." Accessed May 20, 2019. https://data.wto.org/.

Young, Cristobal. 2017. *The Myth of Millionaire Tax Flight: How Place Still Matters for the Rich*, reprint ed. Stanford, CA: Stanford University Press.

Zucman, Gabriel. 2013. *La richesse cachée des nations: Enquête sur les paradis fiscaux.* Paris: Coédition Seuil–La République des idées.

———. 2014. "Taxing across Borders: Tracking Personal Wealth and Corporate Profits." *The Journal of Economic Perspectives* 28 (4): 121–48.

Index

Note: Page numbers in italic type indicate tables or figures.

ABA (American Bankers Association), 88, 101
adjustment costs: government choices and, 41–42, 44, 47–48; shifting of, 3–4, 11, 25, 36, 62–63, 132, 143, 144
AEI (automatic exchange of information): adoption of, 93–100; within EU, xi, 2–5, 34, 89–91, 93–97, 133–34; FATCA as driver of, 23, 82, 93–100, 133–34; US reciprocity, lack of, xiii, xv, 5–6, 18–19, 100–105, 131, 132–33, 143
Amazon, xv, 121, 128, 139, 153n17
Andersson, Per, 37
Antigua, 73
Apple, xv, 127–28, 139
apportionment. *See* unitary taxation
arm's-length standard (ALS), 46, 53, 115–21, 124–25
asymmetric prisoner's dilemma, 6–11
Austria: ending of bank secrecy by, xi–xii, 2–5, 98–99, 103, 133–34; EU level AEI and, 2–5, 34, 90, 93–97, 133–34; foreign capital in, 3; foreign portfolio investment, 29; Model Tax Convention and, 86; share of financial services pre-FATCA, 9
automatic exchange of information. *See* AEI
avoidance *vs.* evasion. *See* evasion *vs.* avoidance

Backus, Jenny, 67–68
Bahamas, 73, 99
Bakija, Jon, 69
banks. *See* financial sector
Basinger, Scott J., 37
Baucus, Max, 111
Belgium, 2, 9, 29, 94, 99
benefits principle, 106, 119, 137, 149n13
Bentsen, Lloyd, 50
BEPS (base erosion and profit-shifting) program, 106–30; context to, 107–12; corporate opposition to, 107, 113, 117–21, 129–30, 144–45; country-by-country reporting and, 121–22, 126–27; implementation of, 124–29; Obama administration and, xiii–xv, 16–21, 41–42, 107, 113–15, 119–24,

129–30, 144–45; original purpose of, 114–15; PE definition and, 121–22, 125–26; transfer pricing and, 115–21, 124–25
Beramendi, Pablo, 37
BIAC (Business Industry Advisory Council), 55, 56–57
bilateral agreements: CbCR template and, 123; diffusion of, 153n20; EU most-favored-nation clause and, 96–97; FATCA and, 20, 90–91, 99, 132–33; on information exchange, 45, 74, 79, 132–33; OECD soft law and, 124–27; PE definition and, 17, 122, 125; Swiss bank secrecy and, 90, 92–93; US power and, 21, 35; on US tax withholding, 62, 149n13
binding arbitration, 125
Birkenfeld, Bradley, 85
blacklisting: by EU, 5, 23–24, 34, 132, 134, 135; by G20, 82, 90; by Global Forum, 1; by OECD: FATCA/AEI, 82, 86, 90; HTC, 54, 55, 64, 65, 73, 75; by US, 14; of US, 5, 24, 135
Branson, Mark, 85
Brazil, 28, 29
Brunetti Group, 93, 97–98
Buchanan, James, 72
budget deficits: Bush (G.W.) admin and, 69, 71; Clinton admin and, 50–51, 63; as predictor of government preference, 147; shifting of to foreign countries, 143
budget surpluses, 67
Bush, George H.W., regressive tax policies of, 50
Bush, George W., administration of: HTC program and, 11–12, 13–14, 23, 66–67, 71–81; regressive tax policies of, 23, 38, 67–71, 80, 83
business. *See* multinational corporations (MNCs)

Cadbury Schweppes ruling, 109, 113
campaign contributions, 39, 40
capital gains taxes, 69–70
capital mobility: as assumption of model, 44; as brake on tax cooperation, xii, 53; as justification for regressive taxation, xiv, 17, 36–37, 42; removal of barriers to, 51, 53

Cayman Islands, *29*, 98, *99*

CbCR. *See* country-by-country reporting

CCCTB (common consolidated corporate tax base), 109–10, 128, 132, 137, 138–41, 146

CFA (committee on fiscal affairs, OECD), 16–17, 56–58, 73, 80

CFC (controlled foreign company) rules: CCCTB and, 138; check-the-box regulations and, 58–61, 87, 108, 110–11; IRS authority and, 35; limitations of, 113–14; Obama admin and, 16, 19–20

CFP (Center for Freedom and Prosperity), 69, 71, 72, 73, 74, 76

Chamber of Commerce, 69, 71, 72, 103

check-the-box regulations, 58–61, 87, 108, 110–11

Cheney, Dick, 70

child tax credit, 67, 84

China, *28*, *29*, *31*, 126–27. *See also* Hong Kong

Citizens for Tax Justice, 67, 68

Clinton, Bill, administration of: CFC rules and, 58–61, 64; HTC program and, 52–53, 54, 55–58, 64–65; progressive tax reforms of, 12–13, 50–51; QI (qualified intermediary) program, 13, 20, 22–23, 51–52, 61–63, 147

Clinton, Hillary, 83

Club for Growth, 70

coercion, 6–18, 142–44; BEPS and, 122, 129, 130; definition, 48; drivers of use of, 42–44; FATCA and, 4, 7–11, 12, 18, 87–88, 90, 96, 105; great power status and, 22; HTC program and, 11–13, 52, 54–55, 65, 73–75; Iran sanctions, 135–36. *See also* power; sanctions and penalties

common consolidated corporate tax base. *See* CCCTB

common reporting standard (CRS), 1–6, 34, 98

conservative politics, 36–38. *See also* Republicans (US)

constitutional reforms, xi, xii, 2

constructivist narratives, xii, 11–15

consumer market size, 27–28, 30–32, *31*

contractualist narratives, xii, 6–11

controlled foreign company rules. *See* CFC rules

controlled transactions, 115–17, 118, 120, 130, 139

corporate taxation: adjustment costs and, 47–48; BEPS program, 16–21, 106–30; Bush's (G.W.) policies on, 12, 69–71; CCCTB, 109–10, 128, 132, 137, 138–41, 146; Clinton's policies on, 50–51; country-by-country reporting (CbCR), 16, 17, 20, 106, 121–22, 123, 126–27, 153n23; deferred tax payments,

60, 86, 87, 110–11, 113, 128–29, 150n2; EU anti-avoidance proposals, 136–41; foreign tax credit, 21, 86, 111; HTC program and, 49, 54–58, 64–65; individual taxation *vs.*, xiv–xv, 17–18, 36–42, 61–63, 87–89, 104–5, 130, 144; legitimization of avoidance of, 57–58, 71–73, 75, 119–21, 131–32; Obama's policies on, xiii–xv, 16–21, 131–32; PTRs and, 13–14, 53–54, 58, 64, 72–73, 80–81; Trump's policies on, xv, 18, 137, 141. *See also* CFC rules; multinational corporations

Council of the European Union, 146

"creative ambiguity," 106–7

Credit Suisse, 3

cross-border deposits, 8–9

cross-border investments, 27–32, 53

cross-border transactions, 53

cross-crediting, 111

CRS (common reporting standard), 1–6, 34, 98

Culbertson, Robert, 59

customer due diligence (CDD) rules, 102

deferred tax payments, 60, 86, 87, 110–11, 113, 128–29, 150n2

deficit reduction, 50–51

DeLay, Tom, 70–71, 77

DeLong, Brad, 51

Democrats (US): conditions for transformative change by, 21, 48, 144–45; global enforcement and, 21–22; interest groups as brake on, xiv, 17–18, 144–45; taxation principles and, xiv, 17–19, 36–38, 82–84, 144–45. *See also* Clinton admin.; Obama admin.

depreciation allowances, 69

digital services tax (DST), 132, 137

discursive power, 39–41, 144; of corporations, 18, 41, 54, 71–72, 76, 110–11, 117–19, 123–24, 145

dividends: profit-shifting and, 127, 128, 150n2; reporting of, 136; taxes on, 28, 38, 60, 62, 69–70, 149n13, 150n2

double taxation, 80, 114, 117, 140, 150n2

DST (digital services tax), 132, 137

earned income tax credit (EITC), 50, 84

ECJ (European Court of Justice), 109, 113

ECOFIN (European Council on Economic and Financial Affairs), 94–95, 97, 98

Edwards, John, 83

Eichengreen, Barry, 51

electoral systems, 37

emerging economies, 112, 114, 125

estate tax, 68

EU (European Union): AEI agreement within, xi, 89–91, 93–97, 133–34; FATCA's legal impact on, 4–5, 83, 91, 95–97; market size, 28–33, *28*, *31*; potential measures by, 136–41; regulatory capacity of, xv, 26, 33–36, 131–34; fiscal sovereignty, 34–36, 143; most-favored-nation clause, xii, 4–5, 83, 95–97, 105; nondiscrimination principle, 26, 125–26; PE definition and, 125–26; unanimity requirement, 2–3, 5–6, 34, 53, 95, 109, 127, 141, 143, 146; state aid investigations by, xv, 127–29, 139

European Commission, election of, 146

European Court of Justice (ECJ), 109, 113

evasion *vs.* avoidance: definitions, 46; FATCA and, 83, 87–89, 104–5; HTC program and, 49, 55, 56–58, 66–67, 76–81; power and, 39–41, 107–8; US capabilities and, 130

exit taxation, 138

ex post adjustments, 118, 120–21

Fabius, Laurent, 75

FATCA (Foreign Account Tax Compliance Act): AEI, as driver of, 23, 82, 93–100, 133–34; coercion and, 4, 7–11, 12, 18, 87–88, 90, 96, 105; constructivist perspective on, 12; corporate *vs.* individual scope of, 87–89, 144; definition and provisions, xii, 4, 12, 83, 87, 96–97; intergovernmental agreement, transition to, 89–93, 96–100; legal impact on EU, 4–5, 83, 91, 95–97; reciprocity, lack of, xiii, xv, 5–6, 17–20, 100–105, 132–33, 143–44; sanction threat of, xii–xiii, 4, 83, 87–88, 90, 96, 142–43; tax havens' agreement to, 82; tax havens' share before, 8–11

FATF (Financial Action Task Force), 69, 77

Faymann, Werner, xi

Feldstein, Martin, 68

FFIs (foreign financial institutions). *See* financial sector: foreign

Fiat, 128, 139

financial crisis (2008), 19–20, 40, 82, 84–85, 147

financial sector: bailouts of, 84–85; foreign: lobbying/pressure by, xii, 4, 89, 97–98, 99–100; shifting of burdens onto, 11, 62–63; state power against, 27–33, 105; US, lobbying/pressure by: advantage gained as tax haven, xiii, 5–6, 83, 102–3, 105, 131–32, 133, 143; FATCA and, 23, 88, 100, 101–104; HTC program and, 57; power of, 40, 144

financial transparency, definition, 46

FinCEN (Financial Crimes Enforcement Network), 102

fiscal sovereignty. *See* national sovereignty

Florida, 103–4

foreign direct investment (FDI), 30, 32, 35–36

foreign holdings of US securities, 8–9

foreign portfolio investment (FPI), *29*, 30

foreign tax credit, 21, 86, 111

France, 74, 126, 127, 140

Frieden, Luc, 95–96

Friedman, Milton, 72

G7, 44, 52–53. *See also* HTC program

G20: BEPS project and, 45, 106, 112, 114–15; FATCA/AEI and, 92–93, 97–100; Starbucks and, 110–11

Garrett, Geoffrey, 37

Geithner, Timothy, 16, 86–87, 110–11, 144–45

Germany: capital flight from, 51; CCCTB proposal and, 140, 141; country-by-country reporting and, 122, 123, 126; equalization tax proposal by, 127; foreign capital in, 3; OECD and, 112; Rubik agreements and, 90–91, 92–93; Starbucks tax avoidance and, 110, 129, 145; US, support for/fear of, 24, 122, 123, 132, 135, 137–38, 145–46

Global Forum, 1, 79, 80, 135

Gore, Al, 67

great powers: market size and, 26–33, 96, 104, 105; sanctions and, 15, 22, 25–26; strategic choices of, 42–44; US as only, 22, 26

Green Books of Revenue Proposals, 54, 86, 100–101, 111

Grenada, 73

Guttentag, Joseph, 51–52, 57, 59

Hacker, Jacob S., 70, 151n3

Hallerberg, Mark, 37

Hammer, Richard, 56–57, 71, 73

harmonized interest barrier, 138

hegemony. *See* great powers; power

Hickman, Andrew, 121

Hong Kong, *29*, *32*, 99. *See also* China

HTC (harmful tax competition) project: Bush (G.W.) admin and, 11–12, 13–14, 23, 66–67, 71–81; context to, 44; dilution of, 22–23, 49, 56–58, 64–65, 73–75, 80–81; introduction and provisions of, 11, 53–55; killing off of, 66–67; mistakes of, 49, 56

HTVI (hard-to-value intangibles), 116–17, 118, 120, 124

Hubbard, Glenn, 75

Huizinga, Harry, 9–10

hybrid entities, 59–61, 111

income inequality, 38, 50, 83–84
individuals: taxation of, compared to
    corporations, xiv–xv, 17–18, 36–37, 39–40,
    130, 131–32; FATCA and, 87–89, 104–5, 144;
    QI program and, 61–63; wealthy: policies
    favoring, 67–68, 69–70; power of, 38, 39, 70
information exchange. *See* transparency and
    information exchange
instrumental power, 39–41
intangible assets, 115–17. *See also* HTVI;
    intellectual property
intellectual property (IP), 32–33, *32*, 107–8,
    116–23, 141. *See also* royalty and license fee
    payments
interbank transactions (value), *28*, 30
interest groups, as brake on governments, xiv,
    17–18, 37–42, 144–47, 151n3. *See also*
    financial sector; individuals; libertarian
    lobbyists; multinational corporations
internet trading, 109–10, 121–22, 127, 132, 137
Iran sanctions, 135–36
Ireland: CCTB proposal and, 141; corporate
    profit-shifting and, 35–36, 108, 141; EU state
    aid investigations and, 127–28, 139; new PE
    definition and, 125; royalties collected by, *32*
IRS (Internal Revenue Service): CFC rules and,
    35, 59–61; check-the-box regulations and,
    58–60; FATCA reporting obligations to, 4,
    12, 20; QI reporting obligations to, 13

Job Creation and Worker Assistance Act
    (2002), 69
Johannesen, Niels, 10
Juncker, Jean-Claude, 94, 96

Kennedy administration, 60
Kintner test, 59
KPMG, 117–18
Kudrle, Robert T., 58
KYC (know-your-customer) procedures,
    62–63, 94, 136

Laffer curve, 17, 37
Levin, Carl, 19, 84, 85, 111
Lew, Jack, 128
LGT (Liechtenstein Global Trust), 19, 84, 94
libertarian lobbyists, 11–12, 13–14, 23, 67–78, 146
license fee and royalty payments, 32–33, *32*,
    122–23, 128, 141, 149n13
Liechti, Martin, 85
Lindsey, Lawrence, 67
lobbying. *See* financial sector; individuals;
    interest groups; libertarian lobbyists;
    multinational corporations

look-through approach, 94
losses, refunds on, 69
Luxembourg: corporate profit-shifting and,
    35–36, 141; ending of bank secrecy by, xi, xii,
    2–5, 11, 98–99, 133–34; EU level AEI and,
    2–5, 34, 90, 93–97, 133–34; EU state aid
    investigations and, 127–28, 139; foreign
    capital in, 3; foreign portfolio investment, *29*;
    Model Tax Convention and, 80, 86; new PE
    definition and, 125; non-participation in
    HTC program, 78, 80; royalties collected
    by, *32*, 108; share of financial services
    pre-FATCA, *9*

Macron, Emmanuel, 140
market capitalization (value), *28*
market size: of EU, 28–33, *28*, *31*; state power
    and, 26–33, 96, 104, 105; of US, *28*, *29*, 30,
    31, 32–33, 90, 96, 104, 105, 131–32, 142–43
MCAA (multilateral competent authority
    agreement), 98–99, 100, 132–33
McCain, John, 68
McConnell, Mitch, 71
McDonald, Michael, 121
McMahon, Emily, 90–91
MFE (minimally functional entity), 117
Mirabile, Germano, 96
Mitchell, Daniel, 71, 72, 73, 76
MLI (multilateral instruments), 122, 124–25, 126
Mnuchin, Stephen, 137
Model 1 IGA, 91–92, 100
Model Agreement on Information Exchange,
    79–80, 150n4
Model Tax Convention, 80, 121–22, 124–27,
    149n13, 150n2
money laundering, 52, 69, 77–78
Moscovici, Pierre, 127, 128, 139
most-favored-nation (MFN) clause, xii, 4–5,
    83, 95–97, 105
multinational corporations (MNCs):
    adjustment costs and, 47–48; legitimization
    of tax avoidance of, 57–58, 71–73, 75,
    119–21, 131–32; lobbying/pressure by,
    40–42; on BEPS project, 107, 113, 117–121,
    29–130, 144–45; on CFC rules, 60–61,
    110–11; on check-the-box rules, 61, 87,
    110–11; on FATCA, 18, 23, 87, 88–89; on
    HTC program, 11–12, 13–14, 54–58, 64–67,
    71–78; on QI, 22–23; on tax cuts, 69–71;
    power of, 39, 56–58, 72–73, 107–8, 113,
    119–21, 123–34; discursive, 18, 41, 54, 71–72,
    76, 110–11, 117–19, 123–24, 145; individual
    power *vs.*, xiv–xv, 17–18, 36–42, 61–63,
    87–89, 104–5, 130, 144; structural, 41, 145;

profit shifting by, 15–21, 27; BEPS project against, 106–30; exploitation of EU mismatches, 128–29; hybrid entities, 59–61, 111; loss to US from, 149n9; royalties and license fees, 32–33, *32*, 107–8, 116–21, 141, 149n13; tax havens' aid with, 35–36, 53–54. *See also* corporate taxation

national sovereignty, xi–xii, 6, 11–12, 34–35, 54, 71–72, 105, 141
Naumann, Manfred, 123
Neal, Richard, 88, 111
Netherlands, *32*, 35–36, 108, 127–28, 139, 141
NFTC (National Foreign Trade Council), 117, 118
Nicodème, Gaëtan, 9–10
normative constraints, 11–15, 54, 65, 105, 146–47
Norquist, Grover, 68, 70

Obama, Barack administration of: anti-tax haven efforts of, 4–6, 85–89, 104–5, 110–11; BEPS and, xiii–xv, 16–21, 41–42, 107, 113–15, 119–24, 129–30, 144–45; corporate tax avoidance policies of, xiii–xv, 16–21, 131–32; reciprocity, refusal of, xiii, 5–6, 17–20, 100–105, 131–32, 143; tax fairness and, 83–84, 87, 129. *See also* FATCA
OECD: Clinton admin and, 52–55; corporate sector, accommodation to, 56–58; evolution in campaigns of, 44–45; FATCA's impact on AEI and, 97–100. *See also* BEPS; CRS; HTC
Omnibus Budget Reconciliation Act (1993), 50–51
O'Neill, Paul, 14, 72–73, 74, 76, 78–79, 151n6
Osborn, George, 110
Owens, Jeffrey, 57, 79

partnerships, 59–60
passive income, 60–61, 108, 109, 113, 128
PE (permanent establishment), 16, 17, 109–10, 121–22, 125–26, 149n13, 150n4, 153n23
penalties. *See* sanctions and penalties
Pierson, Paul, 70, 151n3
political campaign contributions, 39, 40
political orientation (US): constructivist narrative and, 12–15; impact on global enforcement, 21–22, 38; interest groups as brake on, xiv, 17–18, 37–42, 47, 144–47, 151n3. *See also specific party*
"politics without conviction," 75–80
power: of corporations (*see* multinational corporations: power of); forms of, 39; of individuals *vs.* corporations, xiv–xv, 17–18, 36–42, 61–63, 87–89, 104–5, 130, 144;

market size and, 26–33, 90, 96, 104, 105, 131–32, 142–43; political barriers and business power, interactions between, 41–44; regulatory capacity and, 26, 33–36, 90, 96, 104, 105; of US *See* United States: power of). *See also* coercion; great powers; sanctions and penalties
profit shifting. *See* multinational corporations: profit-shifting by
progressive taxation: Bush's (G.W.) claims of, 67; Democrat policies on, *xiv*, 12–13, 17, 37–38, 50–51, 83–84, 131, 144; global tax policies as substitute for, 51–52, 63–64; wealth shifting and, 17
Prosperity Institute, 76
PTRs (preferential tax regimes), 13–14, 53–54, 58, 64, 72–73, 80–81
public opinion: on bank secrecy, 3–4; on distribution of taxes, 38, 55–56, 84, 88–89, 145; on tax avoidance and evasion, 84–85, 88–89, 110, 127, 128, 129

QI (qualified intermediary) program: Bush (G.W.) and, 14, 75; business opposition to, 22–23; circumvention of, 20, 84–85; introduction and provisions of, 13, 19–20, 22–23, 61–63; Obama's proposed extension of, 86, 87; responsibility shifting via, 19–20, 62–63, 147
qualified majority voting (QMV), 146

R&D super-deductions, 139–40
Reagan, Ronald, regressive tax policies of, 38, 50
real economic activity, 114–15, 139. *See also* substantial economic activity criterion
regressive taxation: barriers to, xiv, 22, 35, 36–38, 41–42, 145; Bush's (G.H.W.) policies, 50; Bush's (G.W.) policies, 23, 38, 67–71, 80, 83; Clinton's policies, perceptions of as, 51, 63–64; government preferences and, 41–42, 44, 47; political orientation and, 37–38; Reagan's policies, 38, 50; Republican policies on overall, 37–38; tax competition as justification for, 17, 42, 81, 144; Trump's policies, xv, 18, 137, 141
regulatory capacity: definition, 33; of EU (*See* EU: regulatory capacity); power and, 26, 33–36, 90, 96, 104, 105; of US, 33–36, 90, 96, 104, 105, 131–32, 142–43
repatriation tax holiday, 113
Republicans (US): global enforcement and, 21–22; taxation principles and, 17, 36–38, 144, 151n3. *See also* Bush admin; Reagan admin; Trump admin

revolving doors, 40
royalty and license fee payments, 32–33, *32*, 107–8, 116–23, 128, 141, 149n13. *See also* intellectual property
Rubik concept, 90, 92–93, 95–96, 97–98
Rubin, Robert, 50, 51
Rueda, David, 37
Russia, *28*, *31*, 135–36

sanctions and penalties: EU AEI and, 150n6; FATCA and, xii–xiii, 4, 83, 87–88, 90, 96, 142–43; great power status and, 15, 22, 25–26; HTC campaign and, 12, 54, 58, 78–79, 81; against Iran, 135–36; QI extension and, 86, 87
Savings Directive, 94–95, 98, 134
Schaub, Max, 102–3
Schäuble, Wolfgang, 133
securities transactions (value), *28*, 30
separate entity accounting, 106, 114, 119, 131, 138
shell companies, 136
Single European Act, 44, 53
Slemrod, Joel, 69
Snow, John, 80
source *vs.* residence taxation. *See* BEPS program
sovereignty. *See* national sovereignty
special measures (BEPS), 115, 116–19, 120
Special Sessions on Tax Competition, 53–54
Stack, Robert, 113, 119, 122, 123
Starbucks, 110, 128, 129, 139
Steinbrück, Peer, 94
Stop Tax Haven Abuse Act, 85, 86–87
Strache, Heinz-Christian, xi
structural constraints, 6–11
structural power, 39–41, 144, 145
subjective tax determinations, 117–19
substantial economic activity criterion, 27, 53, 55, 56, 57–58, 64, 72–73. *See also* real economic activity
Summers, Lawrence, 54, 58
super-deductions, 139–40
supply-side policies, 67–71. *See also* regressive taxation
SVTDG (Silicon Valley Tax Directors Group), 118
Switzerland: ending of bank secrecy by, 2–5, 11, 13, 98–99; FATCA and, 83, 89–90, 92–93, 97–98; EU AEI opt-out, 94–95; foreign capital in, 3; foreign portfolio investment, *29*; Model Tax Convention and, 80, 86, 90; non-participation in HTC program, 78, 80; royalties collected by, *32*; share of financial services pre-FATCA, *9*

Tanenbaum, Edward, 89
Task Force on Information Exchange and Financial Privacy, 76
tax avoidance *vs.* evasion. *See* evasion *vs.* avoidance
tax competition: Bush (G.W.) admin's support for, 14, 23, 74, 77, 81; business support for, 56–57; in EU, 35–36, 109; as justification for regressive taxation, 17, 42, 81, 144; between small and large countries, 7
tax evasion *vs.* avoidance. *See* evasion *vs.* avoidance
tax havens, definition, 53
Tax Justice Network (TJN), 122, 124, 146, 149n12
Tiberi, Patrick, 88
TIEA (Tax Information Exchange Agreements), 10, 44–45, 77
TRACE project, 89
transfer pricing, 115–21, 124–27. *See also* intellectual property; multinational corporations: profit shifting by
Transfer Pricing Guidelines, 124–27
transformative change, definition and proof of, 44, 46–48
transparency and information exchange, 73, 75–81, 95. *See also* AEI; FATCA; QI, HTC
Treasury Department (US): data on foreign holdings of US securities, *8*; FATCA, powers of under, 33–34, 35, 36; responsiveness to lobbyists, 23, 40–41
Trump, Donald, administration of: bank secrecy policies of, xiii, 103; Iran sanctions and, 135–36; MLI, refusal to sign, 125, 134–35; tax-haven conditions provided by, xv, 18, 137, 141
trusts, 102, 136, 154n5

UBS (Union Bank of Switzerland), 3, 19, 82–83, 84–86, 98
unanimity requirement, 2–3, 5–6, 34, 53, 95, 109, 127, 141, 143, 146
uncertainty, 117–19, 125, 128, 139
unilateral measures, 126–27
unitary taxation, 46–47, 109–10, 114–15, 138
United Kingdom: BEPS and, 145; diverted profits tax, 125, 127, 154n24; HTC program and, 53, 74; Rubik agreements and, 90–91; Starbucks tax avoidance and, 110, 129, 145
United States: coercion by, 6–18, 142–43; FATCA, 4, 7–11, 12, 18, 87–88, 90, 96, 105; HTC program, 11–13, 52, 54–55, 65, 73–75; sanction threats, xii–xiii, 4, 25–26, 83, 87–88,

96, 135–36, 142–43; power of, 20–21, 25–26, 67, 81, 131–32, 142–44; as impetus to EU, 129, 130, 135–36; market size, *28, 29*, 30, *31*, 32–33, 90, 96, 104, 105, 131–32, 142–43; regulatory capacity, 33–36, 90, 96, 104, 105, 131–32, 142–43; reciprocity, refusal of, xiii, xv, 5–6, 17–20, 100–105, 131, 132–33; rising role of as tax haven, xiii, 5–6, 83, 102–103, 105, 131–32, 133, 143. *See also* coercion; FATCA; *specific administration or interest group*

US Chamber of Commerce, 69, 71, 72, 103

USCIB (US Council for International Business), 56–57, 66–67, 71, 118

UT+FA (unitary taxation and formulary apportionment), 109–10, 114–15

Vestager, Margarete, 127–29, 139

Vincenz, Pierin, 97–98

voluntary compliance, as great power strategy, 42–44, 48

voter attitudes. *See* public opinion

Washington Post, 72

weakest-link problem, 6–11

Weil, Raoul, 85

West, Philip, 51–52, 58

Widmer-Schlumpf, Eveline, 93, 95–96, 97, 98. *See also* Brunetti Group

withholding taxes: EU and, 94, 95, 125, 134, 153n21; FATCA and, 83, 87, 88, 89, 90, 96, 98, 142–43, 150n5; German, 51; on interest and royalty payments, 153n21; in Model Tax Treaty, 149n13; QI program and, 13, 19–20, 61–63, 64, 84, 86; regulatory capacity and, 35, 36

Zucman, Gabriel, 10